1994

TEACHER PERSONAL THEORIZING

SUNY Series, Teacher Preparation and Development
Alan R. Tom, editor

TEACHER PERSONAL THEORIZING

Connecting Curriculum Practice, Theory, and Research

By

E. Wayne Ross

Jeffrey W. Cornett

Gail McCutcheon

State University of New York Press

Published by
State University of New York Press, Albany

For information, address the State University of New York Press,
State University Plaza, Albany, NY 12246

Library of Congress Cataloging-in-Publication Data

Teacher personal theorizing : connecting curriculum, practice, theory,
    and research / [edited] by E. Wayne Ross, Jeffrey W. Cornett, Gail
    McCutcheon.
        p.   cm. — (SUNY series, teacher preparation and development)
    Includes bibliographical references and index.
        ISBN 0-7914-1125-7 (alk. paper). — ISBN 0-7914-1126-5 (pbk. :
    alk. paper)
        1. Teaching. 2. Teachers—United States—Attitudes. 3. Teacher
    participation in curriculum planning—United States. I. Ross, E.
    Wayne, 1956-   . II. Cornett, Jeffrey W., 1952-
    III. McCutcheon, Gail, 1941-   . IV. Series: SUNY series in teacher
    preparation and development.
    LB1775.2.T435   1992
    371.1'02—dc20   91-27209
                                                                    CIP

10 9 8 7 6 5 4 3 2

For Rachel and her friends
E. W. R.

For Vicki
J. W. C.

For George
G. M.

CONTENTS

PREFACE

Teaching is a complex task that demands thoughtful professionals. Teaching cannot be reduced to a merely technical process without contributing to the deskilling of teachers and masking the problematic nature of curriculum decision making. The contributors of this book belong to a community of practitioners from a variety of contexts who believe that the key to professionalizing teaching is the explicit recognition that teacher personal theorizing significantly influences the curriculum and is therefore important to understand. As this understanding evolves, teachers can continue to develop as individuals and as collaborators with other professionals in a manner which rightfully places teachers at the center of curriculum work. This form of teacher empowerment requires that teachers (in all contexts) also accept the concurrent responsibility for critically examining educational theory and research from a variety of perspectives. In addition, educators in all contexts should actively seek to establish a community of reflective practitioners who openly deliberate about what knowledge is of most worth and what processes help stimulate the democratization of schools and society.

The intent of this book is to shed light on teacher theorizing, and the issues and problems surrounding it, in an effort to provide an integrated perspective on curriculum practice, theory, and research. The book is divided into four major sections. Part I discusses epistemological bases for teacher personal theorizing and advances such theorizing as legitimate curriculum inquiry. Part II provides examples of research on teacher personal theorizing conducted in a variety of subject matter and grade level contexts. Part III discusses the implications of this research for the reform of teacher education, school organization, and administrator preparation, with the aim of honoring and suggesting methods of facilitating teacher theorizing. In the final section, two leading curriculum theorists describe their conceptions of the issues and problems associated with such a movement.

We wish to express our sincere gratefulness to both Sandra Mathison and Vuokko "Vicki" Cornett for their constructive and perceptive comments regarding this project. Special thanks are due to Lois G. Patton, Editor-in-Chief, and to Christine Lynch, Production Editor, of the State University of New York Press for their invaluable assistance and advice.

In addition, we would like to thank the chapter authors of this book for the quality of their contributions, for their own systematic personal theorizing about curriculum and the work of teachers, and for their patience as they waited for the completion of this community effort. Most of all, we want to thank the many thoughtful, reflective teachers who provided the inspiration for us all.

I

TEACHER PERSONAL THEORIZING AND CURRICULUM INQUIRY

1

E. WAYNE ROSS
JEFFREY W. CORNETT
GAIL McCUTCHEON

Teacher Personal Theorizing and Research on Curriculum and Teaching

In this book, we examine the relationship between teacher thinking and teacher action as illustrated by the curricular and instructional practices of teachers. During the past decade a number of scholars have investigated a variety of aspects of teacher cognition. The resultant literature can be categorized into three primary research areas: (a) teachers' planning (preactive and postactive thoughts); (b) teachers' interactive thoughts and decisions; and (c) teachers' theories and beliefs (Clark & Peterson, 1986). The research on teacher thinking generally agrees that teachers' personal theories and beliefs serve as the basis for classroom practice and curriculum decision making, yet the nature of this relationship is not well understood.

This book is based upon the assumption that all practical activities, such as teaching, are guided by some theory. Teaching is practical work carried out in the socially constructed, complex, and institutionalized world of schooling, which shapes teachers' actions and gives context to their meaning. As a result, teachers could not begin to practice without some knowledge of the context of their practice and some ideas about what can and should be done in those circumstances. In this sense, teachers are guided by personal, practical theories that structure their activities and guide them in decision making.

The reasons why teachers do what they do are indeed complex and are subject to increasing attention of curriculum scholars and researchers. In this book, we address these issues by bringing together a collection of diverse essays and research reports focused on illuminating how teachers consciously and tacitly use their knowledge, skills, beliefs, and values to make sense of their situations, take appropriate actions, and assess the impact of those actions.

In this introductory chapter, we will discuss the notion of teacher personal theorizing in relation to the broader field of research on teaching. By examining the development of research on teaching in recent years, with particular attention to the dominant research programs within the field we can outline the underpinnings of research on teacher theorizing. Following this is a brief discussion of Dewey's theory of experience as a basis for the construct of teacher personal theorizing.

RESEARCH ON TEACHING

Recent publications, such as the *Knowledge Base for the Beginning Teacher*, the *Handbook of Research on Teaching* (3rd ed.), and the *Handbook of Research on Social Studies Teaching and Learning*; the introduction of the new international journal devoted to research on teaching, *Teaching and Teacher Education*; and the addition of a division within the American Educational Research Association that is devoted to teaching, illustrate the considerable emphasis in current educational research on the development of a systematic knowledge base for teaching.

The burgeoning interest in the research on teaching has introduced a number of theoretical and research frameworks that only a few years ago were not part of the field, particularly critical pedagogy and poststructuralist perspectives. However, two paradigms have dominated research on teaching, and educational research in general, over the past twenty-five years. They are process-product and interpretive research.[1]

Process-Product Research

Process-product, or teaching effectiveness, research represents the mainstream of research on teaching since about 1965. Working in the tradition of applied behavioristic psychology, process-product researchers have attempted to construct a scientific basis for teaching. Key contributors include Dunkin and Biddle (1974), Gage (1978), Brophy (1983), Evertson (1985), and Good (1979). The basic goals of process-product research have been described as attempting

> to define relationships between what teachers do in the classroom (the processes of teaching) and what happens to their students (the products of learning). One product that has

received much attention is achievement in the basic skills . . . Research in this tradition assumes that greater knowledge of such relationships will lead to improved instruction: once effective instruction is described, then supposedly programs can be designed to promote those effective practices. (Anderson, Evertson, & Brophy, 1979, p. 193)

Most research of this type is descriptive and correlational, with field experiments having been conducted in recent years (e.g., Coladarci & Gage, 1984; Evertson, 1985). Shulman describes the typical process-product study as study

conducted in existing classrooms that function normally during the periods of observation . . . Observers ordinarily use categorical observation scales, typically of the "low inference" variety (tallying the occurrence of observable events rather than judging or evaluating the quality of observed activities, which would be deemed "high inference") and most often spread a set of observations occasions (as few as four and as many as twenty) across most of the school year. (1986, p. 10)

In this research, teaching is understood as a linear activity in which the particular teacher actions (such as direct instruction, higher-order questions, or responses to misbehavior) produce particular pupil responses (high standardized test scores or "appropriate" classroom behavior). Teaching effectiveness results from a combination of discrete, observable teaching behaviors that operate independently of time and place. As Shulman notes, there is assumed to be an underlying "true score" for the relationship between a given teacher behavior and pupil outcome measure. Researchers employing process-product models control "context variables" (such as gender, subject matter, and ability levels) so that data from different teachers and situations can be aggregated in an effort to estimate the parameters or laws of teaching. "The problem is to get beyond the limitations of particular teachers, particular classrooms, and particular studies to a more stable generalization" (Shulman, 1986, p. 10). This last effort is represented by advocates of "meta-analysis" of process-product research to discover more stable relationships between specific teacher actions and pupil responses (e.g., Gage & Needels, 1989). Major findings from process-product research are summarized in Brophy and Good (1986), Good and Brophy (1986), and Rosenshine and Stevens (1986).

More recently, and in conjunction with the increased influence of cognitive science, process-product researchers have focused their concern on the mediating processes that occupy the middle ground between teacher actions and pupil responses. The work of Peterson (1988) exemplifies the effort to study teachers' and students' thinking in addition to their behavior and achievement. Although the evolution of process-product research to include cognitions as well as behaviors as part of the effort to create a scientific base for teaching might seem inconsistent with the assumptions inherent in psychological behaviorism, it should be noted that the construct of mediation was developed as part of learning theorists' attempts to understand what processes mediated between stimulus and response. It has been suggested that cognitive science may be able to bridge the differences between process-product and other types of research on teaching.

Interpretive Research

This paradigm, which has been characterized as studies of "classroom ecology," includes a broad and diverse group of studies with foundations in anthropology (e.g., Erickson, 1973), sociology (e.g., Delamont & Atkinson, 1980), sociolinguistics (e.g., Cazden, John, & Hymes, 1972) and other traditions, such as curriculum and teaching (e.g., Doyle, 1977; Elbaz, 1981; Feiman-Nemser & Floden, 1986; Tom, 1984). Cazden (1986) and Erickson (1986) have written recent syntheses of this research.

Studies in this paradigm differ not only in their disciplinary bases but also in their scope. The range is from microanalysis of verbal interactions (Green, 1983) to macroanalysis of entire schools or communities in relation to schools (Peshkin, 1978, 1986).

The key characteristic that makes this collection of diverse investigations a family of inquiries is that each perspective "presumes that teaching is a highly complex, context-specific, interactive activity in which differences across classrooms, schools, and communities are critically important" (Cochran-Smith & Lytle, 1990, p. 3). The central assumptions of interpretive research include (a) attention to the reciprocal interaction between persons and their environments, rather than unidirectional causality from teacher to student; (b) treating teaching and learning as a continuously interactive process, rather than reducing teaching to a few isolated factors; (c) considering the classroom as a context embedded within other contexts (school, community, and culture) that influence what is observed in the classroom; and (d) considering unobservable processes, such as thoughts, attitudes, and perceptions, as important data sources (Hamilton, 1983).

It is important to note the differences between the interpretive and process-product studies of teaching. Often the major difference in these research programs is misunderstood as primarily methodological. That is, process-product research is described as "quantitative" and interpretive research is considered "qualitative." This position assumes that the different research programs are examining the same phenomenon for similar purposes. Teacher effectiveness researchers can be described as conducting carefully controlled correlational and quasi-experimental research, using large samples and employing descriptive and inferential statistics in the development of causal propositions regarding forms of teacher behavior associated with pupil performance gains. Interpretive researchers, on the other hand, employ participant observation methods or conduct extensive and open-ended interviews in a single setting and report their findings in narrative form without making generalizations beyond the context studied.

As Cazden (1986), Shulman (1986), and Erickson (1986) point out, the most important differences between process-product and interpretive research on teaching are substantive rather than methodological. Shulman summarizes these differences as falling into five areas. First, interpretive researchers pose questions not in a search for explanatory laws, but in a search for meaning. Geertz contrasts the positive (e.g., process-product research) and interpretive traditions this way:

> The concept of culture . . . is essentially a semiotic one. Believing, with Max Weber, that man is an animal suspended in webs of significance he himself has spun, I take culture to be those webs, and the analysis of it to be therefore not an experimental science in search of law but an interpretive one in search of meaning. It is explication I am after, construing social expressions on their surface enigmatical. (1973, p. 5)

Geertz continues by describing what ethnographers do and adds that, "cultural analysis is (or should be) guessing at meanings, assessing the guesses, and drawing explanatory conclusions from better guesses, not discovering the Continent of Meaning and mapping out its bodiless landscape" (p. 20).

A second difference can be found in the conception of causality. Process-product research places the teacher at the center of the classroom and treats him or her as the primary data source. Within the interpretive tradition, the matter of causal direction itself is problematic. This is reflected in the central assumptions of this research as noted by Hamilton above. The goal is to understand the nature of an interactive teaching/learning process from the participants' viewpoints.

Thirdly, perspectives differ on the concept of effectiveness. Process-product researchers' conception of effectiveness is decontextualized; that is, criteria of effectiveness lie outside the immediate setting being observed, relying upon measures of achievement by end-of-year standardized tests. Interpretive researchers tend to search for criteria of effectiveness within the situation being studied (see Erickson, 1986), for example, equality of opportunity, indicators of clear communications of meaning between teacher and students, or smoothness of transitions within the classroom.

Although it is not the primary difference between the traditions, methodology is an important one, particularly the unit of analysis used in the various research studies. Process-product researchers typically view the classroom as "reducible to discrete events and behaviors which can be noted, counted, and aggregated for purposes of generalizations across settings and individuals" (Shulman, 1986, p. 20). Interpretive researchers view the classroom and the teaching/learning process holistically. Classrooms are seen as socially and culturally organized environments residing within a broader community in which individual participants contribute to the organization and definition of meanings. Personal meanings are the focal point for inquiry. The concern is for the significance and meanings of the events to the actors themselves, collectively and individually.

Lastly, the logic of interpretive research is from the concrete to the universal, with an emphasis on the construction of detailed cases and analysis of commonalities across detailed particularizations through which generalizations are sought. This differs from the method of the inductive positivists in that interpretive researchers do not sample instances or elements across a wide range of concrete particulars as a basis for inferring universals. As Erickson (1986) notes, the central questions of interpretive research concern issues that are neither obvious nor trivial. They concern issues of human choice and meaning: (a) making the familiar strange, the commonplace problematic; (b) constructing specific understandings through documentation of concrete details; (c) discovering the "local meanings" events have; (d) developing comparative understanding of different social settings; and (e) addressing the need for comparative understanding beyond the immediate circumstances of the local setting.

TEACHER PERSONAL THEORIZING

Despite the great differences between the two dominant paradigms in research on teaching, at least one similarity is important to analyze as we attempt to develop a research program that rises above the constraints of an old dualism. The most recent incarnations of teacher effectiveness research have been heavily influenced by cognitive science research, to which earlier process-product research was immune. With the move away from a strictly behaviorist conception of teaching, teacher effectiveness researchers started to take the mediation of teaching seriously.[2]

The claim has been made that cognitive science and the interpretive tradition of research, particularly school ethnography, are similar in that both "ascribe substantial cognitive and/or social organization to the participants in their studies, and assume that prior knowledge, experience, or attitude frames the new encounters and their interpretation" (Shulman, 1986, p. 22). Despite these similarities, however, research on social and cognitive mediation of teaching has been conducted by two separate communities of researchers.[3]

Newer research, labeled as investigations of teacher cognition and decision making or teachers' thought processes, include two very distinct approaches to research on teaching. The first, cognitive process research, is a direct descendent of psychologically based process-product approaches, and the second, research on teachers' practical knowledge and theories, has roots in curriculum research and teacher education.

Studies taking the cognitive processes orientation have tended to fall into one of three areas: (a) studies of teacher planning (e.g., Yinger, 1979); (b) studies of interactive thought (e.g., Peterson & Clark, 1978); and (c) studies of teacher judgments and decision making (Shavelson, 1976). Each of these genres of research examines a different element of the teaching task in isolation from others and has been heavily influenced by psychological research models, which Shulman cautions "may have driven this program of research into a dead end" (1986, p. 24).

Research on teachers' practical knowledge and theories focuses on social mediation and the influence of social and institutional contexts of teaching. The theoretical framework for this research was elaborated in the work of John Dewey, particularly his concept of experience.

Curriculum as Experience

The notion of curriculum as something experienced in situations is grounded in Dewey's theory of experience (see Connelly & Clandinin, 1988; Ross, in this volume). Experience, from a Deweyan perspective, is much more than passively registering or beholding a phenomenon. Experience for him meant a process "situated in a natural environment, mediated by a socially shared symbolic system, actively exploring and responding to the ambiguities of the world by seeking to render the most problematic of them determinant" (Alexander, 1987, p. xiii).

Dewey's concept of experience emphasizes: (a) the interplay between objective conditions and organic energies; (b) deliberate alteration of the environment by inquirers, leading to new knowledge (e.g., the scientific notion of experiment); and (c) the Peircean notion of meaning, in which our conceptions are analyzed and transformed in terms of the consequences of our actions (Scheffler, 1974).

> In [Dewey's] view, the essential ingredient in acquiring knowledge is the perception of relations, especially the relations between our actions and their empirical consequences. As we gain this type of perception, both our conduct and the environment grow in meaning. To achieve a grasp of relations, we require experience and the ability to store what is learned from experience. Experience . . . involves deliberate interaction with environmental conditions, the consequences of which are critically noted and fed back into the control of future conduct. Such interaction is the mark of scientific thinking . . . but it may be generalized to embrace all varieties of intelligent thinking. Intelligent thinking is, moreover, not a thing apart from the moral life. (Scheffler, 1974, p. 197)

Curriculum as experience has a dynamic quality, focusing on the interactions of the student, teacher, and subject matter (Dewey, 1902). Dewey argued that the child's experience is partial and fragmentary, but not different in kind from that of the human race, which culminated in creating fields of knowledge and disciplined inquiry. He argued that subject matter as contained in textbooks was the logically organized end product of inquiry and as such was important. However, he noted that insisting that students merely recite this body of knowledge is cheating the students of insights and understandings of the process of inquiry that went before. The basic concern in his approach to education was how to relate idea and action toward the end of enriching experience. This meant creating school experiences that would help children grow intellectually, ethically, emotionally, and aesthetically.

In *How We Think* (1933) and the essay "The Relation of Theory to Practice in Education" (1904), we find Dewey's image of the teacher and his or her role in the creation of school experiences. He argued that teachers must be students of both subject matter and "mind activity" if they are to foster student growth. He argued that "a healthy [teaching] profession requires teachers who have learned to apply the habits of critical thought to their work. To do this, they must have a full knowledge of their subject matter, and observe and reflect in terms of psychological and philosophical concepts" (Wirth, 1989, p. 56). Teacher education then should set the stage for professional growth and development over the long term instead of focusing on immediate skill proficiency. Teachers gain the necessary knowledge, attitudes, and skills that allow them to continue learning about teaching and curriculum through personal professional experiences. For Dewey, these personal professional experiences included a role in research and theorizing. Dewey took seriously the injunction that teachers should be engaged in genuine intellectual activity and sought ways to involve them in research investigations.[4]

Dewey's (1900) notion of the classroom laboratory placed the teacher squarely in the center of efforts to understand educational practice and develop educational theory. He sought to join the "objective science" of psychology with the subjective consciousness of the practitioner through a "linking science" or philosophy of education.

> It is the participation by the practical man [sic] in the theory, through the agency of the linking science, that determines at once the effectiveness of work done, and the moral freedom and personal development of the one engaged in it. It is because the physician no longer follows rules, which, however rational in themselves, are yet arbitrary to him (because grounded in principles that he does not understand), that his work is becoming liberal, attaining the dignity of a profession, instead of remain-

ing a mixture of *empiricism and quackery* . . . Shall we seek analogy with the teacher's calling in the workingmen [sic] in the mill, or in the scientific physician? (Dewey, 1900/1976, pp. 136-137, emphasis in original)

The relatively recent growth of the curriculum-as-experience perspective can be attributed to the influence of Joseph Schwab. Parker (1987) notes that Schwab's (1969, 1971, 1973) "practical papers"

turned the attention of some in curriculum away from the field's traditional regard for scientific management and generalized implementation to the project of comprehending phronesis. Schwab thus heralded the old notion that today remains oddly iconoclastic: Teachers are reflective practitioners, their practice is an art, and their curriculum agency is necessarily eclectic and context-bound. (p. 11)

Work by curriculum scholars such as Reid and Walker (Reid, 1978; Walker, 1971, 1990; Reid & Walker, 1975) built on Schwab's notions of the curriculum commonplaces and deliberation and did much to further the notion of curriculum as a practical endeavor. Curriculum problems were defined as practical problems (as opposed to the Aristotelian notion of the theoretical). That is, practical problems arise when an individual or group identifies conditions that it wants to change. A practical problem can only be resolved by an action or a decision to undertake actions designed to eliminate the problematic conditions.

Research on Curriculum and Teaching

Much curriculum research has turned away from positivistic notions of theory making (nomothetic, decontextualized, universal) and become more concerned with ways in which teachers develop practical theories to address the problems they encounter in classrooms and schools. Conceptions of human nature and social scientific explanation have direct implications for the purposes, methodology, and use of findings from social and educational research (Howe, 1990). Examining these conceptions can help us understand the differences between various research programs and can further explicate the position of teacher personal theorizing within them.

The positivist theory of social scientific explanation, which is exemplified by process-product research, "entails discovering mechanistic causal regularities; its conception of human nature entails unthinking Norway rats who are (exclusively) subject to such causes" (Howe, 1990, p. 12). In concert with these tenets, nomothetic research claims to be value neutral regarding moral and political issues, and its ultimate goal becomes technical control (Fay, 1975).

Positivistic technical control is especially vulnerable with respect to the bifurcation between means and ends. Howe (and others) argue that positivistic social research cannot sustain its claimed value neutrality with respect to either means or ends. "Wittingly or unwittingly, positivistic technical control promotes certain values" (p. 13). Thirdly, Howe charges that the rigid means-ends bifurcation is irremediably nondemocratic. "In virtue of (somehow) settling on ends and then relegating the investigation of possible means to these ends to (expert) social researchers, it implicitly dismisses the value of participation in deliberation on the part of those who are affected" (p. 13).

By embracing an intentionalist conception of social scientific explanation and an extreme activist conception of human nature, interpretivism attempts to uncover the beliefs and customs that are the foundations for human behavior, that make it possible for individuals to understand themselves and one another. This, in turn, makes more meaningful and effective participation in deliberation possible. "Respect for individuals as having both a moral claim to and the disposition to have a say in the conduct of social life entails that the findings of social research should be used to facilitate this attempt to work out the details of social life" (Howe, 1990, p. 14).

The interpretivist's exclusive focus on the "insider's" perspective presents problems, just as does the positivist's lack of attention to this perspective. Fay (1975) points out that interpretivism fails to take into account the structural features and causes of social practices and the norms that actors unwittingly internalize and employ in communication and action.[5] The most problematic limitation of interpretivism is its inherently conservative orientation. By limiting itself to the insider's perspective, it commits the researcher to a form of relativism that provides little or no space for external criticism of the social order or educational practice. As Howe notes, "This places the researcher in the position of being a mere data gatherer who then operates as little more than a functionary, withholding, or revising in light of the insider's perspectives, perspectives on the situation that might disagree with those of the insiders" (pp. 15-16).

As an alternative to positivistic technical control and inter-pretivistic facilitation, Howe introduces the "practical social research."

> In virtue of embracing a proper role for technical . . . social sci-entific explanation, critical social research grants to researchers special expertise and knowledge not possessed by lay persons. In virtue of also embracing a proper role for intentionalist expla-nation, as well as an activist conception of human nature, rather than employing this specialized knowledge as a means of technical control, however, practical social research subjects it to critical scrutiny with respect to its accuracy and its implica-tions for social life—both on the part of other social researchers and on the part of lay interlocutors. Practical social research is thus more akin to interpretivism than it is to positivism. Like the interpretivist link between theory and practice, practical social research is inherently participatory and must be ulti-mately grounded in terms of the insider's perspective. The key difference is that practical social research consists in challeng-ing lay interlocutors with (expert) social research findings rather than merely facilitating mutual understanding of the rule of the game. (p. 16)

This type of educational research gives attention to both external and internal value constraints on research practice and requires a collaborative model of that practice. Research on teacher personal theorizing as reported in the chapters that fol-low reflects the conception of human nature and social scientific explanation characteristic of practical educational research. Teaching and curriculum making are viewed as complex, con-text-bound professional tasks. Teachers must select and organize multiple factors in ways that provide educative experiences for particular groups of students in particular settings. Sanders and McCutcheon have characterized teaching as

> practical work carried out in a socially constructed, complex and institutionalized world of schooling. That world shapes action and gives context to its meaning. Educational practices are the media of professional action in that world, and they involve more than simply behavior. Professional practices are manifest in behavior, of course, but they entail thoughts, inter-pretations, choices, values, and commitments as well. (1986, pp. 50-51)

Sanders and McCutcheon continue by noting that teaching "is intentional in that it involves acting in certain ways in order to produce or evoke desired consequences or to create particular conditions" (p. 51). Effective teaching practice is based upon experiential knowledge. Teachers learn to make curriculum decisions primarily through direct experience as both students and teachers. "This knowledge is personal and particular to the actual situation, and much of it is tacit: the teacher knows how to do things he or she cannot explain" (House, Lapan, & Mathison, 1989, p. 58). This knowledge shapes what teachers do as professionals in classrooms and schools, and as a result any strategy for improving curriculum and teaching must work through this basic fact.

Practical knowledge and personal inference structures are required to perform professional tasks. The professional knowledge of teachers is theoretical knowledge, or what has been termed "practical theories of teaching."

> Practical theories of teaching are the conceptual structures and visions that provide teachers with reasons for acting as they do, and for choosing the teaching activities and curriculum materials they choose in order to be effective. They are principles or propositions that undergird and guide teachers' appreciations, decisions, and actions. (Sanders & McCutcheon, 1986, pp. 54-55)

Such theories are important to the success of teaching because educational problems are practical problems (Reid, 1978). Practical problems are defined by discrepancies between a *practitioner's* theory and practice, not as gaps between formal educational theory and teacher behaviors.

> All practices, like all observations, have "theory" embedded in them and this is just as true for the practice of "theoretical" pursuits as it is for those of "practical" pursuits like teaching . . . The twin assumptions that all "theory" is non-practical and all "practice" is non-theoretical are, therefore, entirely misguided. Teachers could no more teach without reflecting upon (and hence theorizing about) what they are doing than theorists could produce theories without engaging in the sort of practices distinctive of their activity. "Theories" are not bodies of knowledge that can be generated out of a practical vacuum and teaching is not some kind of robot-like mechanical performance that is devoid of any theoretical reflection. Both are practical undertakings whose guiding theory consists of the reflective consciousness of their respective practitioners. (Carr & Kemmis, 1986, p. 11)

Educational problems are resolved not by discovery of new knowledge, but by formulating and acting upon practical judgment (Carr & Kemmis, 1986). Educational research, then, must be conceived as a practical activity. The central aim must be to improve the practical effectiveness of the theories that teachers employ in conceptualizing their practice. This aim presents problems in that sometimes teachers may not be conscious of the reasons for their actions. This means that research concerned with teachers' personal theorizing must be sensitive to the tacit cultural environment of teaching—the language, manners, standards, and values that unconsciously influence the classroom and school environment and the ways in which teachers respond to it (see chapters by Pape and Kleinsasser in this volume). As Dewey asserted, the primary factor in education is the culture itself, and culture is not a self-conscious or self-critical medium.

> We rarely recognize the extent in which our conscious estimates of what is worthwhile and what is not are due to standards of which we are not conscious at all. But in general it may be said that the things which we take for granted without inquiry or reflection are just the things which determine our conscious thinking and decide our conclusions. And these habitudes which lie below the level of reflection are just those which have been formed in the constant give and take of relationship with others. (Dewey, 1916, p. 18)

As described in the chapters by Cornett and Associates and McCutcheon, the key is to develop within teachers and their research collaborators critical self-reflection, reevaluation, and explorations of both teachers' practical theories and the actions which they guide. Chapters in this volume by Daresh as well as by Skrtic and Ware address these same issues as they apply to school administrators and other stakeholders in the curriculum-making process. In this effort, the research program illustrated in the chapters that follow reflects a fundamental characteristic of practical social research as described by Howe. The practical end of such research is the creation of a creative-critical culture of teachers, "not as an immediate, isolated base occurrence, as an indefinitely fleeting 'now,' but as the dynamically insistent occasion for establishing continuity or growth of meaning" (Alexander, 1987, p. 269).

This requires that teaching and curriculum making be considered as problematic situations. As Dewey offered,

> In accord with the interest and occupations of the group, certain things become objects of high esteem; others of aversion . . . The way our group or class does things tends to determine the proper objects of attention, and thus to prescribe the directions and limits of observation and memory . . . It seems almost incredible to us, for example, that things which we know very well could have escaped recognition in past ages. We incline to account for it by attributing congenital stupidity to our forerunners and by assuming superior native intelligence on our own part. But the explanation is that their modes of life did not call for attention to such facts, but held their minds riveted to other things. Just as the senses require sensible objects to stimulate them, so our powers of observation, recollection, and imagination do not work spontaneously, but are set in motion by the demands set up by current social occupations . . . What conscious, deliberate teaching can do is at most to free the capacities thus formed for fuller exercise, to purge them of some of their grossness, and to furnish objects which make their activity more productive of meaning. (1916, p. 17)

Research on teacher personal theorizing gives attention to both internal and external value constraints, operates on a collaborative research model, and consists of making problematic the situation under investigation. The focus of such research is not concentrated on teacher behaviors or insider perspectives in isolation. The goal is to understand teaching and curriculum making as universes of activity influenced by personal experiences and interactions among individuals and contexts. As Dewey points out,

> Society not only continues to exist by transmission, by communication, but it may fairly be said to exist in transmission and communication. There is more than a verbal tie between the words common, community, and communication. Men [sic] live in a community in virtue of the things which they have in common; and communication is the way in which they come to possess things in common. What they must have in common in order to form a community or society are aims, beliefs, aspirations, knowledge—a common understanding—like-mindedness as the sociologists say . . . The communication which insures participation in a common understanding is one which secures similar emotional and intellectual dispositions—like ways of responding to expectations and requirements. (1916, p. 4)

Ultimately, research on teacher personal theorizing attempts to develop these common understandings between researchers and practitioners. As noted above, the success of such an endeavor rests upon how ideas are communicated. "Genuine communication is only achieved through creative transformation of experience which involves the combination of a rich cultural matrix, the critical use of intelligence, and the active struggle to establish continuity or growth" (Alexander, 1987, p. 274). Genuine communication about the nature of the teaching enterprise, then, is the goal of this research program and of this book.

2

LYNDA STONE

Philosophy, Meaning Constructs, and Teacher Theorizing

Teaching, as all know who consider it thoughtfully, is both prac- tical and theoretical work, with much of its theorizing being directly practical and thus "personal." The subject of this book is the kinds of "theorizing" that teachers do daily and the forms that these take when reflected upon by the teachers themselves and by their researchers. One way to consider teacher theorizing is in terms of meaning. Teachers construct specific meanings about teaching when, for instance, they describe their roles through metaphors, when they become "entertainers" or "social directors" (Tobin and Ulerick LaMaster, this volume). They also construct meanings about teaching when as curriculum agents they mediate with and through the social structures, practices, and tools of their trade. As Parker and McDaniel (this volume) propose, they tackle daily mediations as "bricoleurs," with prac- tical intelligence that is often both improvisational and efficient. The point of the present chapter is to offer philosophic insight into another kind of meaning about teaching, into the founda- tional meanings that teachers hold that implicitly influence their practical, personal theorizations. This kind of meaning, herein called *meaning constructs*, gets at the beliefs that underpin metaphors or bricoleuric practice. Moreover, as will be explored, forms of meaning underpin even the meaning that teachers make of the various theoretical contexts of the larger education insti- tution, for instance, of the historically dominant "technization of teaching" (Beyer, this volume).

INTRODUCTION

At the outset, it is important to highlight the differences between this chapter and others in the volume and to offer a rationale for its importance to the project of teacher personal theorizing. First, it is written in the voice of a philosopher and out of an emerging social-philosophical tradition in educational theory, a tradition that can offer much insight into teaching practice. The present study is nonempirical, and in form and spirit closest to the significant reflections from Landon Beyer and William Schubert that end the book. Perhaps it is best understood as stepping back from and beneath other kinds of educational theorizing: metatheorizing (Beyer, this volume), research reviews (Ross, this volume), studies of practice reported by researchers (Thornton, this volume), teachers' reports of practice (Chase, Miller, Schrock et al., reported by Cornett, this volume), and individual reflections (Schubert, this volume). Second, it is no less personal than the other chapters—a philosopher's work is "personal theorizing"—but is in a voice that reads differently than the voice of more experientially oriented researchers. It is a voice that develops explanations based both on the thinking of one researcher and on what others of like mind have had to say. This voice is reflected through conceptions and categories that are developed and exemplified.

One other point establishes the importance of this chapter; this is its overall utility for researchers on teaching, for teacher educators, and for teaching practitioners. This utility is established from the following set of premises.

1. As Charles Taylor (1985b) writes, "We are in a sense surrounded by meaning: in the words we exchange, in all the signs we deploy . . . [indeed] in the very shape of the man-made (sic) environment . . . [we] live in" (p. 248).
2. For us, "meaning," as that which is exchanged, expressed, symbolized, and theorized, has particularity in terms of historicized culture.
3. We are enculturated into and personally reformulate worldviews of which, at any one time, diverse manifestations are present and possible (Van Manen, 1977).
4. One kind of worldview (for introductory purposes) is encapsulated in the concept of *meaning construct*, a synthetic shorthand image for the general, dynamic, complex sense making we all undertake.
5. Our own personal constructs, were we to explore them, make sense of the broad time and culture in which we live. Metaphysically they tell us how we take and make the world (Goodman, 1978) and what, for example, we

mean by reality, personhood, truth, beauty, goodness, power, and change.

6. For us, meaning constructs are often taken for granted. They are taken for granted because they underpin the everyday lives we lead, including specific beliefs, ideologies, practices, and institutions.

7. Given their role as foundational, ideational structures, meaning constructs allow us to understand that our lives are not neutral: there are no beliefs or institutions that exist independent of meaning and these founding constructs.

8. Thus, education and teaching, as well as research and personal theorizing, are based in enculturated forms of meaning that can be understood through meaning constructs.

9. Thus, particular practices can be understood through their connection to meaning constructs and through specific exploration of the "web of beliefs" (Quine & Ulian, 1970) in which they are embedded.

10. Thus, changing teaching practices, already tied to notions of changing teachers' beliefs (Fenstermacher, 1986) can be tied to changing—that is to interrogating and reformulating—teachers' meaning constructs.

A final point. At the very least, an understanding of these constructs and of the foundational worldviews that underpin teaching practice seems worthwhile. In the view of this author, endemic to the project of teacher personal theorizing (and to its siblings, the movement in reflective teaching and other reform efforts) are notions of inquiry, questioning, and speculation about teaching beliefs and about the many kinds (or levels) of beliefs that underpin daily practical activity.

PHILOSOPHICAL SITUATING

In this section a first step is taken toward understanding and applying the notion of meaning constructs to reflections about teaching. As indicated, meaning constructs are psychologized, often implicit, belief configurations about foundational aspects of the world. As any single person's "stance toward the world," they have commonsense manifestations. However, for general explanatory purposes, they are best explicated in the language and theoretical situating of philosophy.

An initial and important task is to distinguish philosophical situating from other forms of theoretical contextualizing. One of the latter kinds is "research connecting," regularly done in researcher descriptions of teacher personal theorizing. For instance, Thornton (this volume) constructs meaning out of his investigation by connecting it to a classic study of social studies, the NSF-sponsored work by Shaver, Davis, and Helburn (1980). Similarly, a process of contextualizing is done more briefly by citation, such as that of Tobin and Jakubowski (this volume) of a recent national survey in science and mathematics education (Weiss, 1987). Closer to philosophical situating is another kind of contextualizing or framing, termed "conceptual connecting." This is undertaken either through the mention of a theorist's name and/or a central concept from his or her theory. This is seen in Parker and McDaniel's use (this volume) of Claude Levi-Strauss's term *bricolage*. Wayne Ross's use of the Deweyan concept of experiences is an even more detailed conceptual connection. In his chapter, direct evidence from Dewey supports an analysis of the essentials for "reflective thought" in genuine interest and a social framework. Moreover, in present teacher reform efforts, such as those to develop reflection and personal theorizing, these and other forms of theoretical contextualizing are regularly employed by researchers with their collaborating teachers (Cornett et al., this volume).

As already indicated, philosophical situating is something else. Its purpose is to set out a more general intellectual frame by which to construct aspects of the meanings of research and practice, either in specific studies or in a larger "metatheoretical" sense. Beyer begins the latter undertaking in his commentary on the positivistic emphasis in educational theorizing. His claim, supported by this author, is that a positivist situating results in a false "objectivity," which then provides "precious little opportunity for teacher theorizing." Beyer is helpful also in naming the various contexts—social, political, economic, and ideological in addition to personal—within which this objectivity operates. Philosophical situating, importantly, helps explain the various possible meanings of these general contexts and of their particular "playing out."

A significant condition of intellectual change (Rorty, 1979, 1982b; Bernstein, 1986) situates current theorizing about teaching. Terms of change are variously described, such as from positivism to postpostivism, from epistemological to postepistemological, and from modernist to postmodernist. Philosopher Richard Bernstein (1983) poses this changing condition as a debate between the forces of objectivism and relativism. All too simply put, the first is a search for a universal, transhistorical, and transcultural base from which to make sense (meaning) of the world but which has heretofore escaped "representation." The second is a response that denies that such representation is possible and calls for pluralistic, culture-specific, and time-specific meanings. Taken more psychologically, these seem, on the one hand, to be a longing for a permanent metaphysical anchor as a life foundation and, on the other hand, to be the giving up of such a need, which is then replaced with reliance on a daily "working through" of life (Stone, 1989, p. 190).

The changing situation of *positivism/postpositivism* signals the dominant interest in science in the twentieth century. This reliance on science, reduced often to a scientism, is familiar to educationists. Positivism's aim was to find certain foundational solutions to "problems arising out of the activity and results of the natural sciences" (Rorty, 1982b, p. 211) using methods that were both empirical and nonempirical. One result was the discrediting of other forms of inquiry in which results could not be either logically derived or mathematically proven (with or without observational testing). This then resulted in a change in philosophy itself, at least for Anglo-Americans. No longer were philosophers like Dewey, Alfred North Whitehead, or the German idealists read. No longer, either, was philosophy thought to be a human "science." Instead its models were natural science, logic, and mathematics.

One important and nagging question for positivists was the relationship of the emerging social sciences to the natural sciences. In an aspect of the "debate" that still continues, one answer in the first decades of this century was to posit a theory of "unified science." In it, an intellectual hierarchy was developed with physics at the top and "sciences" like anthropology far below. A widely held belief was that the social sciences were immature natural sciences in earlier phases of growth (Bernstein, 1983, p. 35). The theory of unified science, with its positivist orientation, greatly influenced educational research and practice, particularly in the development of psychology as a behavioral science akin to those "natural sciences," and in its subsequent hegemonic control as the discipline of inquiry—and thus of meaning making—in education (see Beyer, this volume).

The change toward postpositivism has taken several routes, all of which infuse more subjectivity into conceptions and processes of investigation. There is talk of "rhetorics" across all natural and social disciplines and even of the social sciences and humanities as paradigmatic. Mirroring this larger intellectual shifting is the emergence of the "arts of education," and especially of qualitative research. What has also emerged is the kind of attention to teacher thinking central to this volume. An example is the work of Cornett and colleagues, who were socialized as teachers to believe that research was conducted by "experts who were removed from the classroom," but who have come to believe that they can "critically and effectively examine [their] own [teaching] practice," and who believe further that such examinations are central tasks of their professional lives.

Also influencing educational thought is the changing conception of *epistemological/postepistemological* aims in philosophy. Here questions of science were initially tied into questions of knowledge. Taylor (1988) identifies the epistemological aim as the search to clarify "what made knowledge claims valid, and what ultimate degree of validity . . . [to lay] claim to" (p. 464). Two elements which have been and still are central to this subdebate are belief and truth.

Belief has been defined throughout Western intellectual history as some form of internal "representation" of external reality. Rorty (1979) explains that the cultural metaphor of the mind's eye developed, seeking evidence of and justification for ideas, perceptions, images, and the like. In classical theory, belief shared an identity with a form or idea of the external world. In the theory of the Scholastics, form was a sign from God. In the era of modernist science, two formulations of belief emerged. The first was empiricist, in which impressions were imposed upon the glassy essence of the internal mind. The second was nonempiricist or rationalist, in which mind reflected upon itself as nature's mirror in realizing images about which there was no question.

Truth related to belief as the objective ideal, the basic normative frame. Until relatively recently, the philosophical task was to "believe more truths . . . by knowing most about Truth" (Rorty, 1982a, p. xv), a task augmented by the accumulation of truths within philosophy and from other disciplines. Historically, truth also has had several formulations, classically as form, scholastically as God's word, scientifically as tested and proven observations. A significant late-epistemological change has been the reconceptualization of truth as "propositions." At first, their proof from tests was desired; very recently they have come to stand alone. As Taylor (1985a) explains, this has placed language at the center of intellectual attention, not only in using it for epistemological purposes in natural and social inquiry but also in understanding its essential functions and forms.

In the postepistemological change, language which has replaced knowledge in discussions of speech acts and truth-conditional propositions is itself open to new scrutiny, most significantly in projects of poststructuralism and deconstructionism. Giving up language essences means giving up epistemology. This is relinquishing belief in "a priori knowledge and self-evident givenness, in necessity and certainty, in totality and ultimate foundations" (McCarthy, 1988, p. 7). Moreover, the postepistemological move means leaving behind as intellectual deadwood the debate between objectivism and relativism. In educational scholarship, as in many of the chapters of this volume, this change is evident, although theorists such as Schubert and Ross harken back to Dewey for inspiration rather than to the neopositivists or poststructuralists. One particular example comes in Schubert's attention to teacher lore and more precisely in his call for its continual revisiting. This uncertain dynamism rather than dogmatic stasis characterizes postepistemological situating.

Language takes one other "new" form in the broad philosophical shift involving *Modernism/postmodernism*. This concerns man's role as a language animal and his search for intersubjective agreement and its resultant societal consensus. Jean-Francois Lyotard (1988) proposes that the desire for agreement has historically taken several forms as "grand narratives." The ancient proposal is for the "meeting" of rational minds; others include the hermeneutics of meaning (an accepted textual interpretation), the creation of wealth (accepted structures of liberal democracies). All have functioned and continue to function as grand tales told as "truths."

Postmodern situating recognizes the limitations of these narratives. There are many theoretical discussions, one of which comes from Lyotard in a call for localized accounts rather than larger cultural metaphors. This results, as Taylor (1988) and Rorty (1989b) point out, in the construction of a new person (read "new teacher," as empowered *reflecting practitioner*[1]). Gone,

15', 493

in Bernstein's (1983) terms, is the man suffering from Cartesian anxiety who searches for knowledge that he cannot know and a connection to others than he cannot have. Replacing him is someone who no longer searches, who lives within an ambiguous postmodern holism that arises naturally out of culture-specific, sociolinguistic activity. This person recognizes that the latter is all there is.

DEFINING MEANING CONSTRUCTS

The central point of philosophical situating bears repetition and emphasis: no longer is any single, essential, totalizing meaning making possible about life and the world in general or about educational research and practice. In their own consideration and assumption of postures of personal theorizing and reflection, many educationists have perhaps intuitively (and for some time) known about postmodern ambiguity and contingency (see Stone, 1990). Part of this ambiguity is that of language itself (Cherryholmes, 1988), as well as of all other symbol systems. Also related to this is the move away from the need for meaning agreement and singularity. The "meaning of life" is now, at the least, "meanings."

This section defines *meaning constructs*. As premised initially, they are shorthand formulations for basic sense making in the world. They are often taken for granted even as they underpin other symbolizing contexts and concepts in educational life that are also taken for granted. Here is a working definition: Meaning constructs are founding, ideational, multiple, and fluid structures that when explicated help to make sense of more specific beliefs, ideologies, theories, practices, and institutions. Again, one needs to differentiate this concept from similar concepts. The first of these is *cultural worldview*, and the second is *natural mode of knowing*.[2]

Although meaning constructs are kinds of worldviews, it is perhaps best to understand them as undergirding and working across cultural worldviews. The latter are "ways of seeing," of feeling, thinking, and acting in the world, that are tied to the historical, sociopolitical experience of a group of people who identify themselves in a common way. Young Pai (1990) explains that "people who live in . . . [different cultures] see the world differently." This difference is based on two dimensions; the first is culture, the "conception of what reality is like and how it works," and the second is history of the culture, the "certain experiences that enabled a group of people to successfully solve the problems of daily living" (p. 23). These two interact to such a degree that not only are beliefs and social practices differentiated, but so is language, and importantly, so is basic perception (for example, Chinese tonals and Eskimo snows).

In addition to underpinning specific cultural forms of meaning, meaning constructs are related to but not identical with general language structures. These are the forms that language takes to express "enculturated" lives. Jerome Bruner (1985) describes two natural modes of thought or knowing, one paradigmatic and the other narrative. The first is that related to logic and science and is "based upon categorization or conceptualization and the operations by which categories are established, instantiated, idealized and related one to the other to form a system" (p. 98). The second is that related to stories, drama, and history. It is based upon the construction of what Bruner calls "two landscapes." One is "the landscape of action, where the constituents are . . . agent, intention . . . situation, instrument." The other is consciousness, "what those involved in action know, think or feel" (p. 99). Although there will be some subsequent temptation to equate these two modes of thought and the first two meaning constructs, this equation is inappropriate. Meaning constructs are "useful vocabularies" (Rorty, 1989a) that have historically endured and evolved. But however enduring, they are not meant herein as natural kinds corresponding to universal language capacities. That they do not correspond is evidenced by the appearance of the second two constructs.

The foregoing implies that the term *meaning construct* is a new term, which it is. However, it is developed from other usages and has some support in recent philosophic writings. *Meaning* is the word commonly associated with the narrative form of thought that Bruner writes about, with its long tradition in the humanities and especially literature. It is also principally associated with traditional hermeneutics (the study of text) and, as well, with other sociohistorical inquiry of the continental tradition. Interpretive researchers in education often search for meaning. The present usage is more general, expressed by Taylor (1985a) in this way: "How is it that . . . [talk, music, buildings, objects] say something? What is it that we see in things when we understand them as signs . . . [and] which when we do not we fail to apprehend as such? . . . Here . . . [is] the significance . . . [that] things have for us in virtue of our goals, aspirations, purposes"

(p. 218). *Meaning*, with its roots in semiotics, is thus general signification. Tied to *meaning* is *construct*, a term taken from the work of educational psychologists Lee Cronbach and Paul Meehl (1955). It is a postulated attribute of persons that is a construal of experience into potentially testable categories (Cherryholmes, 1988, p. 99). These "potentially testable" categories, when added to the first term, are, in sum, about foundational kinds of signification. As stated previously, they underpin other forms of meaning making, such as ideologies, practices, and institutions (the last-mentioned categories being more closely tied to cultures and to specific social structures such as classes).

From philosophic and other sources, four related functions of meaning constructs are recognized. As posed at the chapter's outset, the first is a fundamental psychological orientation taken about reality, mind and body, beauty, justice and other cultural norms, and about other persons. An example is the person who clings to the belief that he or she "knows" only what he or she sees. The second function is (at least part of) the social locus (i.e., structures) from which persons describe themselves and are described. Here *meaning construct* unites and underpins the categories of race, class, gender, and so on. Sandra Harding (1986) helps us understand this function with her "locating" categories of individual identity, division of labor, and symbolic totemism, the last-mentioned being more generalized meanings arising specifically out of the other two. The third function is the ideological stance of persons—how they consider questions of power and change—as they relate to the first two functions. Michael Apple (1979) and others are helpful here in their discussions of hegemony as the dominant orientation toward power and change that clearly is more founding than any one cultural worldview. The fourth is language competence. Again Taylor (1985b) assists in describing four subfunctions: language that articulates and brings into focus, that defines public space and common vantage point, that helps name human concerns, and that identifies and clarifies moral standards applied to action. Thus, the last function summarizes the other three in the public utterances of persons as they operate from meaning constructs.

CONSTRUCT EXEMPLIFICATIONS

A third step in this chapter is significant: the naming, describing, and illustrating of four meaning constructs. If not emphasized sufficiently previously, the initial task is to understand that *meaning construct* is a human construction that attempts to encapsulate other socially constructed meanings of the world. In the past and future history of human thought and action, untold numbers of others are possible.[3] In what follows, each is named for the *kind of person* the construct represents: the spectator, the storyteller, the conversationalist, and the visionary. In addition to the descriptive value of the title, various synonyms are used.

Meaning of the Spectator

"Spectatorial meaning" is named in honor of John Dewey (1929/1960), who challenged the traditional and dominant view of knowledge, the spectator theory. This kind of meaning is well written about by Rorty, Taylor, Bernstein, and others as enduring across the millennia. Its central idea is of a mental image corresponding to reality, of internal mind attempting to capture external materiality. The spectator's meaning involves a world in some sense ordered; independence of the world from the perceiving subject; the seeking of true representations, designations, and depictions of the world; and the need to control order. In various philosophical formulations, the aim is for control called knowledge.

The meaning of the spectator is most easily located in teacher personal theorizing that seeks truth, universal autonomous agency, and direct correspondences, like cause and effect. It relies on absolute, singular, or unified premises, most often about "world taking" rather than "world making," as discovering a world already out there. Reflective teacher reformer Anna Richert (1987a, 1987b) provides an example of the teacher candidate as spectator in the following journal entry: "I am constantly thinking about how to reach kids . . . how to create a situation where the kids are doing some *real* (emphasis added) learning and thinking" (1987a, p. 9). Likewise, Thornton's (this volume) teacher, Mrs. Nelson, teaches the hidden value of spectator meaning in her questioning of fourth-grade students on their geographic "facts." Researcher Thornton also "slips" into spectator language, even when his meaning foundations may be otherwise, when he seeks "accurate representations" of teacher decision making. One other example extends the "influence" of spectator meaning. It is from Audrey Kleinsasser (this volume), who incorporates spectatorial meaning in her research design in deriving inductive, analytic generalizations of intern practice that are "then subjected to pattern matching" across eight case studies. These last two examples make the important point that representational language dominates Western culture; it is a language that seeks to get *right* statements of images of the world. Plurality and particularity are still representational if they are reductive of complex situations; current quantitative and many qualitative research processes are built on premises of spectator meaning.[4]

Meaning of the Storyteller

"Manifestive meaning," Taylor (1985b) claims, has a long history that pulls in the opposite metaphysical direction from spectatorism. Here artistic subjectivity and the mystery and fluidity of symbolic systems are valued. Storyteller meaning involves a given world controlled by the expressor, powerful subjectivity (as opposed to objectivity) with meaning directly available to the senses, and public recognition of gestalts of feeling that make possible new feelings, self-awarenesses, and social relations. The Romantic philosophers, novelists, and poets of the nineteenth century were relatively recent storytellers.

Whereas meaning for the spectator is over and against something, that is, the match of thought to reality, the meaning of the storyteller is "just there." For the storyteller, the world is also given and expression of *it* is attempted. Manifestive meaning has itself been promoted as a teacher education reform in moves away from the science of teaching toward its arts and poetics. Tobin and Jakubowski (this volume) illustrate this in their theorizing about the use of unconscious visual images in describing teaching. They write, "The interview with Diana suggests that she based her teaching on images associated with her favorite teacher . . . the association appears to have been . . . direct, involving re-presented images [she had experienced]." More explicit calls for expressive meaning are found in Connelly and Clandinin's (1988) creation and utilization of particular "narrative tools" in teacher theorizing. Such terms as *rhythm* and *unity in personal curriculum of teaching* are suggestive of the meaning of the storyteller (Connelly & Clandinin, 1985, p. 192).

Subtle comparisons and contrasts are seen between the meanings of spectators and storytellers. Expressive or manifestive meaning (that of the storyteller) is a subtle "representation" of a given world. Much of the current language of "constructivism"[5] seeks a closed explanation or interpretation rather than more open, fluid forms. In addition, one kind of contrast between the two comes in their least thoughtful forms: the spectator can be a naive objectivist who believes in a "reality" that he or she observes; the storyteller can be a naive subjectivist who believes absolutely in a feeling that he or she experiences. One other important comment must be made about these two meaning constructs. Because each has such a long history, they appear in the psyches of those who grow up and live in the West (at least of those with dominant cultural worldviews). It is no wonder that meaning seems naturally like one of the two modern forms.

However, emerging to challenge modernist meaning are two other constructs that are postmodern. They have more sketchy intellectual histories because they are more recent (approximately from the last fifty years). To look at these final two meaning constructs, consider postmodern meanings as antifoundationalist and antiessentialist (see Stone, 1991a). They are broadly contextualized and particularly situational, that is, both socially constructed and historicized. There is nothing of a world "given" in them beyond some simplistic element of a material reality. In neither of the constructs to follow is there the desire for control as knowledge.

Meaning of the Conversationalist

"Conversive meaning" comes closest to that out of the hermeneutic, interpretive tradition of scholars.[6] Its exemplar is ordinary conversation, or Wittgenstein's language games, and its notions of agreement (to match up text and interpretation, to understand precisely) have changed over time. The conversationalist makes meaning with the following ingredients: the world as constructed, acting subjects with language as their medium, norms as the logic of talk, and temporary unity as "civility rather than by common goal" (Rorty, 1979, p. 318). Recent reformulation includes the creation of an agreement, a solidarity, through difference (Rorty, 1989a). Lastly, this meaning denies the reification of meaning of the first two forms.

The meaning of the conversationalist is *potentially present* in educational settings in which, as Wayne Ross (this volume) writes, the concern is for "interaction between individuals and their particular institutional culture or community . . . [and] with developing critical reflective communities of teachers." Modernist actuality rather than postmodern potentiality remains because of the ties to two modern theoretical frameworks. One, as indicated above, is traditional interpretivist, hermeneutic philosophy and empirical research (Parker & McDaniel; Kleinsasser; this volume), and the other is John Dewey's ghost (Grimmett, 1988) and his own brand of pragmatism (Ross; Schubert; this volume). In both, understanding is formed through interactive rather than solitary processes, through interactions with texts (and situations that are "textualized"), and among persons. However, these remain modernist if a reified interpretation is the aim (Eagleton, 1983) or if a reductive consensus is the ideal (Young, 1990).

Conversationalist meanings are emerging in the educational literature. An important exemplar in teacher education is the work of Zeichner and Liston (1987), who work from and adapt a neo-Marxist base. Other examples are found in the action research literature (e.g., Carr & Kemmis, 1986). In this volume, the collaborative writings of Jeffrey Cornett, Sue Chase, Patricia Miller, Debbie Schrock, Betty Bennett, Alan Goins, and Christopher Hammond provide such an example. Conversational meanings "appear" throughout, in such statements as the following: "All of the co-authors . . . have examined, to different degrees and with different emphases, the literature base," "We uncovered *examples* [emphasis added] of teacher theorizing," "it can be a bit unsettling to encounter evidence that leads us to analyze a question," and finally, "We have begun to appreciate the tremendous complexity of our curricular and instructional decision making." A last comment: just as all other meaning forms are fluid in conception (even if conceptions are themselves posed as static), so too is this one. In the postmodern variant, this dynamism is "taken" as natural, and various definitional treatments are available (see Lather, 1989; Brodkey, 1987).

Meaning of the Visionary

"Transformative meaning" is the latest and least culturally developed of all four constructs. As a result it requires a bit more explication than the other three constructs. This is the meaning constructed by a person seeking fundamental social and intellectual change who construes matters that are postpositivist, postepistemological, and postmodern in broad, fluid, dispersive, metaphysical terms. According to Taylor (1988), this is a new kind of person whose identity is formed from an engagement in self-critical reasoning. This identity, moreover, is continually remade in the world of situated particulars. The visionary constructs meaning with these features: a world as fluid and forming; a centrality and a continual dispersion of marginality, difference, particularity, and pluralism; and change as probably and natural.

As indicated, the method of inquiry for the visionary is criticism, but in a form different from that of the conversationalist. Its "foundation" is one of no privileged meanings or meaning makers (none that are a priori, transcendentally, or historically true or right). Its criticism, as Cleo Cherryholmes (1988) writes, is "that which . . . [analysis, interpretation, and even conversation (author's interpretation)] has omitted, suppressed, devalued, silenced, or opposed" (p. 159). Its aim, lastly, is the mere working through of life armed only with the "norms of the day" (Rorty, 1979).

Given both the newness of visionary meaning and its own ever-conditional status, it is logical to find little evidence of it either in the beliefs and lives of teachers or in their teacher education programs and researchers. What one finds instead are glimpses of it, intuitions perhaps—windows of opportunity for radical change. Right away, the term *radical* offends some. It need not, nor should visionary, transformational meaning. In the chapters of this volume, such glimpses are often found in discussions of aims, in appropriations of new concepts in new ways, and in the idealisms of summations. One example is Parker and McDaniel's understanding of the limitations of present teaching structures and their call for improvisational mediation of those structures; another is Ross's description of experience as challenging the taken-for-granted and his own use of the term *transformation*. Still a third is the commitment of Cornett and his colleagues to "continued professional development." A last is found in many places: in the attention to the ethics of teaching and learning and, importantly, in the depth of this attention.[7] Beyer closes his commentary with the statement that "the choice of theoretical lenses . . . [by which to theorize both the personal and social in education] must be governed by an essentially moral consideration of the kind of world to which it can lead for all of us." Here visionary, postmodern meaning is proposed first in the ethical base and then "precisely" in the multiplicity of lenses and worlds and persons that the statement both encompasses and extends.

CONCLUDING REMARKS

Throughout the chapter a distinction has been made between it and the other chapters of the volume. What has been presented is a philosophic discussion of meaning in terms of a new concept, *meaning construct*. This chapter is not a commentary on the other chapters; rather it uses them to illustrate and exemplify the development of the central concept. It serves thus as a kind of introduction and foundation to what follows in the book and to other writings in the present teaching reform movement(s).

Philosophy, and particularly an understanding of the changing condition of intellectual life, has much to offer those concerned with teaching. It allows for the placement of teaching conceptions, research, and practice in a larger theoretical context—one that moves beyond theorizing that is personal and practical. It also allows for conceiving of teacher practice and its research in new ways. These ways can (and perhaps ought to) move from within modernism to postmodernism. But this requires at least an initial warning about using the constructs of this chapter. They are described in general terms and not as models for direct application: they are *not* new philosophical "isms" like *realism* or *idealism* that teacher candidates learn by memorization, match up to beliefs in a foundations course, and soon forget. Rather, they are broad intellectual lenses by which teachers and their researchers can begin to consider the foundational beliefs of their respective and related enterprises. Such beliefs as the naturalness of contraries (Elbow, 1986) and the premise of socially constructed "knowledge" (Stone, 1991b) are potentially useful to educationists who work in an already postmodern world. Such a world is vital in its complexity and conditionality and is the "new" world of teaching. Were it to be reified and reduced, were it to be discounted in a longing for unreachable certainty, much of the meanings of teaching would be lost. In a living through of daily life, the notion of meaning constructs helps in understanding that meaning permeates and gives form to existence. It is, moreover, meaning that is constructed and used just by us, and that carries with it all of human potential.

3

WILLIAM AYERS

Teachers' Stories: Autobiography and Inquiry

Like everyone else, we teachers tell our stories. We tell stories of tragedy and triumph, of humiliation and rebellion, of subversion, heroism, and moral action. Our stories are comical, self-effacing, often petty and occasionally transcendent. Sometimes our stories are fully articulated and public, but more often our stories are uneven and ragged, private jokes and little anecdotes passed hurriedly to one another in the hallway or the teachers' lounge. Our stories are never neutral or value-free. Because they are always embedded in space and time and people, they are necessarily infused with values, forever political, ideological, and social. Our stories occur in cultural contexts, and we not only tell our stories, but in a powerful way our stories tell us. Interrogating our stories, then—questioning and probing our collective and personal myths—is an important pathway into exploring the meaning of teaching.

WHAT THE STORIES TELL

There are so many teachers' voices, so many stories, so many pathways, so many ways to begin. There are autobiographies, but there are also teachers' journals, diaries, and personal documents. There is research focused on teacher thinking and the voices of teachers, but there are also films, TV shows, and popular representations of teachers' lives. One particularly powerful contemporary story, popularized in newspapers, magazines, books, and film, is the story of Jaimie Escalante, the East Los Angeles high school teacher who reversed the fates of his underachieving math students through hard work, sacrifice, and an abiding confidence that inner-city Hispanic youth could learn. On one level Escalante's story is an example of the difference a fine teacher can make in the lives of students. He believes in the abilities and intelligence of these youngsters; he demands excellence and he draws out the strongest efforts of students. Because he believes in them and cares for them, they begin to believe and care as well. He carries that belief to his colleagues, and struggles against those who assume that these kids cannot learn, and have given up trying to teach them.

There are other meanings, several subtexts, other questions in the popularization of Escalante's experience. Are there ways besides the standardized achievement tests to assess success? Why does Escalante jokingly cast his efforts as competitive with Japan? If desire, and desire alone, is enough to produce school success, does that mean school failure is the result of insufficient desire? Is the measure of a fine teacher the willingness to sacrifice everything—money, personal time, family, and health? Are the goals of education immutable, settled, nonproblematic? Is education potentially transformative and transcendent, or is it always merely the preparation for work and the world as we find it? Perhaps most troubling of the subtexts is the picture of success in Escalante's class (and by extension in work and in life) being a matter solely of hard work and individual will. This being the case, the flip side can also be true: failure is a matter of personal choice too—a comfortable view for those who succeed. Perhaps the multiple readings of the Escalante story explain why it is embraced by both critics and supporters of the schools as they are, by radical reformers and right-wing zealots, by people struggling from the bottom and people satisfied at the top.

The Escalante story is, for me, an experience that provokes a lot of thought about teaching, learning, and the contexts of becoming a teacher. I think about my own teaching, the successful and the unsuccessful moments, the ongoing efforts to become a teacher, to construct a lifelong teaching project. I reflect on the qualities that make an outstanding teacher and the tension between those things that can be taught to aspiring teachers in a straightforward way, and those dispositions of mind that seem almost to be prerequisites to taking those first steps down the pathway to becoming a teacher.

Because becoming a teacher is a complex and idiosyncratic process, reflecting on that process can allow teachers to become more thoughtful and more intentional in their teaching choices. Because education is more than a formal course of work or a planned set of studies, the education of teachers can be conceived as all those experiences that shape a teacher's life. We can look at what is intended in the preparation of teachers as well as what actually happens; we can reflect on the hidden as well as the overt curriculum; and we can consider the larger social, political, and economic forces that impact teachers' lives.

Sylvia Ashton-Warner, author, poet, artist, and teacher, tells another story. Hers is a story of spontaneity, unpretentiousness, and intensity. Her teaching is driven by the same springs that drive her music and her art, springs of caring and love, of passion and dedication.

Her sense of herself as an artist, her sense of her own teaching as inspired—as a piece of her art—is essential for her. Her teaching style, her revolutionary methods, and her efforts become validated as natural outlets for her creative energy. She describes the discovery of her own teaching style as a revelation, a brilliant flash of lightning, like an artistic vision, and she thinks of herself as an artist at work in the medium of the infant room.

Ashton-Warner developed an approach she called organic teaching. As outlined in *Teacher* (1963), organic teaching begins with respect for the richness and authenticity of children's lives. From listening to children's voices and hearing their language, the teacher picks out key words, words of meaning and importance, words that are "captions" to important emotional pictures, and uses these words to build key vocabularies and beginning stories. A child who struggles for weeks over *and* and *the* learns *ghost, kiss,* and *baby brother* at a glance. The teacher's job is to draw out the child, to call on his or her own inner resources, to teach reading as autobiography, reading as power and beauty, because it is so linked with the student-subject, so connected with a real-life need to understand and communicate.

Sylvia Ashton-Warner taught native Maori children in what was basically a colonial educational system, and her methods were suspect, at best, and quite possibly subversive. She saw herself constantly pulled away from the official role:

> They ask ten thousand questions in the morning and eleven thousand in the afternoon . . . And the more I withdraw as a teacher and sit and talk as a person, the more I join in with the stream of their energy, the direction of their inclinations, the rhythms of their emotions and the forces of their communications, the more I feel my thinking travelling toward this . . . key. (1958, p. 59).

When she found the official workbooks destructive to children's minds, she banished them and created her own materials.

In *Spinster* (1958) she confesses to her supervisor and explains: "I can't stand the planning of it. The clockwork detail. I can't bear the domination of it. I hate the interference of it between myself and the children and I resent the compulsion" (p. 101). In place of workbooks, Ashton-Warner developed her individualized key vocabularies and her Maori storybooks. She wrote and illustrated the storybooks herself, and based them on life as she found it in the Maori villages. She worked and reworked the storybooks, and they evolved over years of learning about and from Maori children.

Ashton-Warner's infant room was all disorder, a disgrace to the district, but with an important difference: Maori children learned there. Her success opened some official eyes. What she achieved was an "organic order," a place where "learning is a matter of preference," different from the impositions of petty rules and meaningless rituals. She looked at her little ones and asked, "All this energy . . . Why can't I use it? Why must I curb it?" and discovered that she could, in fact, use it by relating the life of the infant room to the life "of sensuousness beyond" (1958, p. 43).

For Ashton-Warner, there is hope in teaching, and there is pleasure and life. For her, the joy of teaching comes from the children: "I am made of their thoughts, and their feelings. I am composed of sixty-odd different pieces of personality" (1958, p. 22). And the joy also embodies an ever-present urgency: "This teaching utterly obliterates you. It cuts right into your being: essentially it takes over your spirit" (p. 9). Ashton-Warner affirms the dignity of teaching in her infant room, her little dinghy in the storm, courteously kneeling to the level of her little ones, following the "deep breathing of the mind" (1958, p. 226) which is the rhythm of activity and rest, or calling them to attention by softly playing the first eight notes of Beethoven's Fifth Symphony. Her work was based on respect for the Maori culture. She describes her teaching "as a plank in a bridge from one culture to another" (1963, p. 31), and she believes deeply that organic teaching, besides being an effective tool, is a humble contribution to world peace. She writes:

> I see the mind of a five-year-old as a volcano with two vents, destructiveness and creativeness. And I see that to the extent that we widen the creative channel we atrophy the destructive one. And it seems to me that since these words of the Key Vocabulary are no less than captions of the dynamic life itself

they course out through the creative channel, making their contribution to the drying up of the destructive one. From all of which I am constrained to call it creative reading and to teach it among the arts. (1958, pp. 221-222)

Herb Kohl's teaching is also a story of activism. For Kohl (1984), teaching was "a calling" long before it was a job. While other kids had fantasies of heroism and adventure, Kohl thought of being a teacher. Looking back, Kohl remembers two teachers who had impressed him deeply, one for being the respected center of his neighborhood, the other for showing him that there was an immense world of color and depth beyond the Bronx. Kohl argues that practically all teachers are motivated by a sense of altruism, and that somewhere in every teacher, no matter how distorted and beaten down by experience, lies a desire to empower the young by showing what one values:

Wanting to teach is like wanting to have children or to write or paint or dance or invent or think through a mathematical problem . . . It has an element of mystery, involving as it does the yearly encounter with new people, the fear that you will be inadequate to meet their needs, as well as the rewards of seeing them become stronger because of your work. And as is true of the other creative challenges, the desire to teach and the ability to teach well are not the same thing. With the rarest of exceptions, one has to learn how to become a good teacher just as one has to learn to become a scientist or an artist. (Kohl, 1984, p. 16)

Kohl's other early and powerful teachers were his parents and his grandparents. His father and grandfather ran a family construction business from home, and Kohl learned from them the values of hard work and family loyalty. As he worked summers in the business, he learned more specific lessons which he would later relate to teaching: each job is different, there is never a complete or adequate blueprint for construction or reconstruction, you have to probe for uniqueness and specificity, and there can be pride and joy from seeing something beautiful emerge from your own invested labor.

From the beginning, Kohl's sense of being called to teach—his sense of wanting to empower others and to communicate what is of worth and value to him—was in conflict with the role he was hired to perform. He had a sense from the first day in the classroom of being unreal, trapped, and uneasy. As he passed out the meaningless textbooks celebrating "the joys of wealth and progress" to his thirty-six Harlem kids he felt a deep sense of hypocrisy and betrayal. As he struggled to survive the pressures and constraints of covering the curriculum, he meditated on "the tightness with time that exists in the elementary school" (1967, p. 11) without relation to learning or realistic goals. And as he assigned his first homework, heavy with guilt and threat, he realized that his "words weighed heavy and false: it wasn't my voice but some common tyrant" (1967, p. 8).

The sense of unreality was deeply disturbing for Kohl and led him to try something different. When a student suggested a break between lessons, a free time to talk quietly or to do other activities, Kohl reluctantly agreed. Slowly becoming aware that the break was a chance for the children to let down their false covers and roles and bring forth, instead, their more genuine selves, Kohl expanded the break time until it overwhelmed the lessons themselves. What was once the break became the day, organized around interest areas and projects, ongoing studies and passions. Kohl found real learning here, and he found a way to see his children in an authentic mode, one that offered him insights into their lives and that would help him structure opportunities for genuine engagement with materials and curriculum.

Kohl felt that curriculum had to in some way evolve from children's lived situations if any real learning was to take place. He instinctively turned to autobiography, asking the kids to draw pictures of their homes, to write about their neighborhoods. A discussion of names led to a fascinating exchange about the passage of the Jews and the history of African-Americans in America. The use of the slang word *psyched* led to a unit on the growth and development of language. Some of what he learned about their lives was deeply disturbing and filled him with uncertainty because there seemed to be nothing he could do about it. But he hung on, becoming for these kids an honest, reflective voice and presence, not a solution to their deepest problems, but a willing listener, a hand to hold nonetheless.

Searching for his own teaching voice, Kohl connected with his students as whole people with their own dreams, experiences, hopes, fears, desires, and needs. His pedagogy became a pedagogy of dialogue, of whole people in a joint venture. When several of the kids began to write, Kohl was a valuable resource, facilitator and reader but also editor and critic. Interestingly, Kohl's own writing had frozen in fear and uncertainty, and his first book was only completed after a period of watching the kids learn to express themselves with confidence and hope. This locating of one's self as a learner and a teacher is an important part of a pedagogy based on dialogue.

The thirty-six children in Kohl's classroom experienced a terrific teacher during a magnificent year. Toward the end of that year, a colleague of Kohl's said in despair that one good year is not enough. Knowing that it is not the whole solution and that the children "are suffering from the diseases of society," Kohl concludes that he had to "add my little weight to easing the burden of being alive in the United States today" (1967, p. 227). Almost twenty years later he added:

> The time of greatest need for children to be cared for and well educated is during a time of neglect. It is wonderful to be teaching in the midst of a social movement like the civil rights movement, as I did at the beginning of my career. But it is much more important now, when society is indifferent and hope for a decent future for all children is considered romantic and even foolish. The loneliness of trying to teach well during cynical times also promises rewards. Young people and their parents know who cares, and there is a warmth and a sense of common struggle that comes from caring when it's easy to be cynical. And the children themselves can come alive and their minds unfold because of one teacher . . . You can see and feel your students grow, and that finally is the reason to teach and the reward of teaching. Yes, if I were beginning now, I would again put myself through Teachers College to get a credential and find some job teaching in a public school. (Kohl, 1984, p. 163)

Eliot Wigginton's story is also the story of foxfire, "an organism that grows on decaying organic matter in damp, dark caves in the mountains and glows in the dark" (Wigginton, 1985, p. 50). The youngsters who voted to call their fledgling magazine *Foxfire* twenty years ago probably had no idea that their project would soon take the nation by storm, popularizing the details of Appalachian culture, propelling their fantastic and mysterious name into the American idiom, and spinning off among other things a series of best-selling books, a string band, a record company, a press, a cable television channel, a folklore museum, and a Broadway play. But given the keen sense of humor and intelligence many teenagers possess, some may well have had in mind a metaphor for their own situations as high school students, or for that matter, for the entire enterprise of schooling when they settled on the name. In any case, *foxfire* remains a fitting and inventive image, critical without being cynical, hopeful and yet ironic.

Eliot Wigginton graduated from Cornell and began teaching high school in 1966 with an unpolished but sincere sense of being of service to others. He chose Rabun Gap, Georgia, because it was situated near his childhood home in a part of the world where he wanted to settle. His account of his first year teaching in the Rabun Gap-Nacochee School will be painfully familiar to anyone who has stood in front of a group of children and presumed to teach them anything:

> I had never been in a situation before where I was so completely confused by all that was going on around me . . . It was a through-the-looking-glass world where the friendlier I was . . . the more liberties the students took and the harder it became to accomplish anything . . . I'd crack down . . . and the mood would turn sullen and resentful and no sharing and learning would take place . . . It was impossible. I began to regard them collectively as the enemy—and I became the prisoner. (p. 31)

On one particularly gloomy morning, Wigginton confessed to his students his own disappointment and admitted the obvious: his classes were a failure for him and for them. He asked them what they thought they should do together in order to make it through the year. At first there was silence, then awkward beginnings, hesitations, and fresh starts. Slowly, painfully, a conversation began. It wasn't done in a day or a month or a year—it isn't done now—but from that uncertain beginning an authentic dialogue was launched that allowed teacher and students "to look at each other in a different light" (p. 32). Instead of enemies each found whole people; in place of labels and categories each found genuine needs, dreams, intentions, experiences, and powerful inner lives. The discovery of dialogue, neither simple nor automatic, did not make Wigginton's teaching smoother or easier. On the contrary, teaching became messier for him, harder work, more complicated and contradictory, but it was also more genuine, more alive, and more honest, and therefore more uplifting and worth doing.

The conversation grew and developed, spinning off project ideas, readings, and assignments along the way. He asked students to write a composition describing positive or negative school experiences that stood out in their minds. Wigginton was becoming a student of teaching, a researcher into others' auto-biographies, and he had to become the listener as well as the speaker. He had to let go in order to hold on. The student responses awakened his own childhood memories of school, and his personal list of positive experiences included times when vis-itors from the outside world brought interesting and engaging projects into the classroom, times when the students were given genuine responsibilities, and times when their work was pro-jected beyond the classroom to a larger audience.

Other discoveries followed. One day a student—"one of my sixth period losers" (p. 69)—said he'd be out of class for a few days because he was going into the woods to collect "sang" for a "sang bed." Curious and fascinated, Wigginton asked if he could go along. The experience taught Wigginton more than he imag-ined there was to know about ginseng, and more important, it transformed his relationship with the "sixth period loser" into one of mutual respect and deeper understanding. He could see that students needed multiple opportunities to be the authors of their own experiences. He found that when treated with respect, students responded with respect, and when engaged in work that they thought to be of value, they treated it valuably. *Foxfire* was becoming an affirmation of their own lives and culture, an active search for their own voices.

Here and elsewhere Wigginton was willing to use his own autobiography, to reach inside himself, to face himself in order to discover his own uniquely rewarding pathway to teaching. Cyn-ics will argue that Wigginton's teaching style worked for him because of the extraordinary person he is, and that only a super-human could accomplish what he did in the classroom. This criticism begs the question. Before there was a magazine, a book, recognition, and rewards, there was a confused and despairing young man in a high school classroom. What he did then (and what many other fine teachers have done at other times and in other places) can be done by most teachers now if they are will-ing to reach inside themselves and approach students with hon-esty and courage. The great jazz saxophonist Dexter Gordon said, "You don't just go and pick a style off a tree. The tree's growing inside you—naturally." It takes tremendous spirit to dis-cover that tree, and that is just what Wigginton did.

There are, of course, other teacher voices, other stories some-times echoing, sometimes contradicting. In *White Teacher* (1979)

Vivian Paley calls upon her own memory of being a young Jewish schoolgirl in a world of gentiles in order to build a bridge out of the quicksand of assuming that racial differences are unspeakable. Caroline Pratt, the brilliant inventor of unit blocks and founder of the City and Country School, echoes the theme of dialogue between teachers and children. The title of her autobiography, *I Learn From Children* (1948), is a simple statement of her central theme. Many teachers describe discovering their teaching voices in confrontation with standard practices and authorities. Mike Rose (1989) describes the tension of teaching in "the conflict between two visions: one of individual possibility and one of environmental limits" (p. 114).

These are all teachers who are to one degree or another self-critical and self-reflective, teachers who think about their practice in an ongoing attempt to improve. They are teachers who regard children as worthy of their compassion and their intelligence. There is a common discomfort here with the official teacher role, and there is a quest to somehow transcend it in an attempt to reach children. These teachers confront their teaching by reaching into themselves, into their own autobiographies, as sources of strength and insight. This is all part of an abiding struggle to find an authentic teaching voice, a genuine voice that somehow integrates teaching with a deeper sense of being. It is this struggle for authenticity that is most distinctive; it is a quality to uncover, to probe more widely, and to wonder about.

DEVELOPING STORIES

Of course, there is no story that is or could be the last word or the final chapter, no story that could tell all there is to know of teaching. Teaching is not a single story; the attempt to pursue the perfect study of teaching that will once and for all sum it up is a fool's errand. There are necessarily women's stories as well as men's stories, African-American stories as well as white stories, angry stories as well as joyous stories. And more than that, because teaching is more than the action of the teacher, because it is essentially interactive and co-constructed, it is always expanding, always changing, and must always include students' stories. Perhaps rather than trying to sum up teaching neatly, our goal should be to expand the natural history of what teaching is. Making our collective story richer, broader, and more complex may also allow greater intentionality, reflectivity, and thoughtfulness in teaching choices. In *Schoolteacher*, Dan Lortie

(1975) advocates using autobiographies as a way "to increase the person's awareness of his [sic] beliefs and preferences about teaching and to have him expose them to personal examination" (p. 231). This, he argues, will allow the teacher to "become truly selective and work out a synthesis of past and current practices in terms of his own values and understandings" (p. 231). Developing teachers' stories has a personal as well as a collective value, a private as well as a public meaning.

Autobiography is the recent invention of a specific cultural moment: the word was forged in the late eighteenth century from the Greek words meaning "self-life-writing," and was subsequently used to describe an existing literature known variously as memoirs, confessions, recollections, and life histories. The modern interest in autobiography may be linked to the accelerating social, geographic, and political mobility characterizing society. In a world of constant change, of danger, confusion, and fear, autobiography can become an explanation and justification of who one has become. Autobiography can be a response to the flux, motion, chaos, and noise of the environment, something Berger (1963) calls a "global historical phenomenon" and "a real existential problem in the life of the individual" (p. 65). Autobiography is an attempt to ground oneself and explain oneself in the whirlwind.

Of course, any attempt by people to verbalize their experiences results in a kind of fiction. Any ordering, any metaphor, any choice of angle limits even as it illuminates. Just as a work of fiction is confirming of an imagined life and the life of imagination, so an autobiography is confirming of another lived life. In other words, a reader chooses fiction knowing that there will be truths of possibility, and chooses autobiography knowing there will be falsehoods in the explained life. The reader lets the work speak, and must be present to the work in order to co-create its truth or falsity (Mandel, 1980).

Autobiography exists always in the present. Bruner (1983) argues, "The meaning of my own childhood history seems to me now to be dependent less upon context in which events actually happened then, and more upon the context that was created by events afterward" (pp. 4-5). He goes on to note that the "significance of early events seems to be like time running backward," and that the "past is a reconstruction rather than a recovery" (p. 5). Abbs (1974) notes that even memory is intentional, and that the very things remembered are those that serve the present because of our willingness to consider them and to act upon them. And Berger (1963) argues that "common sense is quite wrong in thinking that the past is fixed, immutable, invariable as against the ever-changing flux of the present . . . [rather] the past is . . . constantly changing as our recollection reinterprets and re-explains what has happened" (p. 57).

Allport (1942) dutifully enumerates the limits of autobiography and personal documents in social science: the lack of objectivity and control, the unrepresentativeness, the arbitrariness. But he also describes the invaluable insights of self-report and the importance of discovering what life looks like for a subject. He emphasizes the value of understanding and internal validity, and defends a more personal and activist, less contemplative and aggregated approach to science. Allport writes that "any life . . . can be fitted into a variety of frames" (p. 142) but that "psychological causation is always personal and never actuarial" (p. 187). Personal documents, like autobiographies, become the "needed touchstone of reality" (p. 143).

Grumet (1978) develops a method of teacher autobiography, noting that "autobiography, like teaching, combines two perspectives, one that is a distanced view—rational, reflective, analytic, and one that is close to its subject matter—immediate, filled with energy and intention" (p. 212). For Grumet, autobiography establishes the legitimacy of the teachers' own questions, their "stories, reminiscences of grade school, travel, family relationships, tales of humiliation, triumph, confusion, revelation" (p. 209). Autobiography also establishes a public record, the possibility for dialogue:

> When the stories are very general and muted they bury their questions in cliches and happy endings, and the supervisor's response is to ask for more detail. When the stories are extremely detailed, they often exclude any reference to the writer's response to the events that are chronicled as well as the meanings that have been drawn from them, and then the supervisor's approach is to ask what these meanings might be. (p. 209)

Abbs (1974) argues for a view of education that connects thought with feelings and intentions. Education for Abbs takes place in a knower, a subject, an "assenting individual" (p. 4), and that subject exists in a given world. "It is in individual experience," Abbs writes, "that I and the many interacting worlds of

Nature, Time, Relationships, History, come together in an intricate, creative, and largely unconscious manifold" (p. 4). The dialectical interchange and experience of a subject in an objective world provide for Abbs the "foundation we are seeking for the discipline of autobiography" (p. 4).

This sense of persons interacting in a world, creating and recreating through experience a sense of reason and meaning, is a central purpose of education. Abbs writes that education "must return again and again to the person before us . . . the [assenting and autonomous] individual who is ready . . . to adventure both further out into his [sic] experience and further into it . . . to risk himself in order to become more than he now is" (1974, p. 5).

This has implications for moving away from teacher training as methods courses preoccupied with facts and techniques toward a deeper model that can somehow relate being and knowing, existence and education. For this, Abbs sees a central role for autobiography:

> How better to explore the infinite web of connections which draws self and world together in one evolving gestalt than through the act of autobiography in which the student will recreate his [sic] past and trace the growth of his experience through lived time and felt relationships? What better way to assert the nature of true knowledge than to set the student plowing the field of his own experience? . . . may he not discover that "education" [is] that action of the inward spirit, by which . . . one discovers who one is? (1974, p. 6)

Looking backward, clarifying the unclear, and discovering the unknown, create the conditions for imagining a future different from today. Asking "Who am I? How did I get here?" opens the door for asking "Who will I be? How will I get there?"

Teachers have a special responsibility for self-awareness, for clarity and integrity, because teachers are in such a powerful position to witness, influence, and shepherd the choices of others. In dialogue with a student, a teacher can "underscore his subjectness—encourage him to stand personally related to what he says and does" (Noddings, 1984, p. 178), but only if the teacher is aware of his or her own "subjectness," able to stand personally related himself or herself. Autobiography allows us to understand teaching within the situation itself; it is a kind of "phenomenological description" or "hermeneutical understanding" or "existential psychoanalysis" (Denton, 1974, p. 101). The result will be a grounded situation-specific knowledge of teaching, not a substantialist or functionalist definition of teaching. Seeing, then, is akin to experiencing, something more than observing, something more than either a camera or an outsider can do. This kind of experiencing insider, this teacher, must struggle toward a self-awareness that is always limited, always changing, always mysterious.

Autobiography can become an act of telling and listening to each other's stories, an exercise in understanding and extending our own social history. The telling of life stories gives us clues to the present as well as hints of the future. It provides the possibility of becoming more conscious, more intentional. As people bring forth their own adventures (as well as the tales of those around them) and as they wrestle with the meaning and interpretation of actions and events, they become aware of specifics and particulars, they claim their own lives, so to speak, and in claiming they begin to take responsibility for a future. Being fully present to one's history can empower one to take responsibility for choices.

This is perhaps the deepest lesson from Paolo Freire (1970), whose literacy work among peasants was based on people coming to see themselves as intentional constructors of culture, history, and society. In Freire's work, peasants "naming the world"— seeing themselves as actors, as agents, as subjects—is an essential step in "naming the word." His dialogical method, based on cooperation, unity, organization, and cultural synthesis, has become a model throughout the world of people grounding their teaching and their learning in a serious study of setting and self. From this ground consciousness, reflection, and true education can flower.

Freire utilizes metaphor and image, but he sees metaphor not as analogy nor as a poor cousin to empiricism. Metaphor becomes "a set of terms that permit one to speak of experience and possibilities, and the mystery and hiddenness of their fundamental reality" (Denton, 1974, p. 107). As Abbs (1981) puts it: "Metaphor is not a clumsy or archaic or precious way of stating a truth that could be expressed more simply through a series of propositions. Metaphor is, on the contrary, a unique and enduring and irreplaceable way of embodying the truth of our inward lives" (p. 491).

An assumption here, of course, is that the truth is never final, never fixed. People are always in process, growing, understanding, changing, developing, disintegrating, reincarnating, choosing, and refusing. There is a sense of incompleteness, of striving, of moving into the future. Autobiography is a useful piece in this movement, for autobiography creates the possibility for a dialogue grounded in different realities. Telling lives and hearing lives can enrich our history and make possible our future. It is, perhaps, particularly important in discussing something as complex, holistic, and immediate as teaching, something for which we lack an adequate, embracing language. Lacking language, many people are willing to reduce teaching to isolated behaviors, to fractions, to numbers. Autobiography is an antidote. It is unabashedly personal, connected, alive, struggling, and unfinished. It is the foundation upon which we can build what we will.

II

RESEARCH ON TEACHER PERSONAL THEORIZING

4

AUDREY M. KLEINSASSER _____

Learning How to Teach Language Arts: A Cultural Model

INTRODUCTION

"It was good for me . . . I put in my dues . . . did my time in the barrel."
> "It's going through the fire."
> "jumping in"
> "getting your feet wet"
> "sink or swim with them"
> "trial by fire"
> "thrown to the lions"

The above descriptions are from eight language arts teachers summarizing their preservice learning-to-teach experiences (Kleinsasser, 1988). Their descriptions of intern teaching seem strangely out of place, almost anachronistic, when juxtaposed against recent proposals calling for a revamping of teacher education to emphasize professional decision making (Holmes Group, 1986) and a restructuring of teacher education to emphasize professional development (Goodlad, 1990a, 1990b; Goodlad, Soder, & Sirotnik, 1990).

The statements introducing this chapter describe cultural or social rite-of-passage experiences. They allude to rituals that preface adulthood or demonstrate courage as one faces a daunting but necessary milestone. The descriptions echo Veenman's (1984) depiction of beginning teachers' work as a "harsh and rude reality of everyday classroom life" (p. 143). Absent are the descriptions of professional practice as portrayed in teacher education programs. For example, in the case studies from which these descriptions came, there are few references to a language arts teacher's use of literary criticism. There are few references to theories of language arts pedagogy or general learning theories and how to implement them, even though it would seem reasonable for preservice language arts teachers to articulate such questions or concerns about pedagogy, particularly for these teachers who were graduating from an extended teacher education program.

An increasing number of teacher education programs are characterized as extended or five-year professional preparation periods. Recommendations by the Holmes Group are partially responsible for the increase in the length of professional education. In this chapter, the analyses from a set of eight case studies utilized to develop an argument that learning-to-teach experiences are dominated by knowledge of and adherence to the culture of schooling. By contrast, professional knowledge, which the preservice teacher is supposed to learn in teacher preparation courses, seems to be impotent. The conclusion of the chapter examines the power of the school culture in relation to longer periods of professional preparation.

REVIEW OF THE RELEVANT LITERATURE

The teacher-thinking literature base provides a data-rich source of the beliefs of teachers and the images teachers have of themselves (Clandinin, 1986; Connelly & Clandinin, 1984). Research findings illustrate how teachers' personal, practical knowledge affects educational decision making (Cornett, 1987; Elbaz, 1983) and describe how they teach English (Clift, 1988; Kleinsasser, 1989). The research indicates that teachers with different levels of experience think about practice differently (Berliner, 1986, 1987). Finally, the research demonstrates how teachers' personal, practical knowledge has been examined using a range of research methodologies (Bullough, 1989; Weinstein, 1988).

A teacher-thinking research focus (see Clark & Peterson, 1986, for a review of the literature) has contributed to the picture of teachers and teaching that the sociology of teaching literature leaves incomplete. See, for example, Waller's 1932 classic, *The Sociology of Teaching*, or Lortie's (1975) *Schoolteacher: A Sociological Study*. Specifically, teacher-thinking research contributes a description of practice and an articulation of teaching ideals and beliefs in the words of teachers, providing an emic perspective of the experience. The research base also helps explain why process-product research has not had the effect on teachers and schooling that was initially promised. Process-product research has not produced technical and operationalized definitions of effective teachers' behaviors correlated to academic and affective change in groups of students.

Identifying the personality variables of those who choose to become teachers and measuring academic and affective student outcome variables still did not provide a complete picture of what it means to teach or how one learns to teach. Process-product research efforts resulted in less than powerful, let alone applicable, theoretical propositions about classroom life. As Ross, Cornett, and McCutcheon describe in the opening chapter of this volume, some educational researchers (e.g., Clark, 1979; Erickson, 1986; Shulman, 1986) suggest that this realization fueled the growing interest in naturalistic studies of teaching.

The analytic framework for the study reported here is a culture of schooling perspective (Feiman-Nemser & Floden, 1986). The findings suggest that a novice language arts teacher's articulation of teaching knowledge is anchored in cultural rules and roles. Within the classroom, teaching rules are defined by the role of the teacher as a benevolent but powerful authority. Abiding by the rules and trying out the teacher role produces the "test of fire" described by novice teachers in this study. The rules of classroom culture overpower formal professional preparation and theories of pedagogy.

BACKGROUND OF THE CASE STUDY INVESTIGATION

Eight secondary language arts teaching interns (four male, four female) participated in the study. They were baccalaureate graduates of a major teaching and research university in the Midwest. Seven of the interns were twenty-two or twenty-three at the beginning of the study, and the eighth intern was thirty-one years old. The final year of their five-year teacher education program consisted of a six-week student teaching experience followed by on-campus graduate courses in school law, historical and philosophical foundations of education, classroom management, and language arts methods. After the on-campus study, the students returned to the field for a fourteen-week teaching internship.

The seven-month investigation was anchored by a fourteen-week teaching internship at a second site, during the final semester of their program of study. Although one of the teaching interns returned to the same building where he completed his student teaching, his internship was in another subject area with a different cooperating teacher. In some instances, the student teaching field experience was in a subject-matter minor, like social studies, or with a different age group than the intern had hoped to teach. The teaching internships represented middle school (grades 4-8), junior high (grades 7-9), and senior high (grades 9-12) classrooms. All of the language arts subfields were represented: grammar, literature, writing, speech, drama, and forensics.

Structured interviews at the beginning and end of the study, weekly unstructured interviews, twice-weekly journal entries, and classroom observations constituted the data base. The investigation yielded two separate products, both derived inductively (Corbin & Strauss, 1990; Glaser & Strauss, 1965). The first product was a set of separate case studies for each teaching intern. The eight case studies were then subjected to pattern matching to identify common themes. The case study pattern matching produced analytic generalizations of the knowledge of practice articulated by novice language arts teachers. Table 4.1 describes the themes common to all eight cases.

TABLE 4.1
Themes Emerging from Pattern-Matching Case Studies on
Language Arts Teaching Interns

I.   The task of becoming a real teacher
     A.   Classroom ownership/constraints of the
          student teacher role
     B.   Gaining experience

II. Interpersonal relationships
     A.   Positive interpersonal relationships, caring,
          and rapport
     B.   Making language arts fun
     C.   Literature and composition as subjective,
          different from math or science .

III. Curriculum and Instruction—planning driven by time
     A.   The rhythm of school, constraints of time,
          instructional pacing (technical control)
     B.   Planning by thematic units, activities,
          daily plans

The themes developed from the case studies are contextualized within a culture of schooling that is bounded by place and time.

COMPONENTS OF A CULTURE OF SCHOOLING

The tools of an ethnographer—interview, participant observation, and interpretation—are particularly useful in understanding the culture of formal schooling. Specifically, cultural anthropologists observe and interview members of social groups to interpret meanings and to create a thick description (Geertz, 1973). Geertz suggests that two components of a culture that an ethnographer wants to describe and interpret are ideals and beliefs. Knowledge of belief systems provides a way to understand formalized individual and group actions.

A web of shared meanings makes up a culture, according to Geertz. Ethnographers identify and describe the roles of different members of the culture, the artifacts of the culture, and language use. To understand a culture of schooling, one must examine the use of time and space as well as role differentiation. In the following sections, two examples of cultural knowledge in the schooling culture will be presented. The first two examples discuss the physical and structural commonality of school settings and time use. The third example examines classroom roles.

Commonality of Place and Space

In most American communities, large and small, rural and urban, school buildings are easy to identify. Usually, older brick structures are a short walk from the original community center or town hub. School buildings are identifiable by their surroundings: a flagpole, fenced-in playgrounds, parking lot, gym. Newer, one-story buildings with spacious playgrounds or campuses follow the growth of a community to its sprawling edge. Inside, most school buildings share physical similarities as well. School buildings have long hallways, classrooms of similar size and shape, and a central office area symbolizing a hierarchical control and authority. Often, particularly in older buildings, the principal's office is on the top of a two- or three-story building. In modern buildings, the central office is typically the first stop inside the front doors, straight ahead. This physical placement illustrates control and management. If the district is large enough, the chief administrators and business managers are not even on site. They are ensconced in their own office building, a building that looks different from the school building.

Other similarities among formal school buildings abound. Schools are peopled by many more students than teachers and filled with literally millions of common textbooks distinguished by their publishers, if not their content. Classroom equipment purchased from nationally known companies gives learning settings more similarity: green chalkboards, plastic world maps, and plastic and metal student desks with work space for a notebook and a book. Each desk or table and chair sets limits for a student's space or range of activity. In most classrooms, the teacher's desk—larger than a student's desk and fitted with locks and many compartments—is not different than it might have been one or two hundred years ago. Now, however, it is likely to be metal, not oak. In summary, despite geographical, ethnic, and socioeconomic particularities, school across America is more similar than different.

Commonality of Time and Scheduling

Time and scheduling are a second commonality in a schooling culture. The boundaries of time give American schooling universal meanings. For example, most school beginnings and endings are anchored by Labor Day and Memorial Day holidays. Other time constraints include a 175- to 190-day school year. Time (in years) identifies a student's role in school; for example, students identify themselves as first graders, fifth graders, or sophomores (tenth graders). In the American culture, we have at least some common understanding of what is meant by grouping students by the number of years they spend in school: elementary, middle, and secondary grouping. Parents, students, and teachers plan the school year and school day according to time allocations: eighteen-week semester courses, nine-week evaluation periods, five-day weeks divided by hours—first hour, last hour, lunch hour, before school, after school. Classroom control or management is defined by time as well, by detention hour, time out, and time-on-task. Put simply, perhaps obviously, place-space use and time use are two salient components of the schooling culture.

In this investigation, one of the key characterizations of the language arts intern teachers' articulation of teaching practice was an acknowledgment that teaching and learning occur in a particular culture. Part of a teacher's role in the culture of schooling, in the view of the participants in the investigation, is to engage interpersonally with students. The content, language arts, is the vehicle, not always the destination, for interpersonal relationships with students. Simon, one of the participants in the case study, said this about his ideal image of teaching: "I want to exemplify, most of all, an interest in and excitement about literature. By doing this, I feel I can best encourage the same in my students." In essence, actualizing the ideal for novice language arts teachers like Simon is to personalize an institutional experience through the language arts and the teacher role.

Acknowledging Classroom Roles: Ownership and Artifacts

For the novice teachers in this study, it was through *ownership*, an umbrella concept meaning responsibility, authority, and autonomy, that a *real* teacher did his or her work in the culture of a school. One lesson preservice language arts teaching interns learn is that a real teacher knows how to exercise ownership. Components of ownership include students, curriculum, physical space, and ultimately, teaching experience. In this investigation, the comparisons of a classroom to a community or to a family were pervasive. Thus, one characteristic of ownership is a kind of familylike responsibility. Greaser's description is representative of the way all of the participants in the study viewed their classroom teaching:

> We're in someone else's house or in someone else's classroom and we live by their rules . . . I think that these are his or her students and the students know that. They know that you're not the teacher . . . They [the students] can make you feel that you are not the teacher and that wasn't true in my case. But, I think that can be true and I can see that as being a problem.

Throughout the course of the fourteen-week internship, the teaching interns described themselves as comfortable or uncomfortable, feeling at home or not at home in their intern teaching role. Feeling "at home" is a result of the amount of time in the classroom (experience) and some real activity, that is, being in charge of something to teach. Students reminded intern teachers of their transitional roles, as illustrated by an interview excerpt from Terry's case study:

> Even though my cooperating teacher isn't in the room 100% of the time while I'm teaching, I think that maybe her presence is still felt by the students. But I think slowly they're coming to realize that if they have a problem they need to come to me and not to her . . . a boy was picking on another boy in class, not physically, just verbal shots . . . the boy who was being

picked on came up to me after class and said, "If [student's name] says one more thing to me during the next class, I'm going to get up and hit him." And I looked at him and said, "Not in my class you're not going to." And he said, "This isn't your class. This is [cooperating teacher's name] class." And I said, "No, this is my class when I'm teaching, this is my class. And anyway, I think she would agree with me that she does not want you to fight in her class, either."

The teaching interns claimed ownership of students in several ways. They referred to learners as "my kids," "my girls," "my juniors," "my third hour." For Chris, a drama and forensics intern teacher, the ownership of students was manifested through rehearsal time, talent development, and student loyalty. During Chris's induction year of teaching (a year after the study described here was completed), confrontations with other teachers in competition for the participation and loyalty of students in music, journalism, and science fairs produced a dilemma: they won students but lost the support of colleagues. Although Chris's drama and forensics students were successful competitively and were well supported by the school and civic communities, a heightened level of participation in drama or forensics meant less participation in other co-curricular activities for the students. At the end of the first year of teaching in a small, rural community near one of the state's regents universities, Chris realized that her relationships with teachers who were competing for the talents of the same students would suffer. This single problem demonstrates Chris's success as a beginning teacher (recruiting and keeping students) and her greatest challenge, negotiating the ownership of students with other teachers who had similar claims in the schooling culture.

Students are a human artifact of the teaching culture. Material artifacts further delineate the unique role of a schoolteacher, for example, the grade book, teacher's desk, mailbox, daily announcement bulletin, parking space, building and room keys, content area specialties, and committee assignments. By "owning up" to the responsibilities teaching artifacts symbolize, teachers create a place or belong in the classroom culture. The intern teachers struggled to belong or "own up to their responsibilities" within the constraints of a fourteen-week assignment and found it almost impossible to achieve. Ilsa's description of her internship experience is particularly poignant:

I have not yet been a real teacher in this experience . . . Things like . . . teacher appreciation breakfast yesterday. I had absolutely no desire to go. Absolutely none. On the one hand, I don't feel like a real teacher in this building. Number two, I wouldn't know anybody.

Linus described himself as a "big kid that hangs around" in the classroom, a characterization buttressed by similar qualifiers from the other teaching interns: a second-in-command, copilot, sidekick, someone followed by a cloud, someone who's on the bench. Clearly, even as novices, these teachers recognized the traditional teacher role. Their knowledge of role differentiation intensified the impact of verbal and nonverbal reminders of an intern teacher's transitional classroom role and lack of status: the superior base of experience a cooperating teacher has, the student barbs, and the artifacts of teaching. Sean called her nonposition a "lack of place":

When I tell them to be quiet or sit down and do their work, they'll do it for a little while, maybe, or . . . they'll push me a little further than they would somebody else, just because they know that it's not my place to discipline them at this point. Not as long as there's somebody else in the room in the back . . .

Sensitive to the roles played out in a classroom—learner, intern teacher, cooperating teacher—the language arts teaching interns honored their cooperating teachers' role at the same time that they bridled under its limitations. Near the end of the fourteen-week internship, several of the interns described their cooperating teachers as being "antsy" to reclaim their classes. The teaching interns, despite disappointing professional and personal relationships with their cooperating teachers, voiced deep appreciation for a teacher who "took me in," a teacher for whom this was "a chore," someone who "let me wreck their class." Classroom ownership, manifested by experience and the artifacts of teaching, endows status to a teacher, in the context of a classroom. In the end, although it proved onerous to the teaching interns, the interns held that idea of ownership as a legitimate part of the teacher's role.

In summary, one cultural component of learning to teach and of teaching is ownership: of students, of curriculum, of the artifacts that define teachers. The intern teachers in this investigation readily acknowledged that their cooperating teachers held ownership and deserved it. More importantly, the intern teachers knew that they also had to establish ownership of students, curriculum, and school space.

INTERPERSONAL RELATIONSHIPS

Across grade lines and content areas, the practice of novice teachers has been characterized as being more concerned about interpersonal relationships than student achievement (Hunt, 1988; Weinstein, 1988, 1989). Analyses from this investigation strongly support that claim. In general, research on preservice and induction-year teachers suggests that eventually novice teachers move away from that concern, demonstrating what Weinstein argues is part of the developmental process of learning how to teach. One of the findings from this investigation is that the teaching interns thought that the demands of language arts provided a unique teaching challenge that related to the development of positive interpersonal relationships with students. It is a uniqueness that separates language arts from math, for example. In this section, the importance of developing interpersonal relationships in language arts classrooms is developed.

Concern about interpersonal relationships was intensified by the language arts subject matter. The desire to promote positive, caring interpersonal relationships with both students and colleagues emerged as the dominant theme across all cases in the study. Subsumed within the dominant theme is a secondary theme that teaching language arts is a unique challenge. The teaching interns in this study contrasted the instruction of language arts to the instruction of math. They said that effective language arts instruction includes attention to teacher-student and teacher-class rapport, student risk taking, and interpretive judgments. All directly impact the creation of a classroom culture. An excerpt from Chris's case study, the forensics intern, provides a clear example:

> I don't think that it [superadult stuff] necessarily builds the best rapport . . . a lot of them [students] are incredibly nervous. They put up a tough front. This is one of the classes where you see the nerves come out in people. And they need help in this class . . . it's not like math, where they could succeed in not doing a thing all year, just flunk everything and nobody ever knows it. But if they don't have their speech ready, everybody knows.

Public speaking, whether in a class or in competition, is not the only instance during which a student becomes vulnerable.

Writing, specifically personal writing in journals, exposes student feelings. Sharing feelings has the potential to build rapport between a student and a teacher at the same time that it demands sensitivity and trustworthiness from the teacher. Two examples illustrate this point:

> I think one added benefit [has] come out of it [journal writing] I didn't foresee . . . I really know the kids now. And they write just about everything in those journals . . . everything that's happening in their lives, what they think about other teachers, what they think about [teacher's name], what they think about me . . . that's been interesting . . . I think I know those students . . . I make comments . . . that's developed a good rapport. (Greaser)

Anne calls journal monitoring "read and worry time":

> I found that they wanted to write more about things going on in their lives than the things that I suggested so I would try to limit that to once a week where I would have a required response to things, where I would give them a question that they would have to respond to; otherwise, they could write whatever they wanted. (Anne)

Language arts instruction focuses on oral and written communication. It involves two obvious tasks: taking the risk to communicate and presenting a meaningful idea. The novice language arts interns in this study addressed both tasks by articulating the importance of building rapport, respecting all opinions as valid, and promoting creativity and flexibility, since there seldom is one definitive answer in oral and written work in a language arts class.

> In math, it's just concrete and the answer is 2 . . . it's not like that in English a lot of times. (Sean)

> Math and science are so exact, or almost. Well, math for sure. If you have a problem, there's one answer for it. In literature and writing there's so much room for free thinking that, you know, there, there isn't just one answer, so you want . . . the student to be able to . . . be original and at the same time you want someone else to be able to understand that original thinking. So . . . you have to work on both. (Terry)

> In English [as opposed to math] especially in literature, two people can read the same book and come out with totally opposite opinions of it . . . accommodating all those different opin-

ions in class, rather than having absolute answers to things makes it a little tough. (Ilsa)

In English, you have Johnny who thinks this and you've got Suzy, who thinks this, and somehow, out of all these opinions you have to find some common ground to build on. In my classes, especially, and maybe this is not good, but I build so much on what my kids say. (Ilsa)

In math class they have the answer right or they don't. In English, students have the freedom to learn to express themselves, right or wrong. (Anne)

Near the end of his first year of teaching, Greaser argued that one of the problems with the language arts is that *students* incorrectly perceive learning as coming up with the "one right answer": "their hang-up," he says.

CONCLUSION

Clifford Geertz, in *The Interpretation of Cultures*, says that "if you want to understand what a science is, you should look in the first instance not at its theories or its findings, and certainly not at what its apologists say about it; you should look at what the practitioners of it do" (1973, p. 5). As excerpts from the data and the accompanying analyses suggest, the element that characterizes the beginning practice of the novice language arts teachers in this investigation is perhaps the most obvious but the least attended to in teacher education programs: the culture of schooling and the knowledge preprofessionals bring to their preprofessional courses and field experiences. The components of a culture of schooling are the aspects of teaching that a teacher, especially a novice, is the least able to change: place and space, time use, and the traditional teacher role. A culture-of-schooling perspective is a way to examine the limitations of field experiences. In the analyses presented in this chapter, the teaching interns reflected more about their *cultural* roles and expectations than their *professional* roles and expectations.

It is unlikely that extended or five-year teacher education programs will change powerful elements in the culture of schooling like time, space, and teacher role, particularly if the programs are more of the same and divorced from practice. A radical restructuring of teacher education may be one solution to the problem. John Goodlad (1990a) and his colleagues at the Center for Educational Renewal at the University of Washington are the policy developers behind one set of restructuring proposals. They urge the creation of a socioemotional climate of support for a beginning teacher that is systemwide at the same time that it is focused on the professional development of the inductee. The restructuring proposed by Goodlad and his colleagues confronts the powerful culture-of-schooling model by opening it up for discussion.

Goodlad and his colleagues have developed a list of nineteen postulates, the essential presuppositions to guide teacher education (Goodlad, 1990a, 1990b; Goodlad at al., 1990). Three of the postulates are particularly relevant to a rethinking of field experiences like intern teaching or student teaching. The three postulates are listed below.

> Programs for the education of educators, whether elementary or secondary, must carry the responsibility to ensure that all candidates progressing through them possess or acquire the literacy and critical-thinking abilities associated with the concept of an educated person. (Postulate 7)

> Programs for the education of educators must be characterized by a socialization process through which candidates transcend their self-oriented student preoccupations to become more other-oriented in identifying with a culture of teaching. (Postulate 8)

> Programs for the education of educators must assure for each candidate the availability of a wide array of laboratory settings for observation, hands-on experiences, and exemplary schools for internships and residencies; they must admit no more students to their programs than can be assured these quality experiences. (Postulate 15) (Goodlad, 1990b, pp. 191-192)

It is hardly a novel idea to suggest that preprofessional teachers should be able to think critically, transcend an interest in self, and receive preprofessional experience in an exemplary school setting. The idea has failed in the implementation stage because the learning to teach occurs in a cultural model, not a professional model.

Teacher educators need to heed Geertz's advice: pay attention to the way practitioners make sense of their experiences. Some of what beginning teachers tell us is painful to hear, particularly in light of teacher education's aims at developing professionalism. More importantly, what they tell us rings true: learning to teach *is* a test of fire. As teacher educators and educational researchers, we need to do two things. First, we need to own up to the power of the school culture in learning to teach and better prepare preservice teachers for the transition. Second, we need to rethink and restructure learning to teach experiences so that the professional knowledge constructed during preprofessional education has a chance to thrive and create its own culture within the existing culture of schooling.

5

SHARON L. PAPE _____

Personal Theorizing of an Intern Teacher

This chapter discusses personal theorizing from a constructivist perspective and outlines research findings on the beginning development of a third-grade intern teacher's personal theories about how students learn, the value of what is learned, how instruction is organized, how to identify individual differences, and what classroom climate is appropriate for learners. Findings concerning one case study participant's view of the nature of knowledge and her implementation of this view in the content areas of reading and mathematics are discussed via excerpts from the case study. All names in this paper have been changed to provide anonymity.

CONCEPTUAL BACKGROUND

Much has been written about the ways in which humans make meaning out of their worlds, their views of knowledge and how it is created, of values, and of themselves. A rationale for the inquiry discussed in this chapter is based on a synthesis of the theoretical views of Jean Piaget (1970), George Kelly (1955, 1963), and William Perry (1968, 1981). Piaget, Kelly, and Perry each held a constructivist view of the nature of knowledge; that is, they held that individuals construe the world in terms of their own perceptions, perspectives, and judgments. Piaget developed the basic epistemology of thinking which undergirded both Kelly's and Perry's work.

While investigating scientific knowledge Piaget (1970) hypothesized that there is a "parallelism between the progress made in the logical and rational organization of knowledge and the corresponding formative psychological processes" (p. 12). Because knowledge is in constant evolution, thought, in this case scientific thought, is in a process of continual construction and reorganization. He described the processes by which humans come to know through action on an object (simple abstraction, figurative knowing) and consideration of the action itself when acting on an object (reflective abstraction, operative knowing). To Piaget humans' knowledge was essentially active. Knowledge constituted a person's own repertoire of thoughts, actions, connections, predictions, and feelings. The individual tried to make sense of new experiences and new information by relating these to his or her own knowledge. The problem Piaget identified concerned how an individual moved from a lower to higher level of knowledge. He maintained, however, that experts in the disciplines must determine whether a particular state of knowledge is superior. Piaget's later work shows repeatedly that individuals have difficulty accepting data or evidence that goes against their firmly held beliefs.

Kelly's (1955, 1963) theory of personal constructs elaborated Piaget's position about how individuals come to know. Kelly defined constructs as interpretations placed on persons, events, or things gleaned through interaction between an individual and his or her environment. He postulated that some constructs were permeable; that is, once formed, constructs were subject to change as the individual experienced new situations and gained new information. Impermeable constructs, on the other hand, like the Piagetian concept of 'figurative knowing', represented a closed system. As Piaget had demonstrated, Kelly stated that individuals were unlikely to change beliefs and assumptions about reality in domains contained by impermeable constructs.

Perry's (1968, 1981) theory of cognitive and ethical development continued the elaboration of Piaget's concepts. According to Perry, individuals filtered their actions, feelings, and perceptions about events through a set of assumptions learned as they developed cognitively. The structures of meaning the individual created were sequential, hierarchical, and recursive in nature, progressing from relatively simple to complex understandings. They shaped an individual's ways of learning and colored his or her motives for engagement or disengagement with an event, person, thing, or idea (Perry, 1981). The higher levels of thought on Perry's scale, representative of Piaget's concept of 'operative knowing', constituted one source of individual and cultural change. These levels of thought constituted a source of individual and cultural stability (Kelly, Brown, & Foxx, 1984). In other words, individuals not on a growth path might respond to perturbing experiences by maintaining status or even retreating to a less cognitively mature but emotionally more comfortable position.

Indoctrination, or past overlearning of a construct, is one example of a pattern which does not allow individuals to grow or change. An individual perceiving reality from such a stand might choose to ignore or fail to see evidence which does not fit his or her construct. For example, a student teacher who believes that children must say the pledge of allegiance every day to inculcate a love for his or her country may fail or refuse to see that his or her students develop something other than patriotism. It is unlikely that actions based on indoctrinated beliefs will stimulate inquiry; thus the belief may go unquestioned and simply be accepted as truth.

Each of these three models differed in focus, although each was concerned with how individuals come to know. Piaget was interested in the development of logical scientific thought, explaining conflict resolution in terms of accommodation and assimilation. Perry's model focused on the development of reflectivity. He described conflict resolution in terms of relativistic thinking. Kelly explored the nature of constructs, suggesting the concept of permeability. He explained the manner in which conflicts were resolved once they were acknowledged.

From a constructivist frame, interaction between individuals and their environment provides opportunities for their meaning making. Integration is required for individuals to fit together past and present experiences to build a repertoire of understandings for future experiences. Some matters are attended to or selected for inclusion in the mental system of the individual, some for exclusion, and others for merely acknowledgment. These inclusions, exclusions, and acknowledgments form patterns of qualitative and contextualized judgments that are often based on simple abstractions from concrete experiences and may provide the groundwork for higher levels of reflective abstraction, yielding theories. Theories result from consolidating what is known and understood with new information and new experiences.

Theories become metaphors or models of reality (Perry, 1968). They represent beliefs about relationships between and among assumptions, and form the basis for developing both instructional strategies and patterns of classroom organization (Sergiovanni & Starratt, 1983, p. 304). Teachers' personal theories about the nature of classrooms, students, and curriculum constitute maxims and principles of "good teaching" that guide teachers' professional actions. In short, these personal theories learned through experience constitute professional knowledge. More succinctly, McCutcheon (1982) states that teachers' theories are "integrated clusters of understandings, beliefs and analyses which account for the idiosyncrasies of the teacher's specific situation" (p. 21). In other words, teachers' theories are influenced and bounded by the contexts within which they individually work. Each experience builds on the individual's repertoire of personal theories. The practical value of theories is in providing a framework against which actions are justified and explained.

The reflective teaching model presently attractive to teacher educators assumes that prospective and practicing teachers' theories are permeable despite evidence that only some of an individual's theories may be open to change, or reorganization, whereas others are impermeable (Perry, 1981). Reflection refers to the mental process or level of thought at which a reorganization takes place (Piaget, 1970). In other words, reflectivity encourages transformation, that is, a change or reorganization in an individual's belief system as a result of assimilating new experiences. The transformation system represents a tentatively held new model or metaphor which is slightly more adequate to explain an individual's experiences than the previously held model. In the work of Piaget, Kelly, and Perry, when change occurred, it resulted from thinking about conflicts the individual experienced between a belief and perceptions, a belief and actions, or a belief and an idea, word, or formula.

Positive consideration must also be given to the figurative aspects of knowing; its adaptive imitative state may be quite necessary in the development of novice into expert, for the novice's survival in the classroom. In one respect, it makes little sense for novices not to learn through imitative behaviors some of the routines and management techniques which are both pedagogically sound and effective. However, although these serve an immediate purpose, some individuals, particularly those described by the lower levels of Perry's scale, become rule bound, applying a learned rule or routine even in the face of contradictory data or evidence.

In fact, the case study participant described here (named "Nicole") appeared to be acting from a split perspective. On one hand, in mathematics she exhibited figurative knowing, accepting the authority of the textbook publishers and using imitative behaviors to cope with the complex uncertain context of teaching mathematics in the third-grade classroom. On the other hand, in reading and writing, her self-selected area of expertise, she regularly drew abstractions from her own actions: that is, she was able to think representatively without actually acting. Within the reflective teaching model, it would seem appropriate to include many opportunities to strengthen operative knowing, that is, transformations from one state to another.

The intern student teacher's theories were illuminated and explored through the constructivist frame developed. During our conversations, I would describe, interpret, and question what I saw and heard. She would puzzle over my questions, reflect, reinterpret, and question us both. Frequently, I asked her to justify her actions in relation to her stated beliefs or constructs. For example, I asked questions such as "What do you mean?" "Why do you think that?" or "How does that [action] fit with your belief?" In this way, the interview itself seemed to create perturbations arousing reflectivity. On many occasions she greeted me with "I've been thinking about that question you asked me yesterday."

If, as Carr and Kemmis (1983, p. 111) suggest, anyone engaged in teaching already holds some theories which guide his or her practices, then student teachers must also hold their own theories which guide their practices as novices. This intern student teacher definitely held her own theories which guided her practice as a novice. Some of her theories were permeable, open systems dealt with relativistically. For example, her belief that children learn to write by writing was tested, revised, and retried. Others were less permeable, enmeshed in deep-seated beliefs. She referred to her religious beliefs often when talking about how children ought to be treated. Indeed, influences on teaching practices may come primarily from strong assumptions garnered through experiences as a student (Deal & Chatman, 1989). How were these personal theories constructed? What was the content of those theories? On what knowledge were the theories grounded?

The intern student teacher's development of personal theories was stimulated by the activities of her intern experience. Watching, reading, writing, listening, talking, and experimenting were employed in her theory development. Her experience provides an example of how reflective thinking develops and manifests itself in the classroom.

Nicole, a student teacher intern in a large midwestern university, participated as the primary case study respondent in this inquiry (Pape, 1988).[1] In the following sections Nicole's views about the nature of knowledge, teaching, reading, and mathematics are addressed.

Nicole's View of the Nature of Knowledge

The following narrative illuminates the content of Nicole's personal theories from her perspective as an intern student teacher in an inner-city third-grade classroom. Statements identified as personal theories contained theoretical knowledge elements (understandings of Maslow's hierarchy, for example), contextual knowledge (particular and unique to this classroom), and personal knowledge (values and beliefs). Additionally, classroom events and interactions were used to provide insights into Nicole's tacit or unarticulated beliefs and values. She presented a clear picture of her awareness of the changing or dialectical nature of her own growth by her responses to the final account of their theories: "Yes, that's fair. That sounds like me—a month ago. I keep changing, you know, cycling through things."

Nicole actively sought knowledge with which to structure her experiences in the classroom. She was aware of the need to respond to the situation at hand, although she did not consciously acknowledge changes in her thinking as responses to the exigencies of the classroom. "My biggest qualm with teaching is that there is no black and white. It's all a massive grey, some quagmire of quicksand which has no 'beware' signs."

Journal entries between October 1987 and February 1988 were peppered with the titles of at least ten different books on education. These ranged in content from how-to techniques in subject areas, particularly reading and writing, to classroom management and discipline models favoring improving self-esteem. Nicole's journal entries became like heart-to-heart talks with a good friend. A pattern developed and remained consistent throughout the journal. First Nicole introduced a problem related to classroom interactions and discussed it. She explored a reading concerning that topic and compared the theory she read, her own belief, and what actually happened from her perspective in the classroom. In her journal, she reflected on the readings, evaluating their usefulness in her particular context or on the basis of her own knowledge. In some instances, reflective passages were followed by plans in outline form for changing the immediate classroom situation based on the weight of evidence gleaned from the readings and experiences in the classroom. For example, on September 30, 1987 she wrote:

> I am quite frustrated. The children do not listen. They aren't belligerent or outwardly rebellious; they simply ignore my voice.

and later in October:

> Hello! I have a problem. I have been reading *Dare to Discipline* and I feel Dobson's theories are viable and definitely workable. Moreover, I am seeing a great discrepancy between his theories and our classroom; i.e., our kids need more discipline! They do not listen, instead wait for the instructor to stop nagging. I believe that through neglect, we have taught them that we don't really mean what we say . . . They think we're a couple of Alzheimer's patients who forget our demands and requests. My proposed solution: BE [sic] consistent & follow through on our requests . . . they must be aware of our expectations and they must be sure we will enforce all we propound.

Finally in January:

> Wow! It was a great morning. I feel really good about being stricter on discipline . . . I think structure is very necessary and valuable. My children have so little in life that they can count on. School should give them structure and comforting routine.

Nicole's practice of framing problems, exploring alternatives, and suggesting actions to herself in her journal continued throughout her internship. Often, after the deliberation sequence in her journal, she would present her ideas verbally to the researcher, usually as a conversation opener. She might say, as she did in February, for example, "I'm deviating in reading today," inducing the predictable response, "Tell me about it." "Well, I had this idea for a big book from Byrd Baylor's book *Guess Who My Favorite Person Is.*"

When a puzzle was encountered or a discrepancy noted, Nicole turned to texts almost automatically. Because of her experiences and beliefs about herself as a learner, learners in general, and the meaning of education, Nicole sought the contributions of others who possessed certain kinds of knowledge. The following passage is cited exactly as Nicole spoke it during a discussion about her extensive reading. The interviewer is designated by (I) and Nicole by (N).

> (I) Why do you use so much of your time to read books about teaching?
> (N) Because they "*know.*" [emphasis in the original]
> (I) How do you use them?
> (N) They give credence to my ideas. Affirm or reject what I know. So I don't stagnate. You don't keep growing without ideas. You forget why something was important enough to use.

Later in April, the same question was asked concerning the persistent use of written texts. The original answer was augmented, but not changed significantly:

> To know . . . I read so I can sound intelligent when people ask me questions. So I can explain what I do, why I do things. Just to be exposed to more things. Because it's interesting, it's fun, it's better than T.V.

Nicole explained that observing others and reading also gave her confidence that her experiences were not uncommon to teachers or teaching. If the sources gave conflicting information, Nicole weighed and evaluated the evidence against her growing knowledge about her own style, her classroom, and the children in it. Although books represented valued access to knowledge, practicing teachers, although less accessible than books, were also subject to her persistent search. Nicole held the view that knowledge must be accumulated, thought about, sorted for usefulness, and restructured by the individual forming an integrated whole from all the pieces.

> It's overwhelming. I'm fascinated by the discipline and the classroom management and how different teachers approach it. I want to develop my own style and like right now I'm kind of silly putty. Whatever I am next to is what I become. Because of being in someone else's classroom I adopt their styles and then I'm in other rooms and then I become her. Is that right? When do I develop my own? So that is kind of what I'm going through. I think you take whatever you experience. You take a little bit from that or whatever you spend the most time with I guess. That's why I'm into observing. I want to see how it works.

Nicole described collecting and choosing pieces of information from which she constructed her views. She held these views tentatively and was open to changes as new ways of being were discovered. Her expressions of concern for developing her own style suggested an internal learning orientation. Student teachers with internal orientations who viewed learning to teach as a process of self-guided discovery possessed the metacognitive skills of comparison, evaluation, and self-direction which enabled them to set their own criteria for evaluating their own practices (Calderhead, 1988, p. 5).

A letter she recorded, but never sent, to her cooperating teacher asked for the opportunity to be an independent learner, to test out what she knew against the models she collected from observation, analysis, and experiences. "Let me try . . . And 'spoz I fail? Let me suffer the consequences. I'll survive." Phrases like "I'm still feeling things out" and "whatever feels right" or "I'm pleased with it, but I'm thinking . . ." were scattered repeatedly throughout interview transcripts and journal entries. The reluctance implied by these statements to be held captive by any one premise indicated a tacit understanding that what is most fitting in the immediate context may change in future ones.

Nicole's Views on Reading

Nicole believed children learn by doing what they are trying to learn. For example, "Children learn to read by reading. The more they read the better they read." In practice, Nicole provided many opportunities for children to read. The diagnosis and remediation of one student's difficulties led to a book-sharing program for her reading groups. Every day, every child chose a book to take home and read. Every day, every child shared one special thing about his book in reading group before the books were collected and redistributed, before the basal readers were opened.

In the fall, when she first began her internship, Nicole had suggested to Mrs. Mandell, the principal, that she might use a literature-based approach to reading. Mrs. Mandell thought Nicole was an excellent student teacher who unfortunately "had ideas" and she refused permission for "throwing out the basals." Mrs. Mandell maintained close control of the reading program in her school, regularly reviewing skill tests and conferencing with teachers about scores and children's progress.

When Nicole discussed her ideas in February about a literature-based reading program, she became animated and excited. In March, one reading group began using multiple copies of a book titled *Soup*. Although the book was judged difficult for some of the children, they were reading and enjoying it. "It's real long and really hard for them, but I don't tell them and they seem to do okay." By April a literature-based reading program was established for her reading groups, though the cooperating teacher's groups continued to use the basal readers. The tension between the ideal she believed in and the reality of her practice appeared to be resolved.

Nicole ascribed her attitudes about basal reading texts to being "indoctrinated" through a summer class about the "dangers and evils of basals." She explored integrating subject matter areas, particularly reading, writing, and social studies, through the writing-across-the-curriculum model. Eventually she merged the writing process with the literature-based curriculum model. Integrating subject areas using literature was possible but "messy" to reorganize. "How can you call this a social studies grade when you kind of mesh it all together?"

Nicole's View of Mathematics

Mathematics instruction presented quite a different picture. Nicole did not exhibit her same interest or excitement during mathematics lessons and complained of having difficulty holding pupil attention and keeping them on task.

> Addison Wesley does math, I do writing. I never questioned it. I don't know. We have the textbook and I use it. We just *do* math. Maybe they have the same attitude because I do. I know my children, but they [textbook] know their math. You can't go off on tangents in math."

Mathematics lessons followed the text pattern with little variation and presented a view of mathematics as a manipulation of numbers. Examples and explanations came directly from the teacher's manual. The assignments followed the text page by page. Every child was on the same page and same problem set, although Nicole identified those who "knew their work" better or caught on faster. Variations were mainly in the number of problems assigned. Nicole seemed to base the number of problems assigned on the relative difficulty of the work as she perceived it, the amount of other homework, and the text's recommendations. Work was graded daily, sometimes by an eager pupil using the teacher's manual to mark incorrect answers with large red circles. Incorrect answers were expected to be corrected as homework and returned for reevaluation the next day.

As Nicole experimented with integrating subject areas, mathematics remained an independent unit. The only expressed consideration of integrating math appeared during a recorded discussion about the use of texts in literature based on reading: "I wonder how you teach math without a text?" Possibilities for experiments or alternative activities in mathematics were not pursued in her journal or planning. She did not read "how-to" texts or discuss theories of teaching math to young children. Nicole's room contained many attractive and interesting charts, pictures, learning centers, and materials, but none focused on mathematics. For example, the largest display in the room, the Featured Authors display, presented biographies and pictures of authors and illustrators of children's literature and poetry books, classical musicians, and occasionally a scientist, but not mathematicians.

Learning mathematics was an independent activity of study for the pupils. Children were not encouraged to explore mathematics together, to create alternate or new solutions, or to justify or explain their reasons for work. There was no display of creative mathematics work, no collection box for mathematics puzzles children had found to share or created on their own such as there was for writing samples. Nicole did not conceive of using the conference corners set aside for pupils to discuss writing themes or books as places for pupils to also hold mathematics conferences. Reading games and materials proliferated on the shelves and in the conference corners, but mathematics materials were few. Nicole did not question the authority of the text or seek outside views of mathematics teaching. When she reported her reactions to observations in other classrooms, no journal entries or interview discussion focused on mathematics.

Nicole was an honors student throughout high school and her four years of undergraduate education in a large midwestern university. Although as competent in mathematics as in any other subject as determined by her grades in courses, she *felt* less knowledgeable in mathematics.

SUMMARY

This account of Nicole's engagement with the phenomena of her own practice was told from the belief that individuals construct their own knowledge and must in some manner make sense of new experiences in light of their existing knowledge. The objective of the inquiry was to understand how Nicole was thinking about her teaching, what sense she was making of new experiences, especially those new experiences that seemed to contradict her beliefs.

Questions about her practice and thoughts stimulated Nicole's curiosity even in areas which appeared to be impermeable. Both Piaget and Perry attend to décalages, or the use of analogy between different areas of experience. Individuals can transfer more advanced patterns of thought in one area to areas in which they have been thinking more simplistically (Perry, 1981).

Each day Nicole faced a host of complex, context-specific problems in the third-grade inner-city classroom about which there were no easy certain answers. No singular right course of action was available, although certain courses of action seemed better than others. In facing classroom problems action has to be taken, often immediately. Underlying these actions is a personal guiding theory based on the unique beliefs, understandings, and assumptions which represent an individual's explanation and justification of experiences.

In some domains, Nicole's uncertainties were a source of learning for her. She understood that others in same or similar situations held relevant knowledge. She was interested in and actively sought alternative ways of seeing the phenomena, assuming it was both normal and legitimate to compare approaches. She was not threatened by models that did not fit hers. She questioned, explored claims, weighed evidence, and enjoyed the discovery of creating her own knowledge about the phenomena of her own practice.

> (N) I have a new discipline practice.
> (I) What's this one called?
> (N) My own! It's a composite.

These statements (Perry's levels 6 and 7) reflect the belief that an objective reality probably exists, that reality is sought through evidence, and that evidence is weighed and evaluated to determine the most rational or more correct judgment.

In other domains, Nicole held a less relativistic position, indicated by such actions as acceptance of authority without question and imitative behaviors. When provoked by a discussion with the researcher, she initiated exploring her attitude and its effect on her pupils in mathematics. Nicole demonstrated that she was capable of operational thinking even in mathematics, an area she felt less expert about. She began to change her understanding of teaching from content boundaries to a larger view which was organized around the similarities of instructional technique for her image of "good teaching."

In developing her theories she recognized, at least in language arts, her areas of expertise, that the knowledge she held was one way of looking at something, yet it would probably change as new information came in. Nicole used the questions and interview summaries as opportunities to weigh yet another perspective. Initially, Nicole saw mathematics as a closed system: "You can't go off on tangents in math." The text publishers represented an authority who knew how mathematics should be taught. Despite the evidence she cited about the pupils' attention and understanding, she did not question her methods of teaching or seek alternatives to the text's patterns. The interview questions stimulated her thinking about her teaching of mathematics. "I wonder if they do [have this attitude] because I do?" Changes noted in Nicole's attention to her attitude about mathematics and its effect on her pupils are interesting in light of the accepted belief that figurative knowing is resistant to change and operational knowledge is content bound. Kelly, Brown, and Foxx (1984, p. 278) suggest that to "use formal structures in a significant way requires high level familiarity with the content." With some contents not all formal structures are required. They continue, "the use of higher structures is partially dependent upon appropriate perturbations of lower structures." Dewey (1933) similarly described the dependence of higher thought processes involved in reflective thinking. He urged weighing and evaluating evidence from perturbing experiences to project the consequences of further actions.

IMPLICATIONS

Through her internship, Nicole's personal theories of teaching continued to evolve, building a framework against which actions were justified and explained. This is perhaps one explanation for the popularity of field experiences among society in general and the participants of teaching field experiences in particular. Practical experiences give an individual the opportunity to investigate the dispositional and situational factors of professional action. However, As Perry (1968, 1981) noted and Dewey (1933) warned, education does not always foster higher-level processing. Some students retreat to earlier-held indoctrinated values rather than progress toward more relativistic understandings. As may be seen among student teachers, some adopt and mimic the actions of their clinical teachers without question. An example of this is Nicole's preliminary unquestioning adoption of her clinical teacher's attitudes toward mathematics.

The reflective teaching model assumes that an individual's personal theories are open to change. Indeed, Piaget's (1970) theory of genetic epistemology suggests that change is adaptation to environmental disturbances of the individual's belief systems, and is not dependent on cultural learning. However, other research (cf. Doise & Mackie, 1981; Perry, 1968, 1981) indicates that social cognitive conflict contributes to the development of higher thought processes. College students exposed to the value clashes that are inevitably part of the pluralistic environment of the university may advance *or* retreat along the reflective judgment continuum. It would seem appropriate for teacher education to deliberately provide a continuum of "environmental disturbances" to precipitate the desired changes in a forward direction. These disturbances must occur over time and in relation to the student's present level of thought (Knefflekamp, 1974). Further, research suggests that *time for reflecting* and opportunity for testing newly acquired processes are required to internalize changes. The challenge for teacher educators is to design and implement a curriculum which incorporates these ideas.

Instruction throughout the teacher education program that deliberately focuses on the mental system of concepts, memories, motives, and reasoning patterns of individuals would increase the opportunity for encountering, reflecting, testing, and internalizing new ways of thought. This focus can be obtained by asking students to explore ill-structured problems that affect education and educators. Providing class time for students to exchange beliefs and opportunities to share thought processes while moving toward individual resolution of the ill-structured problems enhances growth.

Supervisors, including clinical teachers, can enhance reflective processes by demonstrating habits of reflection in their own practices. For example, clinical teachers could question their own interpretations of the curriculum, instructional practices, and influences of the instructional materials as a shared activity with the student teachers. Clinical teachers also might engage the student teachers in their own practice-centered inquiries to create sound experiential learning that reaches beyond the accumulation of technical skills.

University supervisors can also provide student teachers with data about their teaching. They can establish and maintain a reflective dialogue with the students, encouraging them to use metacognitive skills to examine their own practices. Opportunities for students and clinical teachers to meet and discuss problems of practice with university supervisors can encourage inquiry. A shared investigation of how school policies shape teaching opportunities and beliefs about what is possible requires the inquirers to play an active role in constructing knowledge.

In summary, as present evidence indicates, it may be unreasonable to expect development of truly reflective thought, thought in which we abstract knowledge, at the *end* of the teacher preparation program. Rather, there should be a coordinated effort *throughout* the program to provide the "disturbing" experiences, time, opportunities, and interactions that encourage individuals to reexamine and/or reorganize their constructs. If experiences that create reflective abstraction occur only at the end of the program, it may in fact be too late for some prospective teachers. For Nicole, there continues to be a happy "beginning" thanks to her extraordinary habit of persistent reflecting.

POSTNOTE — A ONE-YEAR UPDATE

The following unsolicited journal entry from Nicole arrived this week:

> Hello. I thought I'd write and give you a one year up-date. Actually, I really wanted to let you know how much I appreciated being part of the research. Through questioning and reflecting, you have helped me to inquisitively track down the thoughts that flit around in my head. You have helped me to trace surface reactions to their roots in my underlying fears, hopes, and dreams. Your project also helped me to recapture the joy of curiosity and discovery as we probed beneath the humdrum epidermis of experience into the dark underworld of whys and wherefores. Thanks! You taught me to ask why . . . and to expect an answer . . . from myself as well as others.

6

STEPHEN J. THORNTON _____

How Do Elementary Teachers Decide What to Teach in Social Studies?

In the spring of 1987, a research associate and I investigated how elementary school teachers decide what to teach in social studies. We were well aware of the litany of reports noting that elementary social studies curricula emphasize recitation of low-level knowledge and disconnected skills (e.g., Goodlad, 1984, pp. 210-213). We were also aware, however, that there were few answers to the question of how and why teachers make these curricular choices. Consequently, over a period of two months, we interviewed three experienced fourth-grade teachers who had been identified as competent in instruction and management by their principal. We observed forty-two 30-minute social studies lessons taught by the three teachers. The following description of one lesson typifies the kind of curricular emphasis that was evident in most lessons. The description is included to provide a context for a discussion of how and why these teachers frequently selected this curricular emphasis. (For a fuller discussion of these teachers' instructional practices, see Thornton & Wenger, 1990).

It is an unseasonably hot afternoon in early May. The daily 30 minute period scheduled for social studies is about to begin. Along the back wall of Mrs. Nelson's classroom are arranged yesterday's corrected worksheets. At 1:30 sharp, the children file into the room. Despite the oppressive humidity, the youngsters seem to have a bounce to their stride.

Mrs. Nelson: [sympathetically but with a no-nonsense air] I know you're hot.

The teacher checks that the children have brought back their tests with parent signatures affixed. The teacher's guide to the textbook is open on her desk. One boy is tossing a coin; in her typical firm but unthreatening way, Mrs. Nelson tells him to stop and the child immediately complies. Mrs. Nelson asks Todd to summarize yesterday's lesson for two students who had been absent. This review technique — which personalizes the process by identifying it with particular individuals — is a practice Mrs. Nelson often employs.

After further reviewing the previous day's lesson, Mrs. Nelson announces, "Today, Texas. You read about Texas this morning [during English]."

Mrs. Nelson: You'll be looking for climate, products, resources . . . as we've done with other states. [The teacher distributes "Sheet 10," an outline.] [This is] to organize the material for you. On page 156 [of the textbook (Kaltsounis, 1986)], pull out the important things on climate.

Mrs. Nelson begins to explain and question about Texas' climate. She notes that Texas has a warm and humid summer.

Mrs. Nelson: When did we deal with humid [sic]?

Student: The Soviet Union.

Mrs. Nelson: No. What other area . . . ?

Another student: Tropical.

Mrs. Nelson acknowledges that this answer is correct and proceeds to contrast the mild Texas winters with winters in the Great Plains region and in the tropics. "Is 50 inches a lot of rain?" the teacher asks of no one in particular. A few students indicate, by raising their hands, that 50 inches is a lot. The teacher asks, "Where is it very dry?" and a student answers, "Arizona." Mrs. Nelson goes on to explain that 50 inches is a "lot" of rain but the amount of rainfall received is not uniform across Texas. As this question-and-answer session proceeds, the teacher records information on the board while students write it down on their worksheets. The children are on-task and the classroom is orderly — the teacher's demeanor is simultaneously businesslike and warm.

Discussion of Texas continues. The students answer some questions about hurricanes and Mrs. Nelson relates that her youngest sister was born during a hurricane. A couple of students relate that they were born during blizzards. The teacher explains how hurricanes "come along the coast" and some students narrate their experiences with hurricanes. Mrs. Nelson then asks what is grown given Texas' climate: "Do they grow cotton in the Great Plains? Do we grow rice here?" The children are responsive to these comparisons. Momentarily, however, Mrs. Nelson returns to less open-ended questions. Holding the teacher's guide, she asks, for example, "What type of animals do they [Texans] raise on farms?" Again, she prompts students with comparisons: "Do we raise poultry in [this state]? What types?" The teacher then refers the children to particular pages in the textbook to find the industrial products of Texas.

She queries the few students as to why they are not checking their books and encourages them to do so.

A few moments later, and still concerning industries, Mrs. Nelson turns to oil production in Texas. Again, she raises what is familiar to the students: "Do we have any oil refineries in [this state]?" Some children say "yes," and others "no." To break the impasse, Mrs. Nelson asks, "Does anyone live near [a nearby town where an oil refinery is located]?" Scott volunteers that "my daddy used to work there a long time ago." Several other students then offer their own accounts of their knowledge of refineries.

Finally, the class turns to some remaining questions concerning Texas' manufactured products. Tina suggests, as an example, that Texas produces "raw materials." Mrs. Nelson replies, "That's not a product. What products come from wood?" There is no indication of reproach to Tina here—as throughout the lesson, good feelings prevail. The students now provide a few examples of manufactured goods made in Texas and Mrs. Nelson assigns the remaining three worksheet questions for homework.

As I believe this lesson shows, Mrs. Nelson had earned her reputation for effective instructional organization. First, Mrs. Nelson's style was simultaneously no-nonsense and warm—she and the students seemed comfortable with each other and classroom management was unobtrusive. This was not a classroom where either voices were raised or harsh glances exchanged. Second, the lesson proceeded smoothly: Mrs. Nelson had prepared materials in advance, and routines were in place. The students seldom had to be reminded that, when Mrs. Nelson wrote answers on the board, they should record them on their worksheets. Moreover, whenever Mrs. Nelson asked a question, some students invariably raised their hands in response. With only minor exceptions, students were on task throughout the 30-minute lesson. Third, the subject matter was arranged in a sensible enough sequence and student learning was monitored. Further, homework was assigned. Fourth, judging from student comments we overheard, and from their writing, it appeared that they were learning the subject matter. In sum, it seems fair to conclude that, by criteria identified in the teacher effectiveness literature (see Stanley, 1991), we were witnessing good teaching.

Still, it is worth asking: Was this good curriculum? The lesson's emphasis was, as in nearly all of Mrs. Nelson's lessons, on geographic facts. The few occasions when geographic relationships (see James & Crape, 1968) were introduced, such as asking what children believed "should" be grown in Texas, were quickly abandoned in favor of more facts. Worksheets and tests reinforced this approach. In brief, the curriculum Mrs. Nelson provided in her room, heavily derivative of the teacher's guide, is reminiscent of Jere Brophy's (1990) characterization of the typical problems found in social studies curriculum materials:

> worksheets that emphasize recall of memorized facts or practice of isolated skills rather than integration and application of knowledge; suggested questions that are likely to focus classroom discourse on factual recitation but not on critical thinking about the content; suggested activities that use content to provide occasions for practice of skills rather than providing opportunities for students to use the skills to apply the content; and evaluation components that provide only minimal attention to higher order applications . . . (p. 395)

CONCEPTUAL FRAMEWORK

In the 1960s and early 1970s, New Social Studies materials were developed in the hope of promoting inquiry-oriented teaching and learning. By the end of the latter decade, however, the New Social Studies movement was widely considered a failure because most American teachers did not adopt the innovative instructional materials. Many researchers drew the lesson from the New Social Studies movement that teachers were at the heart of curricular instructional change (see Thornton, 1991). For example, in their overview of the investigations of social studies sponsored by the National Science Foundation (NSF), James P. Shaver, O. L. Davis, Jr., and Suzanne W. Helburn (1980) conclude that, notwithstanding other factors such as student characteristics, the role of teachers' "reflection and personal inclination" is central in shaping the day-to-day classroom experiences of students (p. 5). Since the NSF-sponsored studies, several researchers have investigated various aspects of how teachers make curricular-instructional decisions. Gail McCutcheon (1981), for instance, studied how elementary teachers planned the social studies curriculum. She found that "practical" concerns such as classroom control and availability of instructional materials were salient considerations in planning. Similarly, in a review of ethnographic studies relevant to social studies curriculum and instruction, Jane J. White (1985) noted that "what works" seemed to be central to what teachers chose to teach in social studies. From these and other studies (e.g., Levstik, 1989; McKee, 1988), it seems well established that most teachers are preoccupied with "practical" questions of "what works."

It is considerably less clear, however, what "what works" means for the various subject matters within the social studies curriculum. Is what "works" for teaching map skills to sixth graders the same as what "works" for taking first graders on a field trip to a dairy farm? Is being "practical" about using *Man: A Course of Study* (a New Social Studies curriculum kit) synonymous with being practical about using drill-and-practice dittos from the teacher's guide? To put it another way, knowing that teachers make decisions based on "practical" considerations of "what works" does not entirely explain why the curriculum in use and accompanying instructional arrangements look the way they do in particular classrooms with particular subject matter.

Several scholars have recently emphasized the central role of subject matter in explaining why curriculum and instruction look the way they do (Shulman, 1987; Stodolsky, 1988). For instance, Susan S. Stodolsky (1988) concluded that the same teacher teaching the same students provided different types of instructional arrangements in math and social studies. Further, and of particular relevance to the concerns that I have raised, Stodolsky noted that different social studies subject matters were associated with different types of instructional arrangements. In other words, if we want to understand how social studies teachers decide "what works" or is "practical," this understanding partly depends on the particular social studies subject matter under consideration.

We chose to study fourth-grade social studies, particularly the lengthy segment of the curriculum devoted to world regions such as forestlands, deserts, and plains, for several reasons. First, beginning in the fourth grade, social studies appears to have a secure place in the elementary curriculum and to employ basal textbook series. Second, this grade level is the first where the topics are fairly clearly defined and are standard in most parts of the United States. Third, the topics are considerably broadened from the heavy emphasis on local concerns of the primary grades (e.g., neighborhoods) to state, nation, and world (Lengel & Superka, 1982, p. 33). Taken together, these three reasons suggested to us that, to a considerable extent, fourth-grade teachers would, implicitly or explicitly, define for their students what social studies (from the fourth grade up) means.

METHODS

This qualitative study is based on observations of, and interviews with, three female fourth-grade teachers (Jackson, Nelson, and Swan) in 1987. Each woman had more than ten years' classroom experience and was identified as a "good" teacher by building-level administrators. The teachers' experience and instructional effectiveness were important criteria in their selection for this study because we wanted to minimize influences on their decisions about what to teach such as inexperience in teaching social studies and unfamiliarity with classroom management procedures.

The study was conducted at a school located in a metropolitan area in the Middle Atlantic states. The students came from both urban and suburban areas. Most students were from the lower half of the socioeconomic scale, and approximately one-third were from minority groups, mainly African-American.

After an initial 40-minute interview with each teacher, classroom observations began several times a week during the 30-minute period devoted to social studies. These observations continued over six weeks for a total of twenty-one hours of observation. The initial interview was intended to gauge teachers' curricular priorities in social studies, and especially their views of appropriate subject matter concerning world regions. During observations, field notes—separated into transcription of events and impressions—were taken. Elliot W. Eisner's (1985) notion of educational connoisseurship guided our observations: that is, we attempted not merely to describe classroom life but to discern the educational significance of what transpired. Toward the end of the six weeks of observation, we re-interviewed the teachers (again, for about 40 minutes each). By this stage, it was possible to ask more focused questions concerning why the teachers had made particular curriculum decisions whose consequences we had witnessed. For example, puzzled that Mrs. Jackson continued lessons as planned despite frequent and obvious student misunderstandings, we asked her why she persevered in this practice. Two building administrators were also interviewed in order to obtain a fuller understanding of the priorities for social studies in the school and the district, and the possible influence of these priorities on the teachers' curricular choices in social studies.

Following our fieldwork, interviews and observations were

transcribed and analyzed for purposes of identifying themes across the teachers. In particular, we wanted to understand how and why teachers decided to teach some subject matters and not others.

CRITERIA FOR CURRICULAR-INSTRUCTIONAL CHOICES

In beginning this section, it is important to note that selection of subject matter and instructional strategies, although obviously a common occurrence, was not necessarily in the forefront of the teachers' minds. Rather, like classroom management, it seemed to be a part of the taken-for-granted routine of the daily grind. Nonetheless, when we questioned the teachers about their curricular-instructional choices, they were aware that they did indeed make choices. For example, Mrs. Nelson observed, "Perhaps it's intended [by the designers of the curriculum guide] that you just, you know, pick and choose . . . there's a lot there [so] that you can pick and choose what you want to do more in-depth than what you don't."

Although each teacher described how and what she would ideally teach about world regions, within the constraints of the curriculum guide and available materials, each teacher actually made curricular-instructional choices largely on the basis of three interlocking criteria: (1) a commitment to cover the major facts and skills in the textbook, (2) a consideration of how and what their students would be capable of learning, and (3) their beliefs about social studies subject matter such as world regions.

To some extent, however, the teachers did place somewhat different emphases on these criteria. Two of the teachers (Jackson and Nelson) approached what White (1989) refers to as "technical" teaching: that is, they believed that knowledge is acquired through the accumulation of facts and skills. They perceived their role as presenting information clearly and then asking questions so that students had a chance to master the information. The other teacher (Swan) was more "constructivist." Such teachers believe that knowledge is integrated and problematic. They believe that their role is to set up opportunities in which they and their students can be co-constructors of knowledge. Although "technical" versus "constructivist" should be understood as two extremes of a continuum, Mrs. Swan mostly was toward one end and her colleagues toward the other. As evidenced in interviews and observations, Mrs. Swan generally placed more emphasis, for example, on motivational learning experiences and less on factual recall.

Coverage

Regarding coverage, the teachers were more similar than different; all three teachers believed that coverage of a wide range of content was important. A commitment to coverage, moreover, tends to favor teacher-centered and/or textbook-based instructional arrangements conducive to working efficiently through large amounts of subject matter. It almost goes without saying that this subject matter emphasis, with its accompanying instructional arrangements, has commonly been condemned by curriculum reformers; for instance, it has been accused of causing the lack of student interest in and motivation toward social studies (Hertzberg, 1981).

As one would expect, coverage was consonant with the "technical" views expressed by Mrs. Jackson and Mrs. Nelson. Even Mrs. Swan, however, noted that she would be reluctant to omit entirely any of the units (e.g., plains, forestlands) from the curriculum even if this resulted in only superficial coverage: "I would like children to be exposed to it." As should become apparent below, although Mrs. Swan paid some homage to coverage, it appeared to be the driving force behind the curriculum of her two colleagues. For example, although acknowledging that she could not "think of any way that I'm accountable other than knowing that I'm accountable," Mrs. Nelson said that she should try "to do it [cover the range of topics in the curriculum guide]." Despite this commitment to coverage, Mrs. Nelson complained of the superficiality of the resultant subject matter and recognized the need for at least some trade-offs between coverage and depth. For instance, in the plains unit she largely dealt with plains in the United States: "So then when we do the [plains regions of the] world, it's pretty much I'm going to locate . . . places in the world that are plains." Similarly, Mrs. Jackson observed that "there's not really enough time to develop understandings. If you're going to talk about a region, there's so much involved." Nonetheless, she continued that it was necessary to cover many regions (as opposed to a few in depth) because the regions "would be sort of isolated in that context."

Mrs. Swan was a little more flexible concerning coverage— though not as much as some of her other beliefs might imply. Although she too endorsed covering each region in the curriculum guide, she was more willing to rearrange scheduling to focus on subject matter that she deemed important. In the fall, for example, she recalled that she had extended the unit on state history because "the parents were so into it, the students were so into it! And they knew so little about [this state]."

Children's Understanding

Presumably all teachers take some account of what their students know and are likely to be able to learn. The question is: How well founded and considered are their beliefs about students' understanding? More than was the case with coverage, the teachers could be characterized as "technical" (Jackson and Nelson) or "constructivist" (Swan) concerning their beliefs about student learning. It is significant, however, that their beliefs about learning were based on competing and not always consistent criteria. For example, Mrs. Jackson remarked: "I don't think anybody can read it [the textbook], you know take it home, read this chapter and answer the question and here's the test. I don't think anybody can absorb social studies that way." Nonetheless, she admitted that time pressures often led her to cover more subject matter than her Chapter 1 students were capable of learning. Ideally, Mrs. Jackson said, "I would like to be able to do more activities, projects, hands-on type things, you know, making maps, making globes. I think they would benefit from those kinds of things." Frequently, however, she said that what she did was "just cover it [a topic] lightly and let them just have a basic understanding rather than a mastery of it."

Mrs. Jackson and Mrs. Nelson also strongly believed that facts and skills had to be learned before children could engage in higher-order thinking. As Mrs. Jackson observed regarding the teaching of geographic relationships, "We have social studies books this year that cover this information . . . I found . . . it was difficult for them to grasp that information without any basics . . . [such as] What is a mountain?" Before students can understand relationships, she said, they must have "basic knowledge you can build on . . . It's like the second floor and you need the foundation." Similarly, Mrs. Nelson noted that many of her students did not understand key concepts in the curriculum such as countries and continents: "You can work on it from day one till the last day and some of them still do not get that." Nonetheless, Mrs. Nelson persisted in teaching facts and skills as a "framework" for later understanding. As she concluded, "map skills and geographical terms . . . [take] too much time . . . and yet you need [to spend that time], in order for them to have any competency."

Mrs. Swan was less concerned with learning of facts and skills. Facts, she said, do not matter much because students can always look them up "in the book." Skills, she continued, would develop when her students could "read and write." Relationships, not low-order information and skills, were more of a priority for Mrs. Swan: "I figure the kids are not going to learn every objective, every piece of information in the end." In sum, Mrs. Swan was confident that her children would "have a feel for the people and their way of life when we're talking about a region. Because I think they can relate better to that, how their day goes as opposed to somebody in a different part of the world, I think that's something they'll remember."

Conceptions of Geographic Knowledge

As the foregoing discussion of the teachers' views of coverage and how children learn has shown, the teachers' beliefs were interactive. For example, their beliefs concerning the conditions under which students learn reinforced their belief that coverage is more important than depth. This ecological character of teacher beliefs is perhaps most apparent with how they defined geographic knowledge, and hence what children should be taught about world regions.

Mrs. Jackson and Mrs. Nelson held views of geographic knowledge that contrasted with those of Mrs. Swan. As has already been pointed out, Mrs. Jackson regarded facts and skills as the "foundation" of geographic knowledge. Only after the "foundation" was in place, she reasoned, was higher-order geographical knowledge likely to be meaningful to students. This view, of course, starkly contrasts with the constructivist views of geographic educators (e.g., James & Crape, 1968; Joint Committee on Geographic Education, 1984). For Mrs. Jackson, geographic knowledge primarily concerned "how to read a map . . . know[ing] what country they [her students] live in . . . Really, things that you would think children should know and they must know."

Mrs. Nelson's view of geographic knowledge appeared to be strongly influenced by her pedagogical goals. She said, "I think they're always learning geography. From the time they start learning anything, they're learning about the world around them and plac[ing] it in some frame of reference. I think that's geography." Nonetheless, Mrs. Nelson noted that how knowledge was structured in her classes did not vary much from one subject area to the next. For example, she observed how "organizational skills" were something she emphasized in virtually every subject. Similarly, skills such as "outlining" and "answering questions" were "develop[ed] in reading and language arts but the application is in social studies and science." In Mrs. Nelson's view, social studies knowledge was separated from other subjects as much by the greater attention to "study skills" and so forth than by the particular characteristics of geographic knowledge.

As has already been suggested, Mrs. Swan's view of geographic knowledge was less constrained by a facts-and-skills approach and a study skills approach than those of her two colleagues. Although this was a matter of emphasis (not an absolute difference), it seemed that Mrs. Swan placed more value on a higher-order geographic knowledge and was less concerned with social studies as a vehicle for teaching reading, writing, and study skills: "[Regarding] answering questions in social studies, I try to encourage the children that they need those writing skills to answer but, oh, you know I just am not real critical on them always answering in complete sentences. If they have the ideas and the concepts, that's what I'm really looking for." As with her conception of learning, Mrs. Swan's view of geographic knowledge revolved around students and teachers co-constructing knowledge about topics children found engaging: "I guess I have this philosophy, get done with what you have to get done so you can develop other interests, your own interest, their own interest, a kind of joint interest, I guess."

IMPLICATIONS AND QUESTIONS FOR FURTHER RESEARCH

It is intriguing that Mrs. Nelson and Mrs. Swan, in both their interviews and classroom instructional practices (see Thornton & Wenger, 1990), exhibited great differences (and some similarities, such as a belief in coverage) in how and what they decided to teach about world regions. It is important to note, however, that these differences would not necessarily be immediately apparent to the casual observer. For example, compare the following two remarks they made about the point of teaching world regions:

> I think that what you are after is the main objective: that they understand what the region is you're talking about, what characteristics they have in common, where in the world you could find some places like this, then let's take a look at one and see, how do they live there? (Mrs. Nelson)

[Using deserts as an illustrative region:] . . . locating the deserts, but right now we're just primarily dealing with the southwestern United States and the people that live there and what life is like living in the desert region and almost comparing and contrasting with our own region. I want them to feel what the difference would be like. (Mrs. Swan)

It is striking, I believe, how similar these two statements sound. We have seen, however, that in many ways these two teachers approached world regions very differently. This only serves to underscore that accurate and informative representations of how teachers go about making curricular-instructional decisions must entail careful attention to the nuances of particular teachers, particular classrooms, and particular subject matters.

In this study, moreover, several important questions are raised which cannot be adequately answered and deserve further research. For example, where do teachers' beliefs in coverage originate? How do their beliefs about how children learn evolve? In what specific ways do their beliefs about learning and their conception of geographic knowledge interact? Given that it is generally acknowledged that the overarching goal of social studies is citizenship education, how do these teachers conceive of their curricula contributing to citizenship, and how do they define citizenship? In what ways did their strong concerns for the affective growth of students — a concern not systematically dealt with in this study but clearly evident in each teacher's interviews and classroom behavior — influence their curricular-instructional decision making? (Indeed, Nel Noddings, 1990, has suggested that the centrality of "caregiving" for elementary teachers has long presented a conflict with the so-called professionalization of teaching.) To what extent do teachers' choices depend on the subject matter in question? For example, would these three teachers select subject matter based on the same criteria if they were teaching United States history or *Man: A Course of Study* instead of world regions? And what are the effects of various curricular-instructional arrangements on student learning? (See Stodolsky & Glaessner, 1988.) Since it is plain that the teachers' beliefs did account for much of the significant curricular-instructional differences that we observed, more focused research is needed to attend to these questions.

Two salient conclusions have emerged from this study. First, the teachers' beliefs — even if sometimes mutually inconsistent — were ecological in character. In other words, for example, their belief in coverage was linked to the kinds of instruction they provided. This suggests that curricular-instructional improvement efforts should focus on teachers' curricular-instructional decision making as a whole rather than tinker with parts (instructional materials, new teaching techniques) of the process. Second, it is apparent that the teachers, dedicated and diligent as they were, seldom questioned their assumptions about how children learn, what knowledge is of most worth, and so forth. In these circumstances, consciousness raising about the extent and importance of their decisions would appear to be an important issue for teacher education. Finally, there is a clear need to move beyond merely describing what teachers do to helping them understand what they do, why they do it, and to what educational effects.

7

WALTER C. PARKER
JANET E. McDANIEL

Bricolage: Teachers Do It Daily

The teacher's role in curriculum change has successively been ignored, critiqued, and championed in the post-Sputnik era. When in the 1960s public and private organizations disseminated curriculum materials on a previously unknown scale, center-to-periphery curriculum development was practiced widely. Teachers were to act as conduits in the delivery of new curriculum to students, and fidelity of the taught and written curricula was the hallmark of successful curriculum enactment.

Soon to follow these curriculum change efforts were the curriculum change researchers. Inadequacies of the center-to-periphery model were identified and alternatives proposed (Connelly & Ben-Peretz, 1980; Olson, 1982; Parker, 1987). Teachers were conceived as curriculum agents who mediate curriculum inventions—whose beliefs, principles, relationships, knowledge, and interests all interact with the invention, coming between it and the landscape of daily school practice. The mediation may render the invention unrecognizable to the inventors although finally of use to practitioners, or it may result in its outright rejection.

Investigators of teachers' mediation differ markedly from one another in aim. Some (e.g., Hall, Wallace, & Dossett, 1973) regard mediation as a force to be understood and controlled by the presumably wiser higher-ups who select and dispatch inventions—the school district's curriculum supervisors, university professors, and outside consultants; others (e.g., Elbaz, 1983; Olson, 1982) regard it as an aspect of personal knowledge and professional practice that needs to be understood in its own right, both as a correction to the popular misconception of teachers as technicians and as a basis for genuine dialogue among teachers and other educators. Either way, mediation of curriculum inventions by teacher remains essentially a black box. Much happens, no doubt, but just what happens is largely unknown.

Here, we report a case study of the mediation of curriculum inventions by classroom teachers. Examined were four teachers who mediated a critical thinking skills program that was based on the work of Edward deBono (1975). Although the development of such programs is well reported (e.g., Baron & Sternberg, 1987), the ways teachers make sense of them have been all but ignored. What happens when teachers encounter one of these programs? How do they come between students, program, and milieu? To begin with conclusions, we found that these teachers' mediation was bound up in school structures, practices, and tools; was improvisational rather than formal; and was an instantiation of a bricoleur's *praxis*.

TEACHERS' MEDIATION OF CURRICULUM INVENTIONS

Evidence indicates that the curriculum in most schools in the United States neither teaches nor requires much critical thinking of its students (e.g., Goodlad, 1984), and some argue that it emphasizes quite the opposite—the passive acceptance of reified knowledge and ways of relating to one another (e.g., Apple, 1982). For the present analysis, it should be helpful to understand that the present stable curriculum was itself once an innovation that replaced what was then a stable curriculum (Reid, 1987), and that an innovation is an invention that has been accepted into widespread practice (Westbury, 1984). This should remind us of two things: each new stability is an innovation that has replaced a prior innovation, and each innovation is a social happening, an idea-into-practice that necessarily comprises social meanings and activity. These meanings and activities compose the content of teachers' mediation of curriculum inventions.

Two perspectives should be brought to bear on the subject of teachers' mediation of inventions: cognitive science and hermeneutics. The former contributes the idea of practical intelligence; the latter contributes phenomenological interpretation. Practical intelligence (Sternberg & Wagner, 1986) describes cognitive processes of a nonacademic and often tacit sort. People use their practical intelligence to solve the ill-defined problems that arise naturally on the landscape of daily life. There are typically multiple solutions to these problems and multiple paths for obtaining them. This "everyday cognition" (Rogoff & Lave, 1984) is less hierarchic and systematic than formal reasoning, and

usually more efficient and sensible for the in-flight model building needed in the practical realm (see also Perkins, Allen, &
Hafner, 1983).

Cognitive anthropologists Berry and Irvine (1986) elaborated
this theme in their study, "Bricolage: Savages Do It Daily." Res-
urrecting Levi-Strauss's (1962) term *bricolage*, meaning work of
an odd-job sort done by a do-it-yourself practitioner, they contrasted bricolage to formal work. Bricoleurs tackle a problem
not by reading a manual or taking a course of study, but by
using a personal bag of tricks. They are masters of improvisation,
using whatever tools and devices are on hand or can be invented.
Bricolage in several cultures has been analyzed: the navigational
skills of the Micronesian Puluwat, the visual acuity and memory
of the Australian Aboriginals, and the knowledge of animals held
by Kung Bushmen (Berry & Irvine, 1986). This sort of activity
was denigrated by Levi-Strauss and other anthropologists of an
evolutionist bent: "savages" are skilled at simple cognitions but
incapable of abstract, scientific operations. Berry and Irvine,
however, held everyday intelligence in high regard, emphasizing
that it figures centrally in a community's ecoculture and serves a
basic purpose: survival. The ethnocentrism of outside observers
accounts for the observation that the bricoleur is simpleminded.

The present study presumed a parallel between teachers'
and bricoleurs' talents. Doing so credits teachers carte blanche
with practical intelligence. The teachers in this study were not
presumed to be clerks who transmit curricula, but agents whose
mediative activity is directed toward the best functioning of their
ecoculture—their classrooms. In the classroom context, adapting
and transforming curriculum inventions that originate outside
that ecoculture is the intelligent course of action; delivering them
uncritically is not.

Hermeneutics provides another helpful (and similarly
friendly) perspective on mediation. Hermeneutics, the study of
understanding, assumes there is no such thing as a nonpositional subject, and therefore no such thing as nonpositional
understanding (Palmer, 1969). Knowing cannot be separated
from being. Renewed interest in this field helped to identify limitations inherent in much research on teachers' decision making,
judgments, and other thought processes and, in turn, opened for
study the phenomenon called teachers' mediation (Carson, 1986;
Parker, 1987). Using Gadamer's (1985) distinction between genuine questions and conventional research questions, researchers

interested in teachers' mediation argued that the newer study of teachers' cognition did not signify a genuine break with the earlier process-product research (e.g., Gage, 1963) that its advocates had supposed. The argument advanced by the cognitive researchers had been that process-product studies might tell us which behaviors were related positively to student achievement but not how teachers might appropriately apply those behaviors in the dynamic conditions of classroom teaching. Teachers who had learned these behaviors and stored them in their repertoire of pedagogic know-how still had the awesome task of deciding which behaviors to use, when, and with which students (Shavelson, 1973). Yet these two research programs shared the same genuine (or prior) question, which undermined the latter's claim to progress. That question was, How can teachers be made more amenable to change projects that originate outside their practice? Process-product research answered this question in one way: identify teacher behaviors that increase student achievement and install them in the current teaching force. Teachers' cognition research answered in a slightly different way: identify the better cognitive processing models for both planning and instruction, and install them in the current teaching force. Thus the genuine question underlying both is the generalized curriculum model of school change stated as a question. Realizing this helps identify an underlying interest of much work within these research programs. Hardly neutral, that work is interested in teachers becoming good implementers of others' plans (Parker, 1987).

Both the practical intelligence and hermeneutics perspectives, then, though derived from wholly different traditions, break with much of the research on teachers' behaviors and cognitions by breaking with its prior, center-to-periphery interest. Instead, they ask, how do teachers make sense of their work, and how do their understandings create the curriculum in practice?

METHOD

The case study method is advantageous when contemporary social phenomena over which the investigator has little or no control are the objects of study; when the boundaries between the phenomena and their contexts are not clear; when multiple sources of data are used; and when the investigator's goal is to contribute to the same body of theory that justified the present study (Yin, 1984). Such was the situation at hand.

Examined was the mediation of curriculum invention by a team of four ninth-grade teachers. The invention was a portion of Edward deBono's (1975) *CoRT* program. The mediation of this invention was embedded in another—the teaching team's mediation of a pilot, interdisciplinary (ID) curriculum. The mediation of the critical thinking program was our primary focus. As such, the ID pilot was considered a context feature and is detailed in the findings section below.

Data

Data on these teachers' mediation were gathered in document analysis, observations, and interviews. Documents analyzed were a report on the project written by one of the teachers and handouts created by the team for student use in the critical thinking lessons. Observed were these classroom lessons and the team's collaborative planning meetings. Open-ended interviews, really conversations (Carson, 1986), were conducted at the team meetings, and focused interviews were conducted with each team member and a vice principal. In focused interviews, the respondents were asked to reflect on the progress and current status of the critical thinking program, its problems and promise. Extensive field notes were taken during classroom observations, and nearly verbatim records were kept of interviews. The data were gathered over an eight-month span of the 1986-87 school year, from October to May.

Analysis

Data were analyzed using a variation of grounded theory's constant-comparative technique of qualitative analysis (Glaser & Strauss, 1967). The constant-comparative method provides for alternate phases of data collection and analysis. Early phases are devoted to category construction and later phases to the generation of hypotheses. Newly collected data are constantly compared to categories and hypotheses that emerged in earlier rounds of analysis, and those categories and hypotheses are refined and elaborated or abandoned in light of the new data. In this way, the propositions eventually generated are grounded, or based, in empirical data.

Accordingly, in the present study, similarities and differences were noted in data gathered in the first team planning sessions observed in October. These initial categories were then consolidated. They included, for example, the teachers' frustration over the perceived inadequacy of available materials for teaching critical thinking in classroom settings, their pride at being on the "cutting edge" of curriculum innovation, and their tacit versus formal knowledge of the school milieu. Elaborating and refining these categories was one objective of subsequent classroom observations, interviews, document analysis, and conversation through May. In addition, new patterns were sought and new categories constructed that either had not been present in data gathered earlier or were present but not noticed because of lapses in our "theoretical sensitivity" (Glaser, 1978). As the emerging categories stabilized, they were integrated just enough to suggest theory. These early intimations of theory were elaborated and refined during subsequent rounds of data gathering and during the rereading of documents, interview records, and field notes. In this way, the hypotheses themselves matured into the conclusions put forward below.

Two conventions of the constant-comparative technique were modified for the present study. First, we ignored the convention that theorizing not commence until after data are gathered since we intentionally had derived theoretical propositions prior to beginning the study. These a priori propositions helped direct the analytic activity to data more or less relevant to the mediation of inventions. Second, the convention of theoretical sampling was cut short. This convention requires that the first sample of subjects be selected for theoretical reasons because it is considered a likely source of data relevant to the research question. Then additional samples are selected that are considered likely sources of additional data that will, in turn, refine and elaborate categories and hypotheses generated from the first sample. In the present case, only one sample of subjects was selected because a sample was found that constituted a unique case; consequently, a single-case design was used, and the constant-comparative procedure was used *within* this case (see Yin, 1984).

FINDINGS

Three hypotheses are presented and illustrated below. The intent of this section is not to pile up evidence to verify them but to present and exemplify them sufficiently to ground them in data.

Teachers' mediation of curriculum inventions reveals the local milieu. By local milieu, we mean the organizational structures, practices, and tools of the particular work setting at hand. Each will be illustrated following a general sketch of the work setting.

The observed mediation was of a critical thinking program, the immediate curricular context of which was another curriculum invention—a pilot interdisciplinary curriculum in its trial year. Four teachers at Woodland High School (a fictitious name of a school in the Pacific Northwest) decided to design and conduct a ninth-grade interdisciplinary program. They hoped the program would integrate the standard English, mathematics, science, and social studies courses. Two sections of students (seventy in all) moved through this interdisciplinary (ID) block during the first four periods of the day. The four courses were taught in self-contained classrooms during separate class periods, but coursework was interrelated through the efforts of these teachers, who collectively were called the "ID team." For example, works of literature were selected that lent themselves to analysis in each class: *Tunnel in the Sky, To Kill a Mockingbird, Romeo and Juliet, Flowers for Algernon,* and *Farewell to Manzanar.* In the science fiction work *Tunnel,* "there were obvious bridges between each subject," according to the math teacher, Stan. Metric measurements were discussed in his course, law and population growth were discussed in social studies, relevant experiments were conducted in science, and character and plot development were examined in English. (A detailed account of the ID block can be found in McDaniel, 1987.)

The ID team met often during the summer in order to plan their curriculum for the year ahead, and they met daily throughout the school year during a common planning period. In late October, they joined their principal, vice principal, district staff development director, and a university professor of curriculum and instruction at a weekend retreat. Their purpose was to further plan the ID curriculum and to integrate within it a critical thinking component. The retreat was sponsored and funded in part by the state affiliate of the Association for Supervision and Curriculum Development. Its intent was to support local teams of practitioners who had programs in mind but who needed planning time and assistance from resource persons. At the retreat, the team and administrators asked the professor to help them identify and plan a critical thinking component for the ID block. They were particularly concerned that their ninth graders were unable to see problems from any point of view other than their own. None of the ID teachers had studied instruction on critical thinking, though the vice principal, Margaret, had attended a workshop on the subject during the previous school year.

The professor suggested that the team consider two writers whose work focused on helping students explore other points of view: Edward deBono's *Other Point of View* (OPV) and Richard Paul's (1987) rendering of dialogical reasoning. Both encourage students to develop empathy for others' viewpoints and to bring multiple perspectives to bear on problem solving. The group considered both deBono's and Paul's ideas to be appropriate to an interdisciplinary setting because of their applicability in many subject areas. OPV and dialogical reasoning could be taught directly to students as thinking strategies and then used throughout the year with content drawn from each course. The teachers decided to provide direct instruction on OPV and then apply it in all classes; they would then repeat the process for dialogical reasoning. They used the professor's language, "direct teaching" and "application lessons," to signify these two classroom activities. In response to the team's request, the professor supplied them with OPV material that deBono and Howitt-Gleeson had written (1979) and an article by Paul (1987).

During daily team meetings, the teachers discussed in general terms the plan to implement the critical thinking instruction. Then the actual planning of OPV instruction began. Stan (the team leader and math teacher) and Margaret (the vice principal) worked together to design and conduct the lessons in which students would be taught OPV directly. The other three teachers agreed to take responsibility for the application lessons that would follow in their courses. The direct teaching was accomplished during six lessons, one in early December and five in the first week of February. Stan and Margaret each introduced OPV to one section (thirty-five students) during the first lesson. In the five subsequent lessons, they worked together with all seventy students in a double classroom. During all OPV lessons, the social studies, science, and English teachers were present in the classroom; they served as discussion leaders and supervisors of group activities. Time for these lessons was borrowed from the regular block schedule by shortening two of the classes.

Although the team had planned to follow the direct instruction on OPV with application lessons, this bridging to regular subject matter did not take place. As the school year wore on, teachers felt they must attend to their regular course material; thus the OPV lessons were given ever lower priority. One by one, the teachers dropped the application lessons from their plans. In some lessons, however, all four teachers continued to use informally the phrases "OPV" and "looking at all sides."

Classroom practice, then, fell far short of the plan devised by the team at the October retreat. Only one component, the direct instruction on OPV, took place. The other three—application of OPV to the subject areas, direct instruction, and application of dialogical reasoning—did not.

With this general sketch behind us, three aspects of the context may be highlighted: structures, practices, and tools. The social and physical *structures* of the ID block allowed these teachers to construct a critical thinking program that would cut across the school's academic disciplines (and corresponding departments). The ID block was both the most important and the most local prior structure for the critical thinking invention, providing it with a home base. The ID block brought the teachers together in daily planning meetings, where informal discussions of students' reasoning first took place and where a proposal for the October retreat was developed. And, because she was the building supervisor of the ID block, Margaret's involvement in the critical thinking program was facilitated: "I saw some [positive] administrative visibility coming from . . . seeing kids in another context besides discipline. This is a helping, teaching, positive role. I also offered to lend a hand to Stan [helping him conduct the OPV lessons]. He's got too much to do."

ID block students were taught the OPV strategy in a combined classroom by their math teacher, with their science, social studies, and English teachers helping out. And in preparation for application lessons in each course, these teachers began to rethink their own disciplines. Their intent now was to identify subject matter in their courses that could be argued from several perspectives; that is, they were challenged to perceive their subject matter as inherently controversial rather than resolved.

Most important, the ID block structure allowed for a pivotal *practice*—team planning. These teachers put great stock in their daily planning meetings. There they would, as Stan put it, "lay on the table" their concerns regarding the ID pilot, the critical thinking program, and students' progress. It was also the site for "brainstorming" plans. Dividing up tasks came generally through consensus during team meetings, and all four teachers talked about the mutual warmth and cooperation they felt. A team identity formed which was, one said, "the most important thing" contributing to the vitality of the ID/critical thinking experiment. "We have a near-perfect professional regard for one another," said another. Although they had markedly different personalities and teaching styles, they tried hard to defer to one another's subject area expertise and to avoid imposing their styles on one another.

The team planning meetings were the forum for group decision making and commiserating. Group decisions ranged from moving individual students from one ID class to another (the structure permitted this with ease) to selecting the critical thinking vocabulary that all four would use with students (e.g., "both-sides reasoning") and identifying which member would speak for the team at a school board meeting.

These same structures, however, prevented the very sort of deliberation that might have generated a sustainable invention. The single common planning period was sufficient only for mediating the roughest outline of the ID pilot, with little time remaining for the second invention—the critical thinking program. Each team member was kept very busy just dealing with students' difficulties on the basic course content. "These kids, you know, are not ready academically for us . . . So many are below grade level," was a typical concern.

In addition to structures and practices, available and improvised *tools* shaped these teachers' mediation. For example, from the moment team members improvised the six-step OPV procedure, itself a cognitive tool for considering others' perspectives, they envisioned students expressing their OPV analyses in writing. Thus, from the outset the team thought in terms of a tool—writing—that already had been provided by the social context. Moreover, OPV always was considered a tool that, although initially taught apart from the four subject areas, would eventually be embedded in them. Like writing, these subject matters (for better or worse) are cognitive tools available in the social and historical milieu in which the team worked. The point here is that even as the team was improvising the new cognitive tool, OPV, they were thinking with cognitive tools devised before their mediation had begun.

In these ways, the teachers' mediation was shaped by the structures, practices, and tools that were already given by the milieu or devised by the teachers. Even the devised tools (the OPV procedure) were fashioned with given tools (writing; established subject matters). Similarly, the devised practices (collaborative planning; deference to one another's academic expertise) were fashioned with practices and structures already given by the milieu (the existing schedule of class periods; the team's supervision by the vice principal; the ID pilot). The use of existing social forms in the creation of new social forms reveals the social nature of inventions in general and of cognitive inventions in particular (see Vygotsky, 1978).

Teachers' mediation of curriculum inventions is improvisational. The purpose of the mediation under study was to implement a critical thinking program within a pilot interdisciplinary curriculum. The four ID teachers claimed no expertise in this field; consequently, when their October planning retreat was funded, they invited to advise them a local education professor who had conducted research on students' critical thinking. Hearing at the retreat their concern for students' inability to consider perspectives other than their own, this consultant suggested that the deBono and Paul materials might be a place to start. He recommended further that the team concentrate their efforts first on OPV and then on dialogical reasoning, since the latter was less developed than OPV.

Following the retreat, back in the world of school teaching and daily team meetings, the team discovered that the ideas and materials provided by the professor were "completely inadequate." Stan was extremely disappointed, particularly in the deBono materials on OPV: "I read the OPV excerpts, and I couldn't figure out what was going on. It was obvious to [the professor] what it was, but I didn't know what was going on." There were problems of omission, and the material was "internally inconsistent." For example: "In some places [deBono] calls it Other People's Views and in other places he calls it Other Points of View. There is more than a trivial distinction here. The first is based on the thinker, the second is based on the thoughts."

What was the team to do? Primarily through the mechanism of their daily team meetings and much spur-of-the-moment, seat-of-the-pants bricolage, the teachers gradually brought form to chaos. First, they decided to use the term *Other People's Views*. By sharing information and ideas, they began to conceptualize the OPV strategy and to construct a series of lessons for teaching it to their students. Stan concluded that their product was far from what deBono had in mind. "We probably diverged more than we needed to, but we had to anchor ourselves somewhere."

Available materials and people were marshalled. A deBono

book Stan found in the community library was helpful: "I started reading the book, and all of this [the six-step conception of OPV] kind of flowed by having the OPV excerpts [provided by the professor] in my mind and reading the introduction to the book and looking for a structure." A casual conversation in the hallway during which Margaret offered her help to Stan became the basis for her entry into the OPV project. Together they immersed themselves in the OPV materials provided by the professor and found in the library, interpreting and adapting them from where they stood. Stan saw in the deBono work "little individual strategies, [but] what that meant in terms of student understanding of the material wasn't there." The university professor had been "way off base" and "just plain wrong" in suggesting that the OPV materials could be used pretty much as is and "just taught right off the top" Stan was disappointed at deBono's poor grammar and the "vague admonitions" that deBono called "principles." As an example, Stan cited from a deBono resource: "Try and see whether the other person can see your viewpoint." Margaret, too, was dismayed at the unusability of the material as it was. She complained that deBono had taken the OPV idea and "tossed it up in the air." Furthermore, referring to an article he had read concerning Howard Gardner's (1983) theory that there are at least seven distinct intelligences, Stan complained that deBono failed to account for "an individual's blend of multiple intelligences."

Working before and after school, Stan and Margaret reworked the materials until they were satisfied that they could present "a methodical series of lessons" that would make sense to their students. They planned separately for several evenings, then came together to "package it, systematize it, process it." They devised a six-step procedure for "doing an OPV," and six lessons for teaching the procedure to their students. The procedure was as follows:

1. Identify all the people involved in the issue.
2. "Crawl inside their skin" (Atticus to Scout in *To Kill a Mockingbird*).
3. Select the prime players and seek each point of view. Use the mental MACHINE.
4. Seek solutions seen from the viewpoint of each player.
5. Seek a resolution respecting the needs of all who are involved.
6. Communicate the resolution with a focus on each person.

Note that step 2 quotes one of the works all ID students had read, and step 3 has students use a mnemonic tool (MACHINE) Stan invented for recalling Gardner's seven intelligences. Stan justified the incorporation of that theory into the OPV procedure by citing the team's emphasis on the "thinker" rather than the "thoughts"—their belief, as Stan put it, "that all people are intelligent, but certainly in different ways." After their initial examination of deBono's version of OPV, Stan and Margaret had wondered (in Stan's words),

> How do we get kids to realize that [parents are not all alike], that the parent group is composed of a whole bunch of different thought processes, and that we should check them out . . . from as many angles as possible? So, we though, multiple intelligences seem to be a good way of doing that. So I then went home again, and I developed this mental MACHINE, hoping that it would enhance [OPV] a little bit.

The team improvised not only an acceptable OPV procedure and the lessons for teaching it, but the content to which they hoped to apply it. *To Kill a Mockingbird* and *Farewell to Manzanar* were selected for student reading in part because the team saw in them rich landscapes for exploring other people's views. In addition, the usual brainstorming in team meetings often centered on OPV applications:

> Math teacher (Stan): We want everybody to use OPV.
> Social studies teacher: I've got an issue coming up in social studies. I can do it.
> Math teacher: So, we need to talk about one another's coursework. What about science?
> Science teacher: No controversies now. We're studying chemistry.
> English teacher: It doesn't have to come from every class at the same time.
> Social studies teacher: I took Reagan's side on the Iran arms deal [because] the kids just can't imagine Reagan's side.

Once the six-step OPV procedure had been devised, the team had to design a lesson plan for teaching it directly to students. A series of six lessons was produced. The first three steps of the procedure were taught during the first lesson in early December. The latter three were taught in the subsequent five lessons during the first week of February. The planned application lessons were never taught, although the teachers continued to use informally with students and one another the language of OPV. Neither the direct instruction nor the application lessons on dialogical reasoning were developed.

It is not our purpose to explain *why* the team did not take the critical thinking program as far as they initially had planned, but how they mediated it as far as they did. Let us mention, however, that the data suggest that the strain associated with mediating this invention may have been responsible. By any account, a tremendous amount of work was required by these teachers to teach classes that were not part of the ID block while also teaching the ID classes, planning together the ID curriculum, and, atop all this, planning and conducting the critical thinking component. Team members all complained at one time or another about the increased workload they carried and the accompanying stress. The English teacher worked "harder than [she] ever [had]"; the science teacher rewrote and adjusted "everything" in his curriculum in order to take into account the integration of knowledge from the other three disciplines. The social studies teacher tired of playing the political games necessary to secure support for the ID block: "I feel like Chief Joseph—you know, I want to 'fight no more forever.'"

The emotional toll was never more apparent than during the teaching of the OPV lessons. Stan and Margaret met every day before and after school to make their plans: "We talked late last night and again at six this morning." Stan's nervousness in the moments before conducting the first of the OPV lessons was apparent; he shut himself away in his classroom and likened the experience to "an actor getting ready for a role—you need to concentrate hard." In the midst of the OPV lessons, Stan admitted, "This is more of a strain than I thought it would be." Near the last of the six lessons, Stan admitted to feeling "tired, fed up, and relieved." Having to create new materials, orchestrate the inclusion of the other three teachers and Margaret, and deal with the observing eye of the investigators was "a lot of extra burden . . . I don't want to have too many weeks like that." After the six lessons had been conducted, an exhausted Stan was unwilling to commit time and energy to application lessons. Instead, he suggested that the team "let this hang for six weeks or so and then we'll come back to it." The team did not, in fact, "come back."

Teachers' mediation of curriculum inventions is an instance of praxis. The mediation of a curriculum invention is a knowing-

and-doing activity in which knowing and doing are one thing, not two. Clearly these teachers' knowledge of critical thinking did not come before they planned and conducted the critical thinking component of their curriculum, nor did it come after it. Rather, it came *with* it, dialectically. This is not to claim that these teachers' knowing and doing cannot be discussed as distinct features nor that the knowing and doing occurred simultaneously. Rather, the point is that these teachers' knowing and doing were different aspects of a single process within which each aspect continually transformed the other.

Metaphorically, we are dealing with a circle here, not a straight line. Wherever the circle is entered, for purposes of observing the dialectic, the whole is displayed. We might enter the present case at the point of Stan's creation of the mnemonic MACHINE. After delving into Gardner's and deBono's work, Stan began to construct some sense of it; the six-step OPV procedure, the Mnemonic, and the six-lesson plan followed. We might call the former knowing and the latter doing, but then we recall that Stan's studying of deBono and Gardner was predicated on his earlier doing—the endeavor to "teach right off the top" of the deBono material, which he found impossible. At that point, he had made no sense of the material. Only as he began to do just that could he identify what he considered to be its errors, which MACHINE was, in turn, an attempt to correct.

Note that this knowing and reknowing in action (Schön's [1983] reflection-in-action) occurred within the space of Stan's interests—that is, his normative vision of himself and his work with colleagues and students. To have taken deBono's invention as given would have been *wrong* from Stan's vantage point. Its vagaries and inconsistencies violated his sense of good pedagogy; moreover, it would have foisted on students the mistaken view that "thoughts" rather than the "thinker" were what counts in critical thinking. So deBono's good idea was mediated within Stan's meliorative vision. For his students, he wanted upward and forward movement—toward curiosity and intelligence. Against this horizon, instruction on critical thinking stood out as worthy of much hard work. Doing that work, with only bare assistance provided by inadequate materials, gratified Stan and his colleagues. After the first lesson on OPV, a contented Stan announced, "We got over a hurdle today . . . This is the first time I've seen this taught directly as content." And team members described themselves as "pioneers" on the "cutting edge" of practice.

DISCUSSION

This was a case study undertaken to build theory on teachers' work with curriculum inventions. Little is known about this subject because most research related to it has been wedded to the center-to-periphery model of school change. That model's interest in high-fidelity implementation of imported inventions undermines its ability to tell us much about what mediation is and how it occurs. Although there is a reasonableness to the expectation that teachers conduct themselves according to the canons of recent pedagogic knowledge, this study indicates that the expectation is based on a misunderstanding of what teachers actually do. The top-down epistemology of knowledge production and use is wrong, not only as a model of "what works," but as a matter of fact. These teachers mediated the given invention, OPV, reinventing it in the practical realm of the ID team at Woodland High.

The mediation had three features. It was embedded in the local milieu—the structures, practices, and tools at Woodland; it was improvisational; and it was a unity of knowing and doing. DeBono's, Gardner's, and, to a degree, Paul's "good ideas" were transformed. Using resources on hand and creating others, all the while learning from their doing and doing what they knew, the ID team authored the curriculum invention they eventually implemented. And as authors (as opposed to conduits of others' creations), they were empowered, assessing themselves as thinkers on the leading edge of curriculum and instruction.

We suggest that these findings hold true generally of teachers' mediation of curriculum change, and that they be incorporated into the emerging body of theory on teachers' work. The body of theory that justified this study is the same body to which these findings are now generalized. Of course, caution is needed when leaping from case to theory, particularly when leaping from a unique case to general theory. The leap is justified here, for the unique aspect of this case was its embedded structure (critical thinking within the ID pilot). This allowed a clearer view of contextual factors (structures, practices, and tools) that remain, we hypothesize, even when less apparent.

Moreover, we suggest that the theoretical perspective that guided this study's question and design is the most promising for future inquiry on teachers' mediation. Using the burgeoning theory on practical intelligence, investigators will be attuned to the local and improvisational character—the bricolage—of teachers' *praxis* rather than trying to compare their mediation to nonlocal standards of expertise. And, using the interpretive canons of hermeneutics, they will be interested in understanding understanding itself. That is, investigators will regard their subjects *qua* subjects, not objects—as bricoleurs who construct meaning vis à vis who they are, where they are, and what they want. Both perspectives are suited to inquiry on meaning making and change in ecocultural settings like schools.

But to appreciate these distinctions, investigators will need to reflect on their own interests. Those interested primarily in helping to install new and better practices in schools probably will have little patience for inquiry into teachers' mediation. Many educational researchers appear wedded to an improvement ethic (Jackson & Kieslar, 1977), which may stand in the way of inquiry into teachers' mediation except as it might inform the development of strategies to circumvent or appropriate teachers' mediation (as a general wants to know how the enemy thinks, or as a parent wants insight into a child's world in the hope of controlling it). A serious consequence of ignoring or only strategizing about teachers' bricolage is that researchers and the policy community alike will operate without anything close to a comprehension of what teachers actually do. Working in this vacuum, they will conceptualize teachers' work using not teachers' but their *own* bricolage as the standard. *As a result, researchers and policymakers will discover only what teachers cannot do.*

According to one analysis (Parker, 1989), these discoveries actually are judgments and are of three types, depending on the discoverer's conception of quality in teaching. One type finds teachers' knowledge of the subject matter they are trying to teach more or less inadequate; another finds problems in teachers' ability to design instruction that brings about classroom learning of that subject matter; and another laments teachers' reluctance (or inability) to help their students reflect critically on the status quo. In each case we have something like *dueling bricolage* between the judge and the judged.

Several questions should be addressed in subsequent studies. First, and at the center of the methodological challenge posed by such work, must investigators adopt relativism as their methodological stance in order to inquire genuinely on teachers' mediation? Second, if the school is indeed the empirical, logical, and ethical center of educational change (cf. Sirotnik, 1987), then of what use are the judgments and initiatives of district-level curriculum directors and professors of education vis à vis this center? Third, what theoretically pertinent factors in teachers' mediation of curriculum inventions exist apart from those proposed by this study? For example, what is the role of teachers' pedagogic and academic knowledge (Shulman, 1987) and of alternative school milieus, like "effective schools" (Purkey & Smith, 1983)?

In closing, we will comment on the first of these. Is relativism the best stance for this kind of inquiry? As a rule, the answer is yes. Granted, the move risks relativism's errors (amoralism; romanticizing bad practice), but its benefits are sanguine. As a research stance, relativism affords a generous attitude toward the sense making of others, a "cognitive egalitarianism . . . that makes it easier to credit others, not with confusion, error, or ignorance, but rather with an alternative vision of the possibilities of social life" (Shweder & Bourne, 1984, p. 165). It accomplishes this generosity through its contextualization rule (the natives' behavior makes sense to the observer once its context is thickly portrayed) and its rejection of the deficit hypothesis (once the natives are properly educated and motivated, their cognitive processing will improve). Consequently, relativism is an appropriate ground when the research question seeks descriptive insight into a group's *praxis*. Extraordinary caution is needed, however, lest this stance be used to escape judgment or to dress poor teaching in finer clothes. Clearly, there is a tension here that needs to be negotiated gingerly between, on the one hand, dueling bricolage and, on the other, acquiescence to current practice.

8

KENNETH TOBIN
SARAH ULERICK LaMASTER

An Interpretation of High School Science Teaching Based on Metaphors and Beliefs for Specific Roles

Changes in the quality of science and mathematics learning are desperately needed. Since publication of *A Nation at Risk* (National Commission on Excellence in Education, 1983), more than three hundred reports deploring the status of science and mathematics education in the United States have been written. But can the science and mathematics education community respond to the demands for change? In the 1960s the response was to concentrate on curriculum development in an endeavor to enhance learning. However, what became apparent was that teachers implemented the curriculum in accordance with their own knowledge and beliefs and did not necessarily do what curriculum designers envisioned. Several studies of science classrooms (e.g., Gallagher, 1989; Tobin, 1987) indicated that teachers do what they do in classrooms because of their beliefs about what should be done and how students learn. In addition, teacher perceptions of constraints also mediate the curriculum. For example, teachers respond to pressures to prepare students for the university and provide them with opportunities to succeed on local, state, and national tests. Exacerbating the problem even more is a trend for commercial book designers, in an endeavor to sell books in as many states as possible, to increase the length of texts to meet the varied requirements of particular states. Driven by a belief that the content in the texts ought to be learned by students, teachers feel a need to cover more and more content. Although studies of teacher change have provided some guidelines as to how teachers might change to improve the learning environment, more research is needed on ways to help teachers implement the curriculum in the manner they would like.

Recent work with science and mathematics teachers suggests that a major new direction for teacher enhancement programs would be fruitful. Several studies have highlighted the importance of self-analysis of teaching, receipt of feedback, and observation of models of effective practice. A series of peer coaching studies in middle and high school science and mathematics (Tobin & Espinet, in press; Tobin & Espinet, 1989) underlined the importance of observing colleagues teach, discussing observed lessons with colleagues, and receiving coaching from peers regarded as effective teachers. However, reflection on action was perceived by teachers to be the most useful component of the peer coaching strategies. Reflective thinking enables teachers to consider specific beliefs in relation to the manner in which the curriculum is implemented. The peer coaching studies highlighted the strong influence of teachers' beliefs on what was planned and implemented in both science and mathematics. Other studies (e.g., Gallagher, 1989) have replicated these findings.

Tobin, Kahle, and Fraser (in press) have described how teaching behavior is influenced by metaphors used to conceptualize teaching. For example, a teacher described his teaching role in terms of two metaphors: the teacher as *entertainer* ("Teaching is like acting. You're like an actor on a stage and you've got to sell your performance," p. 22) and the teacher as *captain of the ship* (. . . "the captain of the ship, out in front directing . . . I am the kind of teacher who loves to direct and dominate," p. 23).

The observations and interviews suggest that these metaphors influenced the way the teacher perceived his role and the way he taught. For example, when he was entertaining the class the teacher was humorous, interactive, and amenable to student noise and risqué behavior. The class was regarded as an interactive audience. The teacher as entertainer quipped his way through whole-class activities and socialized with students during seatwork activities. The teacher and the students were relaxed, but little learning was accomplished.

As captain of the ship, the teacher was assertive and businesslike. The class was treated as the crew of a ship. The teacher was in charge of the class and emphasized whole-class activities to maintain control of a teacher-centered and paced learning environment. While the teacher was captain of the ship, he was particularly severe on students who stepped out of line and often scolded them in a strong voice. In this mode he called on non-volunteers and ensured that all students listened and participated in an appropriate manner. In this role more content was covered and the class resembled a traditional classroom with students mainly listening to the teacher perform in an expository manner.

Pope and Gilbert (1983) maintain that personal epistemologies of teachers influence the manner in which the curriculum is implemented. Of course, what a teacher believes about knowledge and learning can have no direct effect on *how* students actually learn, but what a teacher believes about knowledge and learning can be at the heart of curriculum planning and implementation decisions. Because the activities in which students engage can constrain opportunities to learn, learning can be focused by the activities which are planned by teachers. Accordingly, it is important to know what teachers believe about knowledge and learning.

PURPOSE

The purpose of this study was to investigate beliefs, metaphors, and the personal epistemology of a science teacher in an endeavor to construct a grounded theory of teaching with potential applicability to problems associated with teacher enablement. The context for the study was an interpretive investigation involving the two authors and a graduate student. Sarah, one of the authors of this paper, was the teacher studied in the investigation.

The study commenced with a broad question focused on why Sarah could not teach in the manner she intended. As the study progressed, more specific questions emerged and the focus shifted to an examination of beliefs and metaphors associated with Sarah's roles as manager, assessor of student performance, and facilitator of learning. The intended outcome of the study was to gain a better understanding of teaching and teacher change to guide teacher educators, researchers, and policymakers.

SETTING

The study took place at Southern High, a small urban high school in Florida which contained students with diverse socioeconomic backgrounds. The participants in the study were Sarah, four male science teachers from the same school, the school principal, and the students in two science classes taught by Sarah.

DATA SOURCES

The data sources in the study were journal entries from Sarah, interviews with a range of participants, and direct observations of Sarah teaching her two classes. Sarah made journal entries describing reflections on her teaching in the period encompassing the fall and spring of 1987-88. In the spring and summer of 1988 interviews were conducted with Sarah, her science teaching colleagues, the school principal, and students within both classes. All interviews were tape-recorded and transcribed. One member of the research team observed forty-two lessons in the spring of 1988, compiled field notes, and at a later time wrote vignettes from the field notes. The vignettes were used as a data source in the study.

DATA ANALYSIS AND INTERPRETATION

The methods of collection, analysis, and interpretation used in the study were based on an interpretive methodology described by Erickson (1986). Data were analyzed on a continuous basis throughout the study by the research team meeting as a whole and by individual team members working independently. All team meetings were tape-recorded and transcribed, the transcription becoming a data source for the study. The analysis and interpretation process consisted of reading transcripts of interviews, meetings, and vignettes and formulating assertions for which the amount of supporting data exceeded the amount of nonsupporting data.

WHAT WAS HAPPENING IN SARAH'S CLASSES?

When the observations commenced, Sarah had been teaching the classes for one semester. Patterns of behavior and interaction were well established. The first month of observations was characterized by severe management problems in both classes Sarah was teaching. In fact, the magnitude of the problems was such that she had lost confidence in her ability to teach and school administrators and colleagues did not regard her as a competent teacher. These views were shared by the students as well. Evidence of Sarah's management problems is provided below in quotes from interviews with the school principal, Sarah's colleagues, and her students, and in excerpts from Sarah's journal.

> Shirley (school principal): I don't think she was receptive to what we were saying. I think we tried to share with her that she

needed to be consistent with kids. I think there was a real lack of consistency when she came in. The rules were changing all the time, and the kids couldn't keep up with the rules as they were changing.

I think she had a hard time at first asking for help, admitting she was having some difficulty relating to high school students. Before the end of the first six weeks Brian and I met with her trying to give pointers, trying to explain to her that you cannot stand up and lecture to those kids for a solid hour.

I had real reservations at the end of the first semester. I just saw it as absolutely disastrous. She was just very very rigid. There was no flexibility on her part.

Brian (head, science department): When Sarah first started having trouble, which was almost immediately . . . coming down here and slamming her books down, cussing out those kids and crying, going through tissues like an endless supply, and all this was occurring in the first few weeks of school. I saw her as unfit to teach at the high school level.

A basic disrespect for students at first and a basic disrespect for her. It was mutual. It got more and more out of hand.

Frank (science teacher): The way I see it is that initially she was having problems with her classes . . . To me it seems like it was a control problem, class control.

Initially her personality was really terrible. The kids didn't like her. It seemed she really didn't like kids. One thing about teaching is that you have to like kids. You have to adapt. You have to be flexible sometimes, and she wasn't flexible. It goes back to her rules. She would revise her rules every other week or so. And that is not correct. If you're going to set up certain rules, you have to follow it and stay with it.

We gave her suggestions, but it seemed like she never really listened to our suggestions. She did just what she wanted to do. It seemed like any time she asked us, it wasn't like she was asking us to help her out, she was like demanding us.

Kurt (science teacher): She lost her self-confidence. She'd come in so frustrated. I don't think she had self-confidence to begin with, and she tried to go to the other extreme . . . Overcompensate with power. You can't try to force their respect, and she was trying to force respect on them . . . She alienated people . . . you've got to be firm, but you can't be domineering.

The kids are selfish. They are takers. To be a teacher you have to be a giver. If there's a taker teaching and takers learning, it's not going to work out because everybody wants to take from each other.

Student #1: You could tell right away that she was vulnerable. Everybody knew that she was ours. Kind of dangling there for us to pick at. She had a bad group, at first. There were some giving a lot of heck.

It's hard to explain her. She is just . . . one minute she'll be nice to you and the next she'll jump on you. She'll just glare at me or yell at me for asking a question.

Student #2: I figured she would be pretty easy but hard to get along with, because during the first week of school no one could get along with her. Everyone was staying after school. She couldn't control our class. Making a C is like making an A in other classes.

Student #4: She just couldn't control the class. Everyone was noisy, walking around, passing notes. I am there to take notes, pay attention and if I need help I go to another teacher and ask. I could not stand it. She would be explaining something and someone would be talking. I couldn't understand. She would just get frustrated and not bother explaining. That would get me mad.

She would lose her temper. She would get mad. We would say something back to her or argue with her; she was always right. She had this little thing about her, *I'm right*. She was never wrong. She would just blow up at anything. She didn't go in and explain.

Student #5: She'll punish the class because she can't pinpoint one person and stuff like that. It doesn't seem like she really knows what she's doing.

Student #6: Her tests are set up, like if it's out of 50 points and you get a 40 or 43, that's already a C. One or two points off is an A then more is a B and it goes down like that. She doesn't even scale them. Her tests, she doesn't do them out of hundred points like most normal people.

Sarah (8/24/87): I really don't know what I was doing today. I had a minimal plan and it didn't work. Class discussion was nearly impossible without control. I'm not sure how to proceed . . . I honestly question if science education is worth this much trouble.

(9/1/87): I really have no idea how to get them to work constructively.

(9/2/87): I'm being more patient with *myself*—and, hopefully, with the students. I still feel *shrill* more often than I'd like and I lose my temper.

(2/3/88): So today the students were restless and inattentive in both classes. It's not much to go back to. The sense that I'm wasting everybody's time is inescapable and depressing. I really don't like feeling that I'm a bad teacher.

(2/16/88): I have some ideas for changes, but I can't quite convince myself that anything could work at this late stage in the game. It's a shame, too, because I have some very talented students and I'm wasting their talents. I'm ready for some advice. I feel ready to take chances and change things—but I don't know what to change.

(2/17/88): My value/need to "look in charge" has driven my strategies. For example, I will hesitate to make changes or ask student input because it will look like I don't know what I'm doing. (So instead, I do dumb stuff and look like I don't know what I'm doing because I don't.) I hesitate to deal in content areas where I have no knowledge. I am most comfortable speaking to the class—falling back on the lecture style which has been my success. In other words, I have taken very few risks. I have done what I know how to do—whether it's working or not.

WHY COULDN'T SARAH DO WHAT SHE WANTED?

Sarah conceptualized teaching in terms of three roles which were salient to the learning environment in each class. Management of student behavior was a major concern in both classes and prevented Sarah from focusing on enhancing student learning. Assessment was also a problem for Sarah. A significant number of students were failing, Sarah was unhappy about the performance of many students, and the school principal was concerned at the impact of such a high failure rate on the matriculation of students.

Because of the importance of beliefs about teaching and learning in earlier research, we decided to examine Sarah's beliefs in relation to each of the roles she had identified. Perhaps some of Sarah's beliefs were contributing to the problems she was experiencing. Interviews with Sarah soon revealed a puzzle. An important belief that applied to each of the roles was described by Sarah in terms of a distance metaphor. As a facilitator of learning in her "ideal classroom" Sarah believed she should be close to students. These beliefs seemed to imply contradictory courses of action. And to make matters even more complex, the distance metaphor also was applied to Sarah's role as an assessor. Sarah believed she should not get too close to students because, even though they tried hard, many would fail the course and she did not want to be hurt when she explained to them why they had failed. The distance metaphor being applied in different ways to the three roles highlighted a potential problem for Sarah. How would Sarah reconcile these inconsistencies? And were there other opposing sets of beliefs that could lead to problems?

We asked Sarah to provide a written account of her beliefs for each role. This was a time-consuming task which Sarah took seriously. At research meetings we discussed what she had written and searched for beliefs to reveal inconsistencies and provide foci for reflection. We soon realized that the specific beliefs associated with each role were so numerous that the task of listing them all or even the salient ones was enormous. In any case, Sarah might hold a particular belief and not allow it to influence her actions because contextual factors deemed the actions inappropriate. What emerged as being important was the manner in which Sarah conceptualized her roles. It was clear there were inconsistencies between the beliefs associated with the different roles. And the metaphors used to make sense of the three roles seemed inappropriate for the classes she was to teach.

In the subsections below Sarah's three teaching roles are described in terms of her metaphors and beliefs.

Facilitator of Learning

Sarah described her facilitator of learning role in terms of the saintly facilitator, the comedian, and the miser. However, Sarah acknowledged that all three metaphors did not influence how she taught. The saintly facilitator was an idealistic conceptualization which did not appear to influence her planning or teaching. Sarah's own words are used to explain how the three subroles applied to facilitating learning.

> In re-reading the saintly facilitator, I realized that it could not possibly have been a working metaphor. That is, I never actually tried to perform that way nor did I have illusions that I could . . . Nor did I ever totally embrace the miserly position . . . I needed to include the comedian role here also (as well as using a comedian metaphor for management).

The Saintly Facilitator

I am in the classroom to help people learn. I acknowledge that students have differing abilities and interests; and differing levels of intellectual and personal maturity. Students are individuals and must be treated as such.

I would like to work one-on-one more and to establish eye contact with each student as I speak to them. I imagine them inviting me into their "personal space" as a trusted friend and guide.

Patience is a virtue. I need to be flexible, gentle, open, attentive. I need to be creative, to develop appropriate instruction for each student. I need to encourage students to do well, to try harder or try again. I need to be enthusiastic and committed.

This is the role that all other roles should support. This is the way I would want students to see me.

The Comedian

The comedian believes that students will be captivated by charm, humor and well-organized presentations, which they find enjoyable and easy to learn. Any extras like slides or handouts—will be perceived as extra "goodies" from a caring and hard working teacher, who goes beyond the normal effort. Students might get restless in such a class, but hardly ever bored or rebellious.

The Miser

I am a facilitator with limits on my time and energy for the job. I will do only so much. I weigh the results against the hassle. A lot of judgments about students and pay-offs are encompassed in this version of facilitator.

Several sets of beliefs are essential here. One set promotes the value of my time and feelings as an individual. I must place high value on my life outside the classroom to justify reducing my efforts in the classroom. The other set of beliefs expands the unteachable students concept. I must have a large number of unteachable students in order to justify my reducing my efforts in the classroom. A third and more overriding set of beliefs also is involved. These pertain to a general cynicism about the educational system, and life in general—the universal "why bother?" What difference can one person make?

The above excerpts indicate that Sarah viewed her role in terms of being a popular comedian. Although she had some beliefs based on what she had learned in her studies (i.e., the saintly facilitator), she acknowledged that these did not influence the way she planned and implemented the curriculum in either class. Furthermore, she believed she should not expend too much effort in preparing her classes. This belief may have become applicable, in Sarah's view, because students were not cooperating with her and had become "unteachable." In summary, Sarah had most experience with the teacher as comedian role, aspired to be a saintly facilitator, but as her successes became less frequent, she conceptualized her role in terms of the miser to an increasing extent.

Teacher as Manager

The metaphor Sarah used to conceptualize management was *teacher as comedian*. Sarah's beliefs about management as they relate to being a comedian are presented below in her own words.

>It has always been easy for me to use my charm and humor to get people to do as I ask.

>People like humorous, charming and reasonably attractive people.

>People will do things you want them to if they like you.

>Being humorous and charming is a way of showing respect for other people and getting their respect in turn.

>Humor is an excellent teaching tool and appeals to most people; however, it can backfire. When humor fails I fall back on my authority, in whatever capacity it exists.

As the study progressed Sarah's beliefs about management evolved as a result of her inability to manage the students. These changes in beliefs can be interpreted as "depowering," leading to the feeling expressed by Sarah of being unable to cope and wondering if the effort was worth the lack of success. A sample of the changed beliefs is provided below.

>I can't get these kids to do anything. My humor and charm don't work with teenagers.

>Students see classroom behavior as an us vs the teacher and draw attention to themselves.

>Students don't care if they pass or not.

>Disruptive behavior should be dealt with on the spot.

>When all else fails, remove the student from the class. When I initially did the removal strategy, it was probably done more to impress the remaining kids with my "power" than it was to effect any useful outcomes.

As the year progressed, Sarah became preoccupied with management. Her focus was to make it through the day. Management became a matter of maintaining the lowest levels of disruptive behavior as possible. Facilitating learning was less of a concern than covering content, and assessing students was related to rewarding them for appropriate behavior and punishing them for inappropriate behavior. Sarah's three roles were interdependent. What she endeavored to do in one role inevitably affected what she had to do in the others.

Teacher as Assessor

Sarah's beliefs about assessment were associated with punishment. She seemed to worry about assessment and focused on failures rather than successes. Certainly the students in her classes were not as successful as she wanted and Sarah was aware of the problems emanating from such a high number of failures. Yet she did not have the knowledge needed to overcome the problems associated with high levels of failures. Of particular importance was the negative effect of many of the failing students who did not accept responsibility for their failures and regarded Sarah as unfair.

Sarah was least comfortable with her role as an assessor, and it was apparent she did not have the knowledge needed to make changes in the way she assessed students.

> I must assign grades to the students for the work they do. I must be fair and consistent, and give all students an opportunity to get a grade. I must keep good records, not lose papers, get papers back in a timely fashion, and provide feedback on their performance.

> I do not like the fact that students who tried very hard can fail, and students who didn't study at all can pass. I do not like the fact that the test, to be perceived as "fair," is ill-suited to many of my students.

> When students do not do well, I infer that (1) they didn't study; or (2) they don't take tests very well; or (3) they aren't very bright and just can't master the material. It frustrates and depresses me to have the majority of students flunking a test. I read that as a statement that I am failing to serve my students; or, if I can't blame myself any longer, I decide the kids are just "lazy."

Sarah had her problems, wanted to make changes, and recognized she needed assistance. Her journal entries indicated that Sarah was reflecting on practice and did not like what she saw. Further, she reached a point where she knew that she could not solve the problems she was facing without assistance from others.

The research team decided it was time for an intervention to help Sarah overcome her problems. The change strategy had two important components. First, the research team meeting focused on constructivism as an epistemology and its associated implications for learning science. Discussions of learning and teaching were referenced to opportunities provided for Sarah's students to construct knowledge and interrelate learning from different parts of the science program. Throughout the study, Sarah became more constructivist in the way she described learning and teaching and in the way she planned and implemented the curriculum. Sarah evolved as a constructivist throughout the study, and facilitating learning became a role that she regarded as having greatest importance. Brian (the science department head at Southern High) fulfilled an important role in resetting Sarah's expectations and helping her implement the curriculum in the manner she intended. On February 2, 1988 Sarah made the following journal entry describing the nature of the intervention and Brian's assistance.

> In physical science Brian came in and addressed my class for about 5 minutes. That's all it took. I then took over and discussed the two rules we would have and what each rule would mean.
>
> We will be courteous to one another.
> We will be prepared to learn.
>
> I explained what the rules meant as far as my responsibilities to them, theirs to me, and to each other. This was done in a questioning format, with students contributing ideas. The discussion was orderly, as students raised their hands to be recognized to speak. I began to hear from students who rarely had contributed before or who had stopped contributing. About one-third of the class adopted "the same old stuff again" stance in their non-verbals. Three students broke the talking rule and stayed after school.

The intervention gave Sarah the chance she needed. The students were quiet and she could, at least, be heard. Sarah immediately tried to focus on facilitating learning by actively engaging learners. But, her management style was inconsistent with her beliefs about how she should be facilitating learning from a constructivist perspective. Instead of thinking of management in terms of being a comedian, *Sarah decided* to reconceptualize her role as manager in terms of being a *social director*. Sarah described her new role in the following way.

> The job of the teacher is to invite the students to a party (learning event) worth attending; the job of the students, if they accept the invitation, is to learn. We, as teachers cannot make them learn and cannot hold ourselves entirely responsible when they didn't learn *if* we have provided a reasonable invitation to learn—to come to the learning "party."

Social director contrasts with the previous perspectives in its assignment of responsibilities in the classroom. In the previous views the teacher is largely responsible for successes and failures in learning. The weight of this responsibility wears down the teacher, ultimately, and results, for many, in the miserly facilitator. The social director, on the other hand, is responsible for her end of the party arrangements; the students are responsible for what they get out of it, for what they learn, and how they feel about it.

Importantly, Sarah's change in metaphor resulted in the rejection of many beliefs about her role as manager (based on a metaphor of teacher as comedian). As she reconceptualized management in terms of being a social director, Sarah formulated management strategies compatible with her emerging constructivist-oriented beliefs about facilitating learning (these beliefs were adaptations of those associated with the saintly facilitator). The social director metaphor allowed Sarah to manage the class in a manner which supported learning.

When Sarah adopted the new metaphor, changes were observed in the classroom almost immediately. Student misbehavior, which previously was rife, almost disappeared overnight. With management less of an issue, Sarah pursued her roles as facilitator of learning and assessor of students. Numerous changes occurred in teacher and student behavior.

Although disruptive behavior diminished considerably, many students exhibited a latent hostility. The interviews suggested that this hostility might be related to Sarah's role in assessing students. Sarah associated evaluation with a metaphor of "teacher as rewarder or punisher." Since her style of assessing seemed to be responsible for considerable negative affect, a change was contemplated. A relatively high proportion of the students were failing, including a significant proportion of students who had tried to be successful. A change that produced almost immediate results grew from the *suggestion* that she view her role as an assessor in terms of the metaphor of "a window into the student's mind." The next day that science was taught there were significant changes, and over a short period of time the learning environment improved markedly.

Sarah changed her metaphors for conceptualizing management and assessment in different ways. Her management metaphor evolved as she taught in classrooms in which the management system had been reset. Given a chance to teach without having to contend with boisterous student behavior, Sarah reflected on what she was doing and made changes in accordance with her new metaphor of teacher as social director. In contrast, the new assessment metaphor was suggested by a number of the research team. Even so, Sarah adopted the metaphor and used it to understand her assessment role in a new way. Over time she formulated beliefs associated with this new approach to assessment.

DID SARAH CHANGE?

Dramatic changes in teacher and student behavior were observed in Sarah's classes. The following quotes and reflective comments are evidence of the changes that occurred.

> Shirley: I think she expected behavior of those students that they're really not capable of giving at that age. I believe that's one of the beliefs she had that had changed somewhat. I think she improved a great deal.
>
> Body language says a lot to kids. Her body language completely changed from first semester to second semester. She smiled at the kids. She didn't have to have the desk between her and the kids. She could get out and be amongst them . . . I could see a great deal of difference.
>
> She smiles now. It's almost a whole different aura about Sarah when you're around her.

> Brian: I saw her change from a person there was no way I would have hired to teach here next year to one I would hire without any problem. I know as long as she wants to teach here, she has the control in order to do it. I can't believe that so

much could have occurred in that short of a time.

When I observed her the second and third time after this change was occurring I saw someone who was in control of the class, who genuinely liked students, who maybe didn't agree with the entire system and how the thing worked, but saw it as reality. I've seen them all. I've seen all types of techniques. Credibility is something you either have or you don't.

Frank: The problem seemed like it was solved. I'm not sure if she solved it, you solved it, or the kids just gave up . . . She actually lasted longer than they did. I'm not sure if they have learned anything.

Kurt: I've seen some improvement and I've seen things not improving, that have gone backwards. Like less hands-on activities . . . She's not talking at them any more, she's talking to them but you need to get outside and do something. You need to be away from the desk . . . Another thing, she is more open. She's more willing to talk.

Student #2: It's been a little different. She can handle the class better. She's a good teacher. Sarah is a nice lady and a good teacher.

Student #3: Yes, it's changed. From someone she has gotten new ideas. She's changed her way of teaching from the beginning of the year. It has improved a lot. I respect her more than I did before. Now she is a good science teacher. About 7, it has gotten better because initially it was really low—a 1. Now I don't mind going there as a last period.

Student #6: [now] we have to read the book and pay more attention to her lectures. We have to come to a decision between what she says and the book. We have to put it together.

Most observers and participants agreed that changes had occurred in both of Sarah's classes. Vignettes based on direct observation indicated a significant change, student interviews confirmed the observations, and Sarah's colleagues verified that they too had noted differences in her classes. However, there were some differences of opinion with regard to whether the changes that occurred were beneficial for student learning. For example, the graduate student who was a member of the research team did not like the way that order was initially imposed on the students. He felt that the environment had become quiet, but that many students retained a latent hostility throughout the study. Similarly, Frank suggested that the students simply tired of being boisterous and that the noise diminished for this reason rather than any other. However, impressive changes in Sarah's reflective comments and her beliefs were apparent as well.

Sarah changed her beliefs as she reflected on what happened in her classes and pondered ways to improve the learning of students. She noted that her knowledge about constructivism was a factor in shaping her beliefs about facilitating learning, and she ensured that her roles as manager and assessor were consistent with her emerging beliefs about facilitating learning. A list of some of the new beliefs reported by Sarah is provided below:

> Students can be given the responsibility for their own learning.

> Students can be taught to be independent learners.

> Students often need information to perceive and understand the value of certain activities to their learning.

> Students can learn from one another.

> The "party" that works for one set of students or one individual might not work for others.

> Students are more likely to "attend" or engage in a learning event that they have had a part in creating.

> At a good party, the host becomes invisible. When learning is working, the teacher becomes a resource often in the background.

> When kids fail to learn, my job is to find out why and, if needed, re-invite them to a more appropriate "party."

> The right to teach is a negotiated right; management is part of that negotiation.

> The teacher competes with the numerous agendas that students bring to the classroom; to succeed, the teacher's agenda must be more interesting than and demanding than others.

Techniques of management that work for one teacher will not necessarily work for another.

Disruptive behavior and failing marks can become a vicious circle.

The teacher's expectations about behavior are likely to be self-fulfilling.

The above changes in beliefs mirrored what was observed in the classroom. What was most important was that Sarah convinced herself that she could be a successful teacher. She could construct a knowledge base about teaching by focusing on what she did in the classroom and by building management and assessment strategies which were consistent with her role as a facilitator of learning. To be sure, Sarah did not have the knowledge needed to overcome her problems, but she did not have to work alone. The school administrators pledged their support, and the research team continued to act as a mirror for her reflections on practice. Sarah was able to think about being an effective manager and assessor and about structuring potentially good learning environments with the assurance that others would help her maintain order and would provide an emotional support system.

As the year progressed, Sarah grew in confidence and self-esteem. She was able to talk about teaching and learning without becoming upset, and her repertoire of relevant concepts about teaching and learning became noticeably greater. Before the end of the year Sarah's confidence had grown to such an extent that she invited prospective teachers, colleagues, and school administrators to visit her class to observe the improvements.

Not only did Sarah reconceptualize her roles and associated beliefs for facilitating learning, management, and assessment, but she took on two additional roles as well. Sarah readily accepted a role as mentor to her colleagues and prospective teachers and focused her research agenda on teaching for greater student understanding. By adopting these roles Sarah set up a mechanism for continual reflection and change. As the new roles became established, Sarah's beliefs changed to become more consistent with constructivism, which she had adopted as an epistemology to guide teaching and learning.

Sarah continued to improve her teaching by focusing on student learning. Essentially her role as researcher enabled her to examine her beliefs about learning and teaching and to gather data which provided a basis for reflection on practice. Regular changes were made to enhance the learning environment, and over a period of time the beliefs associated with the roles Sarah used to conceptualize teaching became consistent with one another. Learning became the principal goal, and her role as researcher enabled her to systematically examine what was happening and relate her observations to opportunities for student learning. This process resulted in an evolution of sets of beliefs over time and a classroom which emphasized active learning, assessment strategies focused on finding out what students know, and effective management.

WHAT DID WE LEARN?

The significant changes which occurred in Sarah's classes in a relatively short period of time were only possible because of Sarah's commitment to change and the support she received from her colleagues at school and from the research team. Sarah's journal entries and her remarks during the interviews with the research team left no doubt that she was ready to change what was happening in her classes and she knew she needed help from others. From the outset, the principal and the science department head were involved in the decision to help Sarah improve. In addition to providing emotional support and advice on what to try, these two key administrators were prepared to ensure that students could not violate the rules which Sarah had to put in place in her classes. This support enabled Sarah to learn about teaching in an environment that allowed her to interact with students in an orderly manner. In contrast to the first four months of teaching, the classes were relatively quiet and Sarah had a chance to implement the strategies she had decided to try. Effective implementation of the new management strategy gave Sarah an opportunity to concentrate on student learning.

This study provided Sarah with opportunities to reflect on action in a variety of contexts. Initially, Sarah met regularly with her two research colleagues and systematically discussed what was happening in her classes. The interviews focused on seeking answers to why Sarah was doing what was observed. The reflections she undertook were focused by interviews. The process was traumatic at times, and it is probable that without the structure of the interviews Sarah would not have thought through some of the reasons for behaving in the way she did. Further, the interpretations of the research team were important foci for reflections. As the study progressed and became an intervention study, Sarah became self-sufficient in the process of reflection, and the evidence suggests that more reflection in action occurred as well as reflection on action.

Two factors enabled Sarah to assume more responsibility for her own reflections. The first was that she began to develop necessary pedagogical knowledge to enable her to manage and assess the class in a manner that was consistent with her beliefs about facilitating learning. At the beginning of the study Sarah was reliant on others because she did not have the necessary pedagogical knowledge to formulate and consider viable options. The second factor was that as the study progressed Sarah constructed knowledge pertaining to management, assessment, and learning by undertaking research in her classes. She learned how to ask significant questions that related aspects of management and assessment to learning. The answers she sought then became foci for reflection, and changes became institutionalized in her classes.

What we learned from the study is how to consider metaphors, knowledge, and beliefs in relation to teachers' understandings of their teaching roles. Ten points, which constitute a grounded theory emanating from the study, are listed below.

> Beliefs about teaching and learning are associated with (nested within) teaching roles.

> Beliefs within one role can be inconsistent with beliefs associated with another role.

> Roles and associated beliefs are deemed not applicable in given contexts. Thus, teachers can conceptualize a role such as management in discrete context-dependent ways.

> Roles can be compared to see whether the actions they imply are consistent with one another.

> Metaphors are used to conceptualize teaching roles.

The conceptualization of a role, and the metaphor used to make sense of it, is related to the way the teacher frames the context in which learning and teaching occur.

A metaphor used to conceptualize a role can be changed in a process of changing the role.

When a role is reconceptualized, the beliefs previously associated with the role can be deemed no longer applicable to teaching.

Reflection in and on action can lead to change, especially when teaching roles and the metaphors used to make sense of those roles are the targets for reflection.

New beliefs for a teaching role emerge when a role is reconceptualized.

Teaching can be defined in terms of roles undertaken by teachers. And just as metaphors are at the basis of all (or most) concepts, so the metaphors used to make sense of the main teaching roles can be the focus for reflection and change. The power associated with changing these metaphors is that changes in metaphors lead to reconceptualized roles and associated beliefs. Further, a focus on metaphors at this level of generality enables teachers to consider whether or not there are significant conflicts between the way they conceptualize and what they believe about their role as a facilitator of learning. As much as anything, this study provided insights on where to focus questions about change and how to organize information on beliefs and metaphors.

Prior to the study, we believed that specific beliefs would have to be changed in order to change teacher behavior. For example, teachers who believed that a short wait time was most appropriate for high-level learning would have to come to believe that a long wait time is necessary for high-level learning. This was a problem because there are so many beliefs that have to be changed and all of the evidence pointed to the resilience of beliefs. Yet this study of Sarah indicated that beliefs can be changed when roles are reconceptualized. In this instance it was not a case of changing specific beliefs one by one, but of making sets of beliefs no longer applicable to a specific role and developing others that are consistent with a new conceptualization of a role. The futility of attempting to change beliefs one at a time became clear as the potential of using metaphors about roles as a master switch emerged.

Assisting teachers to adopt new metaphors to understand their roles appeals as an important strategy for helping teachers improve aspects of teaching they would like to change. Such an approach rests on the assumption that teachers need to be cognitively prepared to make necessary changes in beliefs about their roles. Consequently, teachers should be involved in observing their own teaching, observing colleagues teach, reflecting on practice, and discussing, analyzing, and interpreting data from classrooms. It is assumed that such activities facilitate cognitive restructuring and subsequent changes in teaching practices.

Reconceptualizing roles and implementing the curriculum in accordance with emerging sets of beliefs can be a traumatic process. In this study, Sarah needed support as she evolved from a teacher who had to concentrate on management to one who emphasized her role as a facilitator of learning. Without a high level of support, it is doubtful that Sarah could have been as successful in changing her beliefs and practices. Many "topdown" approaches to change ignore the cognitive restructuring teachers need to undertake if they are to change as intended. This study suggests that it is desirable to provide opportunities for reflection with colleagues, administrative support, and access to resources such as advisory personnel to focus reflection and provide assistance as required.

CAN THESE FINDINGS BE APPLIED ELSEWHERE?

Questions concerning the generalizability of the findings of this work can be legitimately raised. The purpose of this study was to construct a deeper understanding of teaching with a particular focus on teacher change. The purpose was not to catalogue and generalize specific beliefs that Sarah might have had or specific strategies she might have used. And the intention is not to generalize what Sarah believed and did. In the first place, there probably are few teachers like Sarah and the circumstances under which she was teaching are not like those under which most teachers teach. Although significant changes of similar magnitude are undoubtedly possible for teachers in other schools, the level of support available to Sarah is unlikely to be available to most teachers, and without that support it is unlikely that changes will be as comprehensive or successful. So, rather than generalizing from Sarah, the purpose of this study was to develop a grounded theory which could be applied to teacher change programs for prospective and practicing teachers. Sarah was selected because she had extensive content knowledge and discipline-specific pedagogical knowledge, but was a beginning teacher with limited pedagogical knowledge. The theory which evolved is grounded not only in this study but also in earlier work undertaken in a five-year period (Tobin, 1987; Tobin, Kahle, & Fraser, in press).

9

JEFFREY W. CORNETT
K. SUE CHASE
PATRICIA MILLER
DEBBIE SCHROCK
BETTY J. BENNETT
ALAN GOINS
CHRISTOPHER HAMMOND

Insights from the Analysis of Our Own Theorizing: The Viewpoints of Seven Teachers

As the preceding chapters reveal, investigations about teacher theorizing can increase our knowledge about the impact of teacher beliefs upon curricular and instructional practice. In addition, research into teacher theorizing which involves teachers as either collaborators or as the researchers themselves can add to the knowledge of teacher decision making as a whole and to a more informed practice by the individual teacher. This chapter reveals insights from the personal theorizing of seven teachers (the co-authors) whose professional contexts range from the elementary to university levels. We highlight the impact of individual efforts to make our implicit theories explicit and suggest some implications of such activity for our professional development. In addition, the process guiding such identification of teacher theories, the evolution of that technique, and ethical and methodological concerns with this type of reflection are discussed.

All of the co-authors of this chapter have examined, to different degrees and with different emphases, the literature base supporting the notion of the teacher as an important curricular decision maker and of teaching as a highly complex activity. This base includes literature from teacher thinking research (e.g., Calderhead, 1987; Clark & Peterson, 1986; Cornett, 1987; Kleinsasser, 1988; Pape, 1988); studies of deliberation (e.g.,

McCutcheon, 1989; Reld, 1979; Walker, 1971); reflective thinking (Dewey, 1933; Ross & Hannay, 1986); practical and interpretive inquiry (e.g., Parker, 1987; Schubert, 1986; Schwab, 1970); and action research (Carr & Kemmis, 1986; Cornett, 1990; Oberg & McCutcheon, 1987). We have applied insights from these sources to the study of our own contexts, which represent considerable differences in teaching experience (e.g., Chase has twenty-one years, whereas Hammond has one year) and subject matter responsibilities (e.g., Miller teaches second-grade language arts, math, and reading, whereas Goins teaches chemistry).

While investigating our own practices, we uncovered examples of teacher theorizing which increased our understanding of our own decision making and the impact of our theories on what our students have opportunities to learn.[1] For each of us, this was the major finding of our individual investigations, and justified the commitment of the time and thought required for this self-scrutiny.

During this reflective activity, we each experienced some anxiety as we systematically analyzed our practices. For example, it can be a bit unsettling to encounter evidence that leads us to analyze a question we have posed to a class and then realize, "No wonder the students did not understand. I don't know what I was asking there either!" In addition, it can be embarrassing to listen to examples of our communication with students that reveal sarcasm, a lack of patience, boring and/or moralizing commentary, or even anger. It is also uncomfortable at first to read a transcription which reveals teacher talk that sounds "choppy" or "not like my voice" and is sometimes grammatically incorrect. On the other hand, we believe it is also empowering to have the opportunity to reflect on what teaching means for each of us. It is quite productive to confront our practice on our own terms (rather than have someone else tell us what we are doing "right" or "wrong") and to identify the strengths and weaknesses in each of our practices that we had never confirmed before.

We have begun to appreciate the tremendous complexity of our curricular and instructional decision making. We have a clearer framework to discuss with others what we believe, how these beliefs guide our actions, and how we are working to systematically examine the appropriateness of these beliefs as our contexts of teaching continue to evolve.

We have also identified institutional barriers to reflectivity similar to those described in this volume by Ross and also by Skrtic and Ware. It is quite difficult to find the time to analyze classroom practice systematically and to simultaneously concentrate upon our professional responsibility of teaching.[2]

It is also difficult to assume a systematic inquiry stance regarding our own practice because we have been socialized into thinking that others are better equipped to study our practice and to give us direction. We have all been subjected to scientific management approaches to teacher evaluation (e.g., by supervisors, administrators, and/or researchers utilizing tools such as the Florida Performance Measurement System). Although we do not reject these methods as totally useless, we certainly consider them to be insufficient sources of information for meaningful teacher reflection. Prior to our initiation into the related literature and our own self-study, we considered research on teaching as something done by experts who were removed from the classroom. Therefore, this research was not our responsibility—it was the turf of the "experts." This conception led us to believe that we could not systematically examine our practice; instead we relied upon the advice of experts and/or our own implicit personal wisdom to guide our practice. But now we realize that we can critically and effectively examine our own practice and take individual responsibility for clarifying and determining the worth of our personal beliefs about teaching. We also believe it is our responsibility to engage in this task throughout our teaching careers.

In order to gain this understanding, we needed a method of facilitating our understanding of our own theorizing (see chapters by McCutcheon, Tobin & Jakubowski, and Ross in this text). As a result of the collaboration between Cornett and Chase in an investigation of Chase's theorizing and influences upon Cornett's theorizing (Cornett, 1990), a model of teacher curricular and instructional decision making was developed. This model served as the major heuristic device for an action research assignment Cornett implemented in his teaching at the university level (see Figure 9.1). This chapter summarizes the evolution of that model and assignment, presents the findings of our individual investigations, and suggests implications of this type of introspection for other teachers.

SUE CHASE: AMERICAN GOVERNMENT, GRADE 12

Cornett and Chase collaborated on a six-month naturalistic investigation of Chase's thinking about curricular and instructional decision making (Cornett, 1987). Cornett had designed this inquiry to discover, in part, the theories guiding Chase's practice as a high school government teacher. Five major per-

FIGURE 9.1
A Model for Analysis of the Impact of Teacher Personal
Practical Theories on the Curricular and
Instructional Decision Making of Teachers

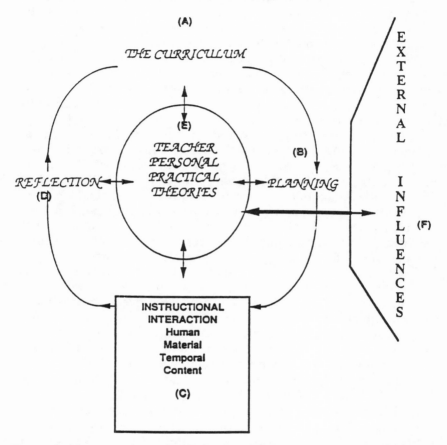

From J. Cornett. (1990). Utilizing action research in graduate
curriculum courses. *Theory into Practice, 29*(3), 185-195.

sonal practical theories were identified for Chase (see Table 9.1).
These were labeled personal practical theories (hereafter PPTs)
because they stemmed from Chase's experiences outside the
classroom (personal) and fifteen years of experiences as a government teacher (practical), and because they were quite systematically guiding her practice (theories).

For example, she would determine the direction of a particular American government lesson by her sense of whether the content needed to be highly structured (often manifested in following the outline of the textbook) or more spontaneous and student initiated (exemplified by student ideas dictating the direction of the lesson, representative of theories 2, 3, and 4 in Table 9.1). In all instances, her theory of unconditional positive regard (theory 1) guided her planning, instructional interactions, and reflections upon her curricular and instructional decision making.

TABLE 9.1
Personal Practical Theories (PPTs) of Seven Teachers

SUE CHASE, Problems of Democracy (12th grade), Hilliard, OH
1. Unconditional positive regard for students.
2. Empathic understanding for students.
3. Teacher as human.
4. Learning and teaching as fun for students and teacher.
5. Teacher provides organized and systematic instruction.

PATTY MILLER, Language Arts, Reading, Mathematics (2nd grade), Wichita, KS
1. Teacher and students work to establish a family environment.
2. Teacher should try to be fair to all students.
3. Teacher should help students learn to handle themselves.
4. Teacher should help students learn how to learn and enjoy the process.
5. Teacher should help students meet objectives.

DEBBIE SCHROCK, Advanced Biology (10th grade), Andover, KS
1. Every student is important.
2. Learning should be interesting, motivating, and enjoyable.
3. Teacher should ensure that every student has the opportunity to learn.
4. Student dignity and humanity should be maintained.
5. Student is responsible for learning process.
6. Teacher has obligation to give 100 percent.
7. Teacher has responsibility to apply validated pedagogy.

BETTY BENNETT, Algebra I (9th grade), Orlando, FL
1. Self- and mutual respect.
2. Not all children are the same.
3. Teacher responsible for more than "three r's."
4. Relate meaning of work to students.
5. Fair evaluation.
6. Ensure opportunity to learn for each student by maintaining

TABLE 9.1 (continued)

good learning environment.
7. Motivate students to learn.
8. Foster atmosphere of student responsibilities.
9. Maintain strong structure but allow for "bends."
10. Offer a shoulder to students, but maintain professional relationship.

ALAN GOINS, Chemistry I Honors (11th grade), Lake Mary, FL
1. Respect and caring are the foundation of all personal practical theories.
2. Teaching understanding over knowing, concepts over trivia.
3. The work ethic is the basis of all success.
4. Personal responsibility in all matters.
5. Learning is independent/individual act; others can only help facilitate it.
6. Firmness and adult decision making set boundaries for appropriate learning.
7. A sense of community is the context for relating to and working with others.
8. Humor and fun relieve stress and demonstrate that learning and working can be enjoyable.

CHRISTOPHER HAMMOND, English III (11th grade), Orlando, FL
1. Teacher should make learning entertaining and fun.
2. Teacher should focus most energy on "average" students, the amorphous center.
3. Practicing classroom discipline instills self-control, which leads to self-discipline.
4. The practicality of knowledge must be shown to the student.
5. The teacher must always allow freedom of thought.
6. Students have responsibility for preparation for class and class atmosphere.
7. The teacher should use examples from multicultural perspectives.

JEFFREY W. CORNETT, Curriculum Theory, STEP IV (University), Orlando, FL
1. Professor as contingency facilitator of learning (for students and for himself).
2. Importance of graduate student's classroom experience, personal experience.
3. Importance of subject matter's basic constructs.
4. Importance of climate concerns.
5. Importance of temporal constraints.

Another significant finding for Chase was her enhanced sense of her role as curriculum developer. Before the study, she viewed this as an activity conducted by a centralized committee, which "took away from [her] real responsibility of teaching" when she served on this committee. Now, Chase understands more clearly the high degree of autonomy and responsibility she has as the most significant curriculum developer. She determines, to a great extent, what her students have the opportunity to learn as a result of her planning, instructional decision making, and reflection.

Since the initial study, Chase has continued to explore her PPTs and has discussed the long-range impact of her participation in the case study, which she describes as quite positive (Cornett & Chase, 1989). In addition, Chase has considered the ethical and methodological implications of qualitative investigations with teachers in their classrooms. Chase identifies trust as the key point in her discussion of ethical elements in naturalistic studies and suggests that

> trust is essential between the researcher and participant, as are ongoing communication about the emergent aspects of the study, the lack of direct value judgment by the researcher about the quality of teacher practice, the establishment of data that allows [sic] the teacher to make judgments about the quality of her practice, and the anticipation and virtual elimination of effects of the ongoing research's impact (in a negative sense) on the teacher's immediate practice and on her students. These qualities were all present in our collaboration and resulted in the highly ethical conduct of the teacher thinking researcher in my classroom. (Cornett, Chase, & Miller, 1990, pp. 15-16)

Her involvement in this topic has continued to expand and is a major source of her ongoing professional development. She is currently authoring a paper on ethics in social studies research in which she addresses her views from the perspectives of both case study participant and a teacher-consumer.

As a result of this research and the desire to apply this work to his interactions with graduate students in curriculum courses, Cornett devised a model of curriculum development (1990) which has the PPTs of the teachers as the core and which illustrates the impact of those PPTs upon teacher decision making during various stages: initial conceptualization of the curriculum, lesson planning, instructional interaction, and reflection upon the enacted curriculum. In addition, the impact of external influences upon those PPTs and each phase of instruction is suggested (see Figure 9.1). This model was devised during a lecture in a curriculum theory class for the purpose of explaining the central role of teachers' thoughts in curricular and instructional decision making to graduate students.

PATTY MILLER: LANGUAGE ARTS, READING,
MATHEMATICS, GRADE 2

Miller was enrolled in the "Elementary Curriculum" course at Wichita State University in the fall of 1987, as part of her master of education program. She read some of the literature described above while in this course, studied the curriculum development model, and participated in an action research assignment designed to enable the student to examine the impact of personal theorizing on curricular and instructional decision making (see Table 9.2). Miller identified her PPTs and their influence upon her practice and indicated that she had gained significant insights into her own decision making and the external influences upon that process.

TABLE 9.2
Action Research Assignment to Make Implicit PPTs Explicit*

Part 1. What are your personal practical theories? (30 pts.)
A) Prior to systematically gathering data on your practice, list your personal practical theories in the order you believe represents their importance in your practice.
B) Define what each theory means to you.
C) Identify possible external influences upon each theory.
D) Draw a diagram or picture of your PPTs which represents their ideal manifestation in your practice (attach as figure 1). In a paragraph, explain the diagram.

rt 2. How are these personal practical theories manifested in practice?
) pts.)
scribe a series of lessons (at least three) which you have implemented nd discuss your thinking during the preactive (planning), interactive nteractive), and postactive (reflective) stages of instruction. Utilize the rriculum development model as a conceptual lens (Cornett, 1990).

rt 3. What is the level of congruence between your theories and prac-
ce? (10 pts.)
Discuss your tentative conclusions about the degree of congruence between your personal practical theories and your practice.

Part 4. Describe an action plan to gain additional insight into an aspect of your practice which has resulted from your analysis of parts 1-3 above. (10 pts.)

Part 5. Summarize how your personal practical theories impact upon what your students have the opportunity to learn through the explicit, hidden, and null curriculum (McCutcheon, 1982). (10 pts.)

* This format evolved at Wichita State University. An addition to the assignment was instituted in 1989 at the University of Central Florida. Students are required to review the literature related to issues/problems they have discovered in their own practice via the PPT assignment. They provide a rationale for the literature review, summarize the major findings in the study and the implications of that study for their own practice, and suggest additional avenues in the literature for future reference.

Because she was working in an elementary school which had a strong competency-based focus, Miller's theorizing (which centered more on what she labeled as "humanistic themes" of family-type student socialization and promotion of students' self-esteem) resulted in considerable tension for her at this work site. Miller therefore sought a teaching position at a school whose philosophy was more in line with her own. Since that time, she indicates that her teaching has been more effective and more rewarding.

Cornett and Miller collaborated on a follow-up study at this new site two years later. The purposes of the investigation were to determine the trustworthiness of Miller's original findings (do action research projects and researcher-conducted studies reveal the same basic categories?), the impact of the new site on her theorizing, and the potential value of the curriculum development model and the original assignment.[3] This four-month investigation revealed the accuracy of Miller's self-study and the importance of the original assignment in the enhancement of Miller's reflectivity. It demonstrated the significant impact of her theories of student responsibility (theory 3, Table 9.1) and family environment (theory 1) on her practice (for example, even when working on academic skills in her curriculum, the main focus, both explicit and hidden, was on learning to get along with one another, caring for each other, and on taking responsibility for actions). Miller indicated that in addition to identifying the presence of her key theories in her practice at this new site, she explicitly confirmed the appropriateness of these theories for her practice.

Self-analysis is an important facet of teaching that could use much more attention, both at the universities and in the classroom. Both the classroom assignment and participation in the follow-up case study have helped me communicate more effectively with students, parents, and administrators. Because I have analyzed some of the interactions of my theories in practice, it has built my confidence and increased my understanding of teaching.

Miller now describes her PPTs to her students' parents at the beginning of the school year and believes it promotes more parent understanding of and involvement with her classroom. Parents have indicated that knowing about her beliefs has helped them be supportive of the curriculum.

In addition, Miller has become more active in mentoring activities as a result of her introspection and new confidence. She has "stepped up many phases of her leadership," such as selecting and ordering curriculum materials and advocating teacher goals with the administration. In addition, she has discussed the ethics of such reflective investigations as a part of her own continued professional development and as an attempt to add to the knowledge base in this area (Cornett, Chase, & Miller, 1990).

The results of Miller's self-study suggested that such an assignment might be of benefit to others as well, and they provided a stronger rationale for the inclusion of the PPT assignment in Cornett's courses as a part of teacher professional development opportunities.

DEBBIE SCHROCK: ADVANCED BIOLOGY, GRADE 10

Shrock enrolled in the master's-level "Secondary Curriculum" course at Wichita State in the fall of 1988. She completed the PPT assignment and identified seven basic PPTs (see Table 9.1). Schrock then devised an action plan and carried out that action plan the following semester as a part of an elective course, "Instructional Process," she took with Cornett. She formulated her own protocols to determine the degree of manifestation of her theories in practice. These included a guide for an external observer (she requested and received classroom visits from a professor from another university and her principal as well) and student feedback sheets which provided student perspectives on her PPTs. She also analyzed audio- and videotapes of her instruction.

From this collective data, she identified the degree of congruence between her PPTs and her practice. After seeing some incongruities, she decided that she needed to emphasize more inquiry-oriented science lessons and that she needed to concentrate on increasing female student participation. This, in turn, led her to read literature on inquiry in science education and student motivation and engagement.

Although Cornett did not visit Shrock's classroom (or those of any of the remaining authors of this chapter), Shrock's use of data collection, analysis, and establishment of data archives (video- and audiotapes) helped to indicate the appropriateness of her findings. It should be noted that the purpose of the assignment was to enable teachers to study personal practice and to apply those findings to an enhanced understanding of curricular and instructional theory. However, the rigor of Shrock's investigation (as well as those by Miller, Bennett, Goins, and Hammond) has warranted its inclusion in this volume. We believe that it can serve as an example of the power of systematic teacher reflection to improve curriculum and teaching practices.

As a result of Schrock's extended study, Cornett incorporated an additional element into the original assignment, a follow-up literature review based upon the findings of the original action research project.

BETTY BENNETT: ALGEBRA I, GRADE 9

Bennett enrolled in Cornett's "Curriculum Theory" graduate course in the fall of 1989 at the University of Central Florida, where the assignment was first modified to include the literature review. Bennett identified ten basic PPTs (see Table 9.1), and, utilizing the image of a sailboat to fulfill section 1D of the assignment (see Table 9.2), described the interaction of her PPTs with her practice as follows:

> I chose a sailboat to illustrate my PPTs because it relies solely on the elements around it to progress along its course; similar to education. The wind (self and mutual respect) is the most important part. Without it, everything is at a standstill. A sail (understanding that not all children are the same) is important to channel the wind for optimum movement. The larger the sail (understanding), the more wind (respect) that expedites our journey. The water beneath (good learning environment, motivation, making student responsibilities clear, strong structure, and a shoulder to lean on when needed) supports us and makes

for smooth travel. However, when there is turbulence in the water, the journey is not so smooth. Finally, our cargo that we carry all through our trip (teaching more than just the "three r's," meaningful learning, and fair evaluation) are in place for a safe trip, providing that all of the other processes are intact. It is an inevitable reality that, from time to time, there will be incidents that will rock the boat. But strong concentrations on maintaining all functions (PPTs) makes our sailboat more resilient. Without these functions operating properly, we could lose some of our crew, or even worse . . . be totally sunk.

Bennett indicates her desire to view her practice holistically, and the sailing imagery that she describes above is one manner in which she tries to visualize the complexity of her classroom context. She works with students to think by using analogies and tends to think quite metaphorically about her algebra instruction.

Bennett's analysis of her PPTs led her to develop an action plan aimed at strengthening the thinking skills instruction in her mathematics curriculum. She examined literature which discussed thinking skills, problem solving, reasoning, and higher-order thinking, because, she said,

> my students were getting the facts but that was about it. I had overlooked a vital skill . . . the skill of thinking. My students had become so dependent upon my regurgitation of basic facts, that they were not developing any new knowledge on their own.

As a result, she searched the literature and critiqued seven sources on this topic.[4] She concluded this phase of the project as follows:

> I never realized that getting students to develop and use thinking skills was such a widespread problem until I began my search for literature in this area. The articles that I found made me see the intensity of the need for these skills.
>
> Considering all of the suggestions offered for enhancing thinking skills, I feel that the best plan of action is to incorporate the basics with problem solving and other higher-order thinking skills. With this, we will continue to teach the ever important basics but do so in a way that they will become part of long-term rather than short-term memory. This could be accomplished by tying the basics to real life situations that require thought and reason.
>
> I would like to try some cooperative learning where the class is divided into pre-selected groups. Each of these groups will contain a student who exhibits good problem solving skills

to act as a model from which the others may gain a little "reflective self-instruction." By developing my own word problems and activities, I can relate students' prior knowledge and experiences to the skills that are intended to be learned.

Bennett believes that the PPT assignment is a powerful discovery tool.

Initially I was concerned about the time and effort that this would take in addition to the other things I was doing in graduate school and at work. However, once I began I immediately saw what a worthwhile type of activity it really was.

ALAN GOINS: HONORS CHEMISTRY, GRADE 11
CHRIS HAMMOND: ENGLISH III, GRADE 11

Unlike the teachers already discussed, who all had a significant amount of practical experience, Goins and Hammond were beginning teachers enrolled in the final phase of a competency-based alternative certification program in the fall of 1989.[5] In an attempt to provide a more holistic view of their practice and to integrate their understanding of the individual competencies they had demonstrated throughout the program, and as a part of their ongoing professional development, Cornett suggested that they might complete a version of the assignment as well (see Table 9.2). Goins and Hammond realized, as a result of this experience, that they had received no direct grounding in subject matter pedagogy as a part of their alternative program. They found that they were concerned about a lack of knowledge and experience with learning theory, curriculum development, and instructional strategies that were directly linked to their particular subject matter responsibilities. Their action plans focused on learning more about components of these areas.

Goins identified eight PPTs (see Table 9.1) and indicated that respect and caring was the "overarching theory encompassing all [his] other theories." He attempted to capture the impact of his PPTs on his decision making by generating data sheets which highlighted his major "steps" in planning, interaction, and reflection on the left-hand side of the sheets and his thoughts about those steps on the right-hand side (see Table 9.3). These notes are included to represent an example of student response to this portion of the assignment, which requires that protocols, including the data analysis sheets, be attached to the summary narrative turned in to the professor.

TABLE 9.3
Personal Practical Theorizing Protocols for Alan Goins, Lesson Plan 1

PLAN

Activity	Rationale from Deliberations
1. Discovery lab: flame test and spectrum tubes	1. Introduces new unit with a fun, hands-on activity that will peak student interest in a new unit.
	Lab will not be graded because: (a) I'm behind in grading as it is and (b) it may engender an appreciation of learning for learning's sake.
2. Class discussion of lab question & answer to develop conclusions	2. Facilitates students' discovery of important concepts that are within their grasp to discover. This should be more effective than simply transmitting information.
3. Brief summary lecture of lab conclusions; notes on overhead	3. Writing down key concepts should aid retention and serve as a basis for further study.
4. Homework: reading in text and definitions	4. Reviews this lesson and previews the next. Having students learn terms independently should free class time for more difficult concepts.

INTERACTIONS

Discourse	Concurrent Thoughts
1. I briefly explain lab and demonstrate. I cannot get the burner lit so I joke about my incompetence. Students laugh. When I get things straightened out, they are attentive but impatient to start.	1. Slight embarrassment—I hope I'm not blushing. I also wonder if they are listening and if they will follow directions.
2. During the lab, I move around and assist. I make few remarks since students are following directions. They seem to be enjoying themselves.	2. I'm glad they are having this fun, but I get the feeling that is all they are getting out of this lab.

Discourse	*Concurrent Thoughts*
3. Students are slow to settle down after lab. I express a little impatience with this and quickly regain control by firmly telling them to settle down.	3. They're stalling. I need to regain control so that I can cover everything I need to.
4. During discussion of results, I have to ask more leading questions than I had planned in order for them to "discover" concepts. Only a few students are actively participating. I tend to ask these students more questions.	4. I need to keep moving, but I also need to draw other students into the discussion and make them think. This is frustrating.
5. During lecture students intently copy notes.	5. Are they listening? I doubt it.
6. When homework is assigned, some students jokingly complain. I joke back about their "bellyaching."	6. This is nice—I think that the students and I have a good rapport.

INTERACTIONS

Initial	*Retrospective*
1. Setting this lesson up required much preparation, but it was really a waste of time. The students had fun but did not learn anything substantial.	1. In retrospect, the students probably learned more from this lesson than I initially believed. I still do not feel that they learned as much as I had originally hoped, but perhaps my original expectations were too high. I also feel that this type of nongraded discovery activity is worthwhile on occasion, especially when beginning a new unit. If nothing else, it seems to increase appreciation—if not comprehension—of the subject matter. It also fosters a more positive, relaxed attitude towards science.

As a result of his self-study, Goins indicated the following:

> It became apparent that my basic instructional goal is to develop in my students a high level of understanding. In analyzing my practice, however, it became equally apparent that I am not always actualizing this goal in the classroom. Insofar as an emphasis upon high-level cognitive learning has been associated with exemplary high school chemistry teaching (Garnett & Tobin, 1988, p. 4), it is clear that much of my professional development hinges upon developing skills that allow teaching for understanding and not just for knowing. To this end, I must address three areas of weakness in my practice that I identified in my initial self-analysis (October 21, 1989). These areas are questioning skills, diagnosis and understanding of student cognitive development, and curriculum development.

Goins analyzed articles related to these topics and summarized his findings in his report of the literature. A very brief excerpt of his discussion is included below to indicate the type of synthesis which can be utilized to find support for and/or contradiction of basic personal practical theories as they are manifested in practice.

> Garnett and Tobin (1988) have noted that exemplary teachers of high school chemistry exhibit an ability to ask appropriate questions (p. 1). According to these researchers, effective teachers use "questions to develop lesson content, to determine student understanding of . . . the chemistry content, to check student performance . . . and to involve students in sharing ideas" (p. 7). Furthermore, the authors indicate that such teachers initiate questions in a supportive environment and do so in order to foster student understanding. While the importance of questioning in teaching for understanding is well documented, so are the problems encountered in initiating questions.

Goins continued his discussion of this issue, and, at the end of his six-page analysis of his literature findings, concludes, "Hopefully, restructuring the curriculum and all it entails will also help me actualize my main personal practical theory—teaching for understanding."

Hammond identified seven PPTs (see Table 9.1). His definition of those theories is given below as an example of the importance of clearly defining the construct prior to actual on-site investigation. It establishes a baseline of personal theorizing which serves as a standard for comparing the findings of the investigation.

1. *Entertaining/Fun:* The teacher should make activities that are creatively humorous whenever possible. Lectures should not only be informative, but chock full of juicy morsels of trivia, witty repartee, and ribald anecdotes.

2. *Amorphous Center:* Rather than concentrating on students of high or low ability in the class, the teacher should focus most of his/her energies on the "average" students in the class. Often this requires a different approach or several approaches to a particular topic.

3. *Self-Discipline:* By following standard procedures daily, students will learn routines. Practicing classroom discipline will instill self-control, leading to self-discipline. This route will add structure to many students who come from aberrant families.

4. *Practicality of Knowledge:* The student must be shown the value of any given task, whether it pertains to skills/knowledge which will be practical outright, or for use at another time/level.

5. *Freedom of Thought:* The teacher must always allow students to disagree or dispute the teacher's theory/practice (provided it is done rationally) without consequence or reprisals. Teachers explain their biases to students, and expose the students to other philosophies.

6. *Responsibility:* Students must be prepared for class and must take responsibility for the atmosphere of the room; homework must be completed; materials must be brought to class daily; and students assist the teacher in maintaining control over the classroom through democratic liability.

7. *Multicultural Perspectives:* The teacher should attempt to use examples, materials, etc., from the cultures of minority students whenever possible.

Hammond then collected data on the congruence between his PPTs and practice. An example of his critique of one PPT is given below:

1. *Entertaining/Fun:* Some of my choices for activities were boring. One selection on how to write a research paper went over like a lead pancake. I did, however, recognize that my reviewing the concept of narrowing the research topic and my interdictions regarding sources were redundant. I allowed the student to go directly to the Media Center. Doubtless, they enjoyed this much more. Usually, I try to be as entertaining as possible in my lectures, but failed to do so during this unit.

A good illustration of the tension that occurred when his PPTs of teaching conflicted with his own personal morals and also his concern with external opinion was when one white male student asked if he could write a research paper on the Ku Klux Klan for this class. This request followed on the heels of Hammond's approval of an African-American girl's request to do a paper on Malcolm X. The male student had openly discussed his support of the Klan, a group Hammond personally found distasteful. Hammond indicated to this student, through both his words and body language, that he could not report on "such a group." However, as Hammond reflected, his PPTs of freedom of thought (theory 5) and responsibility (theory 6) made him tense about his earlier decision. As he thought about it overnight, he decided that the student had a right to report about the group of his choice. Although Hammond was concerned with what the community might think if the report was delivered, he decided that the principles in theories 5 and 6 would form the basis of his decision.

Hammond believes that the ongoing analysis of his PPTs enabled him to deliberate in a more open manner and to look at the process in his classroom in a more holistic fashion. Although he still viewed his decision in this "KKK case" as problematic (as we believe all curricular and instructional decisions are, since we can never be certain we are "right"), he felt more confident that his decision making was the result of professional reflection and not of personal whim.

JEFF CORNETT: CURRICULUM THEORY, UNIVERSITY

As a result of interaction with these teachers, several hundred graduate and undergraduate students, and the co-authors of this book during the past three years, Cornett's PPTs have continued to evolve as well (Cornett, 1990). His PPTs center around the notion of professor as contingency facilitator of learning (for students and for himself) (see Figure 9.2). These PPTs form the central filter through which the facilitation of curriculum and instruction flows in his overall practice, which is represented by the model in Figure 9.1. Through this contingency role the professor as curricular and instructional decision maker interacts with the other commonplaces of the classroom (Schwab, 1970) to determine the most appropriate balance between emphasis on the basic constructs of the subject matter, the personal and practical experiences of students, temporal constraints, and climate concerns.

Cornett views the investigation of teacher theorizing (his own

FIGURE 9.2
A Model of the Interaction of Cornett's Personal Practical Theories

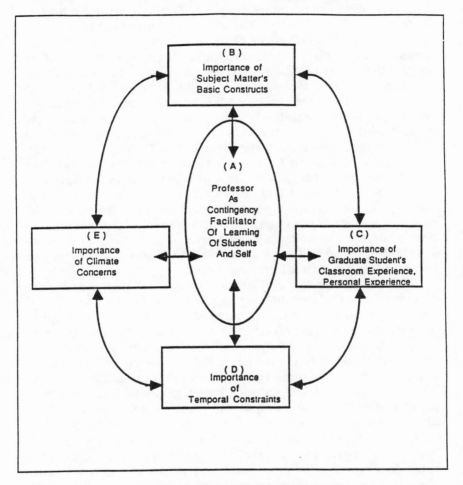

From J. Cornett. (1990). Utilizing action research in graduate curriculum courses. *Theory into Practice, 29*(3), 185-195.

and that conducted with other teachers) as a highly positive experience which enables him to understand more holistically the complexity of teaching. The importance of attempting to understand and explain teacher theorizing is placed at the core of his research and teaching agenda.

CONCLUSION

In each of our investigations, the individuals decided the appropriateness of their PPTs and the value to be attached to the indications of congruence between PPTs and actual practice. Cornett stressed with each teacher that congruence, in and of itself, is not positive. Instead, it is an indication of "what is" and leads to the next questions for analysis, "Is this what should be?" and "What influences have facilitated this congruence?" Each teacher needs to critically examine his or her findings and look to other studies and colleagues for data to spark continued reflection and analysis of the appropriateness of the PPTs. In contrast, if congruence is limited and a critical analysis by the teacher reveals that the guiding PPTs are appropriate, an examination of the forces which resist (e.g., students with conflicting personal theories, inappropriate material resources such as some textbooks, and district pressures for improvement of test scores and deemphasis on socialization, self-esteem objectives) the manifestation of those PPTs is warranted. Subsequent action can be taken to facilitate their implementation.

Although the results of our investigations have been quite empowering for us, we do not suggest that every teacher should engage as a participant in a naturalistic investigation or complete the PPTs analysis assignment. Chase indicates that participation in a naturalistic investigation requires significant trust between the teacher and the researcher, a high degree of willingness to engage in and reveal one's reflections, and a time commitment (in Cornett & Chase, 1989). Shrock was initially so anxious about the assignment that she dropped the curriculum course in 1988. She indicated a concern that she was not ready for such reflection. She still is uncomfortable with elements of the assignment because such introspection makes explicit the fact that "you can't do everything well in teaching, you can't do it all." She states that it can be "demoralizing because you don't have anybody to debrief you on-site." Goins indicates that he believes he would not have been ready to undertake such a project at the beginning phase of his alternative program one year earlier. He states that he was "trying to survive" as a new teacher and did not have the time and perhaps the insight to profit from such a study then.

The concern for ethics in the promotion of such an assignment is a significant one, especially for Cornett. Although the assignment is always mentioned as "an option," students can still feel that it is what the professor really wants and they should "comply." This can lead to what Miller and Martens (1990) refer to as issues of "imposition and hierarchy." Questions such as "Whose interests does this assignment serve?" and "Are teachers better off as a result of this assignment, or have we opened a series of concerns that we cannot address with each individual?" are still prevalent.

However, these issues are tentatively overshadowed by the overwhelmingly positive unsolicited feedback from teachers who appreciate the assignment and the opportunity to reflect in this fashion. The authors of this chapter all believe we are more professional because we have critically examined our practice in a systematic fashion, set goals for our continued professional development, and initiated action plans to increase our effectiveness as teachers. We believe that this increases the likelihood of the appropriateness of our curricular and instructional decision making. If improved teacher decision making occurs and our facilitation of student learning is enhanced, it is certainly worth the effort.

III

IMPLICATIONS OF RESEARCH OF TEACHER PERSONAL THEORIZING FOR EDUCATIONAL PRACTICE

10

KENNETH TOBIN
ELIZABETH JAKUBOWSKI

The Cognitive Requisites for Improving the Performance of Elementary Mathematics and Science Teaching

A large number of influential reports have claimed the existence of serious shortcomings in elementary education and have proposed major reforms in American education (Murnane & Raizen, 1988; Office of Technology Assessment, 1988; Weis, 1987). The problems in mathematics and science education have been enduring. Evidence of increasing concern is the publication of more than three hundred major reports in the United States since *A Nation at Risk* (National Commission on Excellence in Education, 1983) drew the attention of the American public to the plight of mathematics and science education. An insufficient number of mathematics and science students are in the educational pipeline, and existing curricula appear to emphasize rote rather than meaningful learning. The evidence suggests that students learn facts and algorithms to obtain correct answers to exercises of standard format. At a time when knowledge growth in the sciences is expanding exponentially, there are fears expressed by the business community and community at large that the United States is losing its competitive edge. The mathematics- and science-related knowledge and skills of high school graduates are insufficient for today's technologically oriented work force. These deficiencies can be traced to the elementary school and persist in middle and high schools. Not surprisingly, then, strong cries for reform are focused on all educational levels.

Can teachers and teacher educators respond to the calls for reform? If reforms are to be implemented as intended, it is apparent that teachers and students will have to change what they do in their classrooms. Legislative and policy initiatives might facilitate change in the sense that teachers will perceive that the community expects the curriculum to change in a par-

161

ticular way; however, there is an assumption that teachers can and will learn new strategies and plan and implement the curriculum as intended by policymakers. Little attention is given to why teachers currently do what they do. This study assumes that teachers adhere to traditional practices because it makes sense to them to do so. Accordingly, we set out to ascertain how teachers make sense of teaching and how they go about initiating changes in their classrooms. Because of the nonspecialist nature of mathematics and science teaching in elementary schools, we felt we could learn a great deal by beginning this phase of our ongoing studies of mathematics and science teaching (e.g., Tobin, 1990; Tobin, Kahle, & Fraser, 1990) in elementary schools.

METHODS

The study was an interpretive investigation (Erickson, 1986) of elementary teachers and classrooms. Teachers from four elementary schools in Florida participated in the study over a period of one and a half years. A research team consisting of ten science and mathematics educators collected, analyzed, and interpreted the data for the study. Two members of the research team were at each of the school sites for an average of ten hours per week throughout the data-collecting component of the study (fall 1988 and spring 1989). Each week the team met for approximately ninety minutes to analyze data, discuss findings, and reorientate data collecting. Data analyses continued through the summer and fall of 1989.

Structural Characteristics of the Project

Two *coordinating teachers* and an *administrator* from each of the four schools began the project in the summer of 1988. A facilitator (a full-time substitute) was provided for each school to enable teachers to plan for teaching, observe colleagues teach, conduct research, and consult with colleagues. Each school constructed a plan to use the facilitator to benefit the science and mathematics programs at their respective school sites.

The teacher enhancement program commenced with a twenty-day summer program anchored at each end with three days of activities in which all coordinating teachers and administrators were involved. The three-day anchor points enabled all participants to work together and share concerns and solutions to problems. The fourteen days between the two anchor points were planned to address individual needs of coordinating teachers and administrators. Teachers were assisted in planning and implementing individual schedules to enable them to work in their own schools at their own rate, to work at home, and to seek assistance from the research team as required.

The three-day workshops held in the summer and others held at intervals of approximately eight weeks throughout the fall and spring were instrumental in providing foci for reflection and subsequent change. The research team carefully selected topics and scheduled time to allow teachers to share successes, to identify practices and trends to be changed, and to introduce content areas judged by the research team as salient to improving the learning environment of students. Examples of such topics included constructivism, alternative assessment techniques, integrating mathematics and science, collaborative learning, problem solving, conducting research in classrooms, and being a mentor to colleagues. Each workshop topic was designed as a basis for teachers to begin to construct knowledge in a particular area.

By the end of the summer program, each participant had developed a comprehensive plan for a science and mathematics program to be implemented in his other classroom in the fall of 1988. In addition, participants had constructed the knowledge to undertake a program of research and to help colleagues improve their science and mathematics teaching.

After the summer program, participants returned to their schools and implemented their plans. Strategies differed at each school site. However, at all sites the principal and coordinating teachers worked together as a team to carry out a program which emphasized problem-centered learning of mathematics and science. Throughout the year, the research team interacted closely with teachers in their schools, monitored progress, and provided assistance on request. The goal at each site was to initially focus on the curriculum within the classes of the coordinating teachers, and as the year progressed to involve as many faculty as possible in a plan that included observations of one another teaching, discussions about teaching and learning, involvement in research on learning and teaching, and dissemination of successes and failures. To facilitate between-site communication for the coordinating teachers and administrators, regular meetings were scheduled at intervals of six to eight weeks.

Data Sources

Data were collected from all teachers within a school; however, intensive data were collected from the two coordinating teachers, the students in their classrooms, and the principals. The techniques used to collect data included direct observation; interviews of teachers, students, and principals; and transcripts of discussions at meetings of the participant teachers.

Data Analysis and Interpretation

Data analysis and interpretation involved team members carefully examining all of the data and constructing assertions which became foci for subsequent data collection. Endeavors were made to identify data to refute assertions, and explanations were sought for disconfirming evidence.

What we learned from this study is represented in the following sections, which describe five assertions related to why teachers do what they do, and how they change their practices.

WHY TEACHERS DO WHAT THEY DO

The sense-making process is associated with understanding the teaching roles which are of greatest importance in the classroom. Teachers appear to make sense of crucial roles in terms of images and metaphors in which are embedded belief sets and epistemologies. Images and/or metaphors serve as organizers of belief sets. The images and metaphors may be used consciously and have language associated with them, or they might be used in an entirely tacit manner with beliefs being implicit in the actions of the teachers and students and in the use of resources.

Assertion 1: Teachers identified as important the classroom roles of facilitator of learning, manager, assessor, and curriculum designer.

The teachers conceptualized teaching in terms of a number of roles, which included learning facilitators, learner and curriculum managers, student assessors, and curriculum designers. It is not clear that teachers would spontaneously have identified these roles as being most salient if it were not for the intervention of the summer workshops in which we scheduled topics that focused on these roles. Accordingly, as teachers discussed what they were doing in their classes and what they planned, they tended to use the same categories to which they had been introduced.

Perhaps the most obvious shift in teachers' verbal comments and stated goals was their evolving definition and understanding of student learning and student engagement. As a group, teachers identified this change as one of the most important aspects of the entire project. They were conscious of their strong focus on student learning brought about by thinking about constructivism and by conducting research in their own classrooms. All teachers now realized that they could be facilitators of learning but could not do the learning for students. They knew that learning meant a lot more than reproducing facts learned by rote or solving problems using algorithms.

Management of equipment and materials, arranging students for learning, and organizing learning activities and presenting them in a logical order to facilitate learning are all aspects of the management role. A major focus in the study was on the organization of learners in groups so that cooperative learning could be possible. The clear focus of cooperative learning activities was on the negotiation of meaning as students collaborated to obtain solutions to problems. Attention was directed toward ensuring that students understood what they were doing and agreed upon acceptable solutions to problems. Arriving at consensus was an important part of doing mathematics and science.

The management of materials and learners was a topic that arose at each of the teacher meetings. They discussed it in relation to their successes, in relation to their continuing problems, and as a topic they would like to know more about. A significant factor in these discussions was that teachers appeared to be relating management to student learning opportunities. In collaborative learning groups students were more difficult to manage, and because they were expected to be autonomous, teachers had to help them develop new patterns of engaging, cooperating, and staying on task. Misbehavior among students was a problem in most classes, and teachers had to learn strategies to ensure that the classroom environments were conducive to learning. Ideas were gleaned from visits to colleagues' classrooms and subsequent discussions.

The role of being an assessor was identified by teachers as being an important component of their teaching. Our workshops focused on using alternatives to paper-and-pencil tests, and specific attention was given to performance testing and the use of concept maps. Initially teachers perceived assessment as a process in which teachers tested students to find out what they did and did not know. In contrast, we assisted teachers to think in terms of assessment as an opportunity for students to show what they know. As teachers became more constructivist in thinking about their roles, it was observed that techniques such as concept mapping became used to an increasing extent.

As curriculum designers, the teachers began with materials-centered curriculum guides and designed some activities that integrated science and mathematics. Elizabeth was perhaps most successful in this regard. She was determined to have her children learn both mathematics and science in an environment in which the differences between the two subjects were not emphasized. Others, such as Pam, adopted the attitude that mathematics would be emphasized during science lessons and vice versa. Process skills such as measurement, classification, recording, using numbers, and graphing provided a means of achieving this goal. However, all teachers adapted the curriculum they had used in the past, and changes were made to focus on students learning with understanding, not by rote memorization.

Assertion 2: Personal epistemologies influenced teachers' conceptualizations of their roles and associated beliefs. Teachers began the study as realists and gradually became more constructivist as the study progressed.
The coordinating teachers were introduced to radical constructivism at the first of the summer workshops. At this time, the topic was introduced and implications were discussed in terms of what it meant to know, how knowledge was constructed, the nature of reality and how students access reality, possible roles of science and mathematics teachers, and how to assess what students have learned. In most instances teachers had not previously thought about these ideas in a conscious way; however, they found the ideas appealing and intuitively sensible. Soon it was apparent that there would be many constraints to be encountered in implementing the curriculum in a constructivist manner. Fortunately, the teachers had a colleague with them at the summer workshops, and their principals also were involved. Thus, during the planning phases of the project teachers were able to work with a colleague and discuss what they were intending to do with the principal. Accordingly, the opportunities to do something innovative were enhanced because of the support systems built into the design of the summer workshops.

As the study progressed, there was evidence that teachers became increasingly aware of the needs of students to learn with understanding. From the onset of the study, teachers had a realist view of knowledge, and learning was conceptualized in terms of the conduit metaphor, whereby knowledge, having the properties of a fluid entity, is transferred from the teacher's head or books to the empty heads of students. As a result of our program, teachers began to think of knowledge as existing only in the minds of their students. Questions about the nature of knowledge and implications for learning mathematics and science also became the focus for thinking and discussion. Teachers began to focus their planning on what students must do in class in order to learn with understanding. Teachers became more constructivist in their thinking. They focused on the needs of learners and student learning. As a consequence, their own roles changed from teacher as dispenser of knowledge to teacher as facilitator of understanding. They realized that they could not pour the truth into the minds of students, but that students had to have experiences from which they could construct their own knowledge of mathematics and science.

Although all teachers appeared to adjust their beliefs about knowledge to become more constructivist, they did not all shift to the same extent. Some, such as Elizabeth, made immediate changes in the classroom; moreover, as the year progressed she focused on successes, and the reinforcement she received provided her encouragement to make even more adjustments to the manner in which she implemented mathematics and science curricula. On the other hand, the changes in Julie's class were not as evident. She adopted some of the lessons from the materials-centered curriculum guides that were provided, but her approach did not appear to be strongly constructivist. Two possibilities present themselves. Perhaps she did not believe that constructivism was an adequate theory of knowledge, preferring realism as a more appropriate theory. Or she might have believed that constructivism was the best theory of knowledge but also that the context was such that she ought not allow her beliefs to influence her classroom practices. It is possible that the curriculum frameworks provided by the state and district, together with district-level tests, were a sufficient stimulus for her to continue to emphasize learning and testing of facts. To give up reliance on standardized tests and prescribed scope and sequence, one must change beliefs associated with accountability. The focus needs to change from external stimuli (e.g., tests) to internal stimuli (e.g., professional decisions).

It is entirely possible that teachers such as Julie were becoming more constructivist throughout the project as a result of their reflections in and on practice and their discussions with others. Newly developed beliefs about knowledge might not affect practice until some future time when the context seems appropriate.

Assertion 3: Visual and verbal metaphors were a basis for conceptualizing teaching roles.

This study provided numerous instances of teachers having made sense of particular teaching roles (i.e., learned about them with understanding) through the use of metaphors. In previous studies (e.g., Tobin & Ulerick, 1989) the link between metaphors, roles, and belief sets was demonstrated. Belief sets were associated with specific teaching roles which were conceptualized in terms of metaphors. Identification of the metaphors used by teachers to make sense of specific roles was therefore regarded as an important step in helping teachers change their practices. In this study, links between metaphors and roles are demonstrated in excerpts from an interview with Diana, a teacher at Urban Elementary.

Diana used three metaphors to describe her teaching role in different contexts. Sometimes she managed her class as a policeman, in other circumstances as a mother hen, and on other occasions as an entertainer. Her mode of behavior (the metaphor she used to drive behavior) depended on the context in which learning was to occur. Each conceptualization of her role as manager was associated with a discrete set of beliefs. The following quotations selected from an interview illustrate the manner in which Diana conceptualized her role in terms of metaphors.

> I was an MP for three years. So in certain ways that comes out in me when I teach. Sometimes I'm real firm. I guess I behave like a policeman. I kind of give them directions that way. Things had to be done in a certain time, or they had to be done certain ways . . . At certain times I am a mother hen when I have certain kids come in and help in the morning. I get very close with them . . . but it doesn't carry on through the whole day. It only comes out at certain times. I don't think I'm always an entertainer. But in certain ways I do try to do that only to make the

children stimulated to the activity. I think that the way you teach is really a performance in a certain way. I really do my own thing.

As students sit in classrooms, they experience teaching at first hand, minute by minute, hour by hour, day by day, week by week, month by month, year after year. A variety of teachers, some good, others not, implement curricula in diverse ways. Students experience teaching and learn. Images of teaching are etched on the minds of students, and when they recall class-room experiences they do so by reconstructing rich images which contain details to which language can be assigned. These images are representations of sensory data obtained in the distant past. On many occasions the images will be visual re-presentations, on other occasions auditory, and perhaps there are times when images might be associated with touch, taste, and smell as well. What seems to be clear, however, is that when teachers think and talk about teaching, their initial thoughts, at least, seem to involve the construction of images which are used as a basis for assigning language.

When teachers are to described some aspect of their class, they do so by re-presenting segments from the class as an image and using language to communicate the salient elements of the image. The following excerpts from an interview with Diana indicate that she used imagery as a basis for establishing a mind frame in which she could explain how the teaching of a former teacher influenced her own teaching.

> Diana: H was a social studies teacher who taught tenth grade, world history. And he was a real energetic type person. He did different games and contests that were really fun. Hilarious type situations. But the games got everyone involved. It was really stimulating and we would laugh a lot in that class. We all enjoyed going to his class because he was a fun person to listen to and learn from.
>
> Interviewer: Can I ask you a question about what was going on in your mind as you were telling me that? Tell me what was happening with your eyes. They were looking up over there somewhere. What were you doing in your mind?
>
> Diana: I was picturing myself sitting in that classroom . . . The whole class was there. And I was sitting among the group. And he was sitting in the front of the room. Kinda directing the class.

Is it possible that images are used metaphorically to make sense of a new role that is to be adopted by a teacher? The metaphorical use of images would bypass the use of language and could be done unconsciously. For example, the decision to use a policewoman as a metaphor for managing a classroom probably is not done consciously. Something in the context might result in the construction of an image associated with a role which is well understood (e.g., a policewoman) and which will provide a basis for subsequent behavior. Basing action on images associated with another role is analogous to using a verbal metaphor to make sense of a new concept. The interview with Diana suggests that she based her teaching on images associated with her favorite teacher. It is apparent that she did not sit down and meticulously describe in words those behaviors she would adapt and adopt. Rather, the association appears to have been more direct, involving re-presented images of her former teacher. Similarly, Diana's decision to be an entertainer probably was associated with images of entertainers she had experienced and occasions when, in other roles, she had been entertaining.

TEACHERS CHANGING THEIR PRACTICES

Assertion 4: Evidence of change was first seen in adjustments to teachers' role conceptualizations, metaphors, and beliefs, and then in classroom practices.

Although teachers changed what they were doing in the classrooms, the first evidence that changes were occurring was visible in the words used to describe what they were thinking during the workshops. As teachers made sense out of their new emerging roles, they searched for language to describe what they visualized and what they believed. An analysis of this language provides a ready indication of imminent changes in the classroom. Free of the constraints of having to implement what they believed, teachers talked about what should ideally happen and what they intended to do in the future. The language used in the workshops provided ample evidence of changes in the conceptualizations of roles, metaphors, and beliefs.

Before the program began, Bernice was intimidated by science and did not teach many activities. Since then Bernice feels she has done much more, attributing the increase to the summer workshop. "The summer workshop sort of enlightened me to just be yourself. If you have an idea try it." She accepted that a teacher must take risks in her classroom and, as a result, learn by doing. Bernice now feels that she does not have to know everything. However, Bernice still appears to perceive science as a product, a set of facts produced by many experts in the field of science. During interviews Bernice explained how science should be seen everywhere, and it should not be a hard subject for students to learn. Science was taught in a way that was similar to her description of what science was like prior to her participation in the project. Science was introduced with a pretest or oral discussion with the intent of finding out what the students already knew. Films, worksheets, field trips, projects done at home, and reading assignments were the most commonly used activities. Even though her school had a Science Fair, students did not work on their projects in class. Bernice used several activities from the materials-centered curriculum guides, which both she and the students enjoyed. However, most of the time, there was little interpretation of the data collected in the activity. In mathematics, Bernice usually had the students solve a few exercises at the board and then spend the rest of the period working on exercises out of their book. Most mathematics activities were of a drill and practice nature, she assigned few problem-solving activities, and when materials were used, manipulation of them seemed to be regarded as an end in itself. Mathematical ideas rarely were developed from the students' experiences.

Bernice expressed a belief that she had grown as a teacher. She had a "vision" of how she wanted to teach, but her actions had not yet caught up with her beliefs, a situation that resulted in some frustration for her.

Assertion 5: The metaphors and beliefs associated with a specific role are context dependent. As the context changes, roles are reconceptualized and different sets of beliefs guide teachers' thoughts and actions.

Time and lack of self-confidence were probably the main reasons that Bernice opted to utilize her textbook and videotape resources as the main components of her science program. She believed that the best way for students to learn was to utilize materials to solve problems, and she believed that she ought to teach that way. However, when she implemented the curriculum she usually used her traditional approaches. In the context of having to teach a new curriculum using unfamiliar strategies, she was not sure that she could organize the students to learn this way, and she was not able to justify the additional time needed to prepare herself for this unfamiliar style of teaching.

Julie also seemed to believe that she ought to organize her

classes to enable students to learn using hands-on activities associated with problem solving. She had not always believed that, but as the study progressed her beliefs changed to become more constructivist in nature. Although Julie was a hardworking teacher, she often complained about the lack of time to do what needed to be done. She grudgingly gave time after school hours for tasks associated with the project. Julie was a person who had many dimensions to her life and could not justify allocating too much additional time to preparing to teach or helping her colleagues improve their own teaching. Consequently, compromises needed to be made. Her roles were conceptualized in terms of the contextual elements that applied to her, not just as a teacher, but as a person. She gave greatest priority to the program in her own class and did not participate as a mentor or a researcher. The reason for not participating was not that she lacked the knowledge or believed such roles were inappropriate. In the circumstances, she believed that she did not have the time to get involved as a researcher or a mentor. And on occasion she would have to teach in her traditional style because it was better than not teaching at all. For each given context that was constructed by Julie, she had an alternative belief that governed her actions. In other circumstances, it is conceivable that Julie would have been a model mentor and researcher. The main implication for teacher enhancement programs is that special attention should be directed to ascertaining how the context is framed by each participant and to providing assistance to individuals to overcome or reconceptualize constraints.

AN EMERGENT THEORY OF TEACHER CHANGE

The study provided evidence for the importance of three cognitive factors in the change process. Teachers needed to personalize a commitment to the need for change, to construct a personalized vision of what the curriculum could be, and to reflect on thoughts and actions. Each of these elements is discussed below in relation to the study.

Commitment to the Need for Change

Since she began teaching, Elizabeth had a belief that changes could improve the quality of her teaching. The excerpts extracted from a written interview with Elizabeth document some of the changes she made prior to her involvement in the study.

We did have a state adopted science textbook and I decided I was going to teach science using that book. Dutifully I assigned reading, we discussed it as best I could, then I quizzed them to see if they could fill in those blanks and answer those true-false statements correctly. This continued for a few years. Next, I decided I would learn all I could about the different units I was required to teach and impart my knowledge to the fourth grade students. I had become a different kind of teacher, one who stood proudly at the front of the class just filling those little heads with all kinds of information. Now I am doing mini projects, still using films, textbooks and giving my great lectures imparting all this information that I thought was science. This continued for many years until I became involved with the Cooperating Teacher Project during the summer of 1988. From the first day, I remember so clearly hearing we should emphasize learning and understanding over content. I thought, all these years I have been chastising myself for the lack of content knowledge and they are saying sure the content should be there but more importantly [*sic*] is the understanding.

Unless teachers have a commitment to change there is little likelihood they will make changes or be receptive to suggestions that improvements are necessary. Consequently, an important component of any teacher enhancement program is to provide teachers with an opportunity to develop a commitment to change.

Elizabeth quickly decided to make changes in her own classroom, and soon she was the most enthusiastic of the coordinating teachers. She was eager to get her students excited about mathematics and science, and she wanted them to learn with understanding. Elizabeth's following comments provide insights into her enthusiasm for a new approach to teaching.

I started science the first day of school. And also math. I had written a short letter on the board and I had the kids finish it. The best thing about school this week was _____ . And 11 out of 23 of my kids either put math or science. In the second grade we've done three units. The first unit was a process unit on color, and the next unit was on magnetism, and we're doing sound now. And each time, in planning with the other teacher that's working with me, we say, we've got to make it just as exciting or more exciting. Because they are expecting really exciting things because it is all hands on. Very little paper and pencil type stuff.

In contrast, Bernice did not have the confidence to break

away from the textbook-oriented program. The research team endeavored to provide her with assistance to implement activities to augment the content in the text. However, she had not reached the point where she was confident about influencing her peers and did not make assertive efforts to involve them in collaborative exchanges. She did not make the decision to restructure her science and mathematics programs in the way that Elizabeth had. Modest changes were observed in her own class in both mathematics and science.

Construction of a Personalized Vision of What It Could Be Like

Having decided that change is desirable, the challenge is for teachers to construct a vision of what a changed classroom ought to look like. Inevitably teachers will need to construct new knowledge and beliefs in order to do this; however, it is important that the vision be one that is not abstract and free of context. Teachers should be encouraged to consider possible changes in relation to the state, district, and school in which they teach.

Toward the end of the summer component of our study, Elizabeth communicated her vision of what an ideal teacher could be like.

> My ideal teacher would be one who wouldn't give out all the answers at the beginning. My ideal teacher would be someone who showed a love for the subject and would set up learning situations which enabled students to work together to find some answers and allow time for sharing. She would not give the fill in the blank test and would not give boring lectures that would put me to sleep. She would be someone who would give me time to think . . . I would like to have a chance for some input into what I studied or what I didn't study.

The summer workshop was a catalyst for change in the sense that new ideas were introduced. Elizabeth was an individual who searched for ways to improve, and she did not regard herself as an expert in either mathematics or science. Consequently, she came to the workshop willing to consider and learn from new ideas which might facilitate the learning of her children. As she noted in her written comments, she did not necessarily share the research team's goal of adopting new roles outside of her classroom roles, but she did have a commitment to the children she was to teach.

> I envisioned my role as that of a teacher of young children trying to set up the environment in such a way that they would truly learn and understand math and science and love learning and understanding at the same time. I see me as more or less setting up the room environment, groups, materials, and presenting a situation and letting the kids take off with it. Also for more informal learning situations, there are always manipulatives around the room for children to play around with and experiment with.

The above quote indicates that Elizabeth had personalized her vision of what mathematics and science could be like. Clearly she had a determination to make specific changes in her teaching, and these changes were represented in her vision.

Reflections on Thoughts and Actions

Adoption of the role of researcher enabled teachers to ask questions about what was happening in their classes. Consequently, teachers were interested and alert to finding out what worked and what did not. During workshops we continually emphasized that teachers should expect some things not to work on some occasions for some students. Their role as researchers was to identify what was happening, work out why it was happening, and plan changes to enhance the quality of the learning environment. The raising of questions brought teachers to a new level of awareness regarding what their students were doing and the effectiveness of their strategies. Being a researcher stimulated reflection in and on practice. As answers to questions were obtained, teachers could then make decisions about the roles of students and themselves. Raising questions, seeking answers, reflecting on alternative answers, and making changes resulted in shifts in beliefs about what works and what does not. As new strategies were tried and evaluated, teachers' beliefs about learning and teaching changed. And as they made sense of what they were doing, they used new metaphors to describe their roles.

Reflection can be an individual process involving cognitive processes such as the following: raising questions and seeking answers; determining what is working and what is not; identifying perturbations; and resolving cognitive conflicts. However, reflection also can be enhanced through collaboration and negotiation with colleagues. Processes such as the following can enhance reflection: explaining, clarifying, justifying, elaborating, evaluating, reconsidering, and building consensus.

Essential ingredients for teacher change were reflection in and on action and access to resources to provide foci for reflection. Although we knew about the importance of metaphor in conceptualizing roles, we did not provide contexts in which teachers would actively search for the metaphors they were using to make sense of their roles and query whether changes in metaphor were desirable. The emphasis given to this dimension of cognition could have been stronger and more overt. In future teacher enhancement efforts teachers should be provided with opportunities to understand how metaphors relate to learning and how the use of certain metaphors to make sense of a role can constrain thoughts and actions. Teachers can be encouraged to undertake research on their personal metaphors by analyzing thoughts and actions (particularly transcripts of speech). If the personal metaphors of teachers become a focus for teacher reflection, it is possible that changes can be made to metaphors and hence to the manner in which roles are conceptualized and the beliefs that apply to those roles.

Similarly, a focus on the roles that are of most importance to a teacher also should be the focus for reflection. Teachers who give greater emphasis to management than to facilitating learning ought at the very least to be aware of their bias and consider the implications for student learning. Teacher enhancement programs should allocate time for teachers to reflect on their salient roles and consider making changes to the value associated with each role.

CONCLUSION

A factor that emerged in the study that warrants more attention is the role of imagery in learning about teaching and learning. It was apparent that teachers made sense of what they were learning by constructing images which provided a basis for recalling events and assigning language to what is known. It was clear to us that we needed to know more about the role of imagery in learning and teacher change. It is ironic that we endeavor to persuade teachers to make changes on the basis of rational thoughts presented via language when the most powerful method of stimulating the reflection underlying change might be to use visual methods from which images might be constructed. The possibility that teacher knowledge and beliefs are based on verbal and visual metaphors needs to be explored in further research on teacher change.

Finally, we were reminded constantly that it is individuals that need to change. Consequently, when teacher enhancement programs are planned and implemented, special attention needs to be directed to making it possible for each individual to participate in a manner that is personally meaningful and rewarding. If individuals are to be successful teachers of elementary science and mathematics, they have to see themselves as being successful. The self-concept of an individual with respect to teaching mathematics and science needs to be positive, and this is so often not the case. Unless teachers change their self-concept, it is unlikely that they will assume the roles that are implicit in the calls for reform in elementary science and mathematics teaching. Within the context of school-based approaches to reform, designs for teacher enhancement programs should incorporate concern for the self-concept and self-esteem of participants with respect to the teaching of science and mathematics.

This study suggests that suitable objects for reflection include interactions involving teachers and students; images and metaphors used to make sense of teaching; the epistemologies embedded in the images, metaphors, and practices adopted in class; and the discipline-specific pedagogical knowledge used while teaching mathematics and science.

The conditions necessary for the cognitive changes which need to occur if teachers are to change can be attained in a variety of ways. These structural conditions are dependent upon the circumstances which apply to particular classes, schools, districts, states, and countries. In this study there were several structural components that enabled most teachers to change in a significantly positive manner. The most important of these are summarized below. Detailed analyses of the structural components of teacher enhancement programs are provided elsewhere (Jakubowski & Tobin, 1989).

Foremost among the structural components is the location of the program. Although we used a variety of locations, there is little doubt that school-based assistance for teachers is essential. Providing learning experiences for teachers on site enables them to construct images and metaphors that are grounded in the context in which the innovations are to be implemented.

The provision of a facilitator to "free" teachers to observe others, plan activities, and reflect on practice was viewed by the participants as a positive feature of this study. However, the provision of a full-time substitute is an expense that schools and districts might be unwilling to commit. It is possible that this highly desirable structural component is not an essential. Teachers and schools might be able to make alternative arrangements to "free" up teachers to enable them to engage in the manner that has been described. Less costly alternatives should be explored.

Finally, the research team was a resource for the schools. We were able to provide regular workshops on topics we regarded as important. The purpose of the workshops is to enable teachers to construct appropriate visions of what science and mathematics might be like and to help them project themselves into those visions. Similar resource teams need to be available, although they do not have to consist of university researchers. Currently we are assisting teachers to help one another in families of schools where groups of elementary, middle, and high school teachers meet together to discuss mathematics and science learning. Teachers from the high school might be able to offer assistance to their colleagues to overcome science content weaknesses while receiving assistance with some aspect of pedagogical knowledge. Although having access to resource teams from universities and community colleges is a decided advantage, there are numerous advantages to be gained from the collaboration that occurs among teachers at the three school levels. The optimal solution will depend on the specific circumstances which apply to the schools involved in the enhancement program; however, some mix of having families of schools work together with universities and community colleges is appealing as a suitable structure.

The extent to which these changes in science and mathematics teaching will be sustained has not yet been investigated. However, it is already evident that it is desirable to formally document changes that are considered to be worthy of implementing on a schoolwide basis. Schoolwide acceptance of reform necessitates a consensus of the faculty that a particular course of action is to be followed. This consensus represents a change in the culture of a school. Of course, the changed elements of the culture can be transmitted orally to newcomers. However, as faculty are replaced there is a danger of an innovation not being adopted by newcomers if formal documentation is not available.

11

E. WAYNE ROSS ─────────────────────────────

Teacher Personal Theorizing and Reflective Practice in Teacher Education

The project of teacher theorizing proposes a relationship between individuals and the context of teaching such that understanding and transformation of practice is possible. An implication of this stance for preservice and inservice teacher education is that teaching must be approached as an activity in which there is a dialectical relationship between individual action and cultural context. Much of the present research and practice in teacher education derives its framework from the "reflective practitioner" model as developed by Schön (1983, 1987); however, it relies heavily on notions of reflective thought and practice as individual acts.

In this chapter, findings from research on teacher socialization are used to illustrate the limitations of approaches to teacher education attempting to transform teaching practices through interventions at the level of individuals. Teacher socialization research, which focuses on how beginning teachers adapt to the role of teacher, give meaning to their own beliefs, and adapt to the beliefs of others, has demonstrated the influence of institutional contexts as well as personal biography on teachers' practices and the personal theories that guide their practices. In light of these findings, teacher education should be concerned with more than just the transformation of individuals into reflective practitioners, but also with the development of self-critical communities of teachers in the schools. The final section of this chapter explores both a conception of reflective practice based upon the interaction between individuals and the contexts in which they work and ways in which Dewey's theory of experience and conception of reflection might be used to construct teacher education experiences that transform teaching through both individual and cultural action.

CONCEPTIONS OF REFLECTIVE PRACTICE
IN TEACHER EDUCATION

In recent years there has been a surge of interest in reflective teaching practice. Much of the work in this area takes Dewey's distinctions between apprenticeship and laboratory experiences in teacher education (1904) and routine and reflective action (1933) as its starting point. This trend, fueled particularly by the work of Schön (1983), has led teacher educators to reconceptualize their research and teacher preparation programs.

The findings from recent reviews of research on reflective teacher education have illustrated a lack of shared meaning within the teacher education community about the nature and purposes of reflection (e.g., Clift, Houston, & Pugach, 1990; Tom, 1985; Zeichner, 1986). Conceptions of reflection range from those clearly grounded in technical rationality, such as the instrumental reflection of Cruickshank (1985), to perspectives informed by deliberative (e.g., Trumbull, 1986) or critical (e.g., Smyth, 1989) conceptions of knowledge and reflection (Grimmett, MacKinnon, Erickson, & Riecken, 1990).

The call for reflective teachers has led, for the most part, to accommodation within, rather than transformation of, teacher education programs. Although the language of technical rationality has generally given way to the language of reflection in teacher education, technical-mindedness still permeates teacher education practices (Beyer, 1988; Richardson, 1990). Conceptions of professional knowledge in teaching are still powerfully affected by an understanding of professional practice as "consisting of instrumental problem solving made rigorous by the application of scientific theory and technique" (Schön, 1983, p. 21).

This is evidenced in a number of ways: (a) the "technologizing" of the idea of reflective thinking (Beyer, 1984; Ross & Hannay, 1986); (b) the reliance upon a linear, positivist framework for research and evaluation of reflective teacher education programs and the development of a "knowledge base for teaching" (Richardson, 1990); and (c) an emphasis on reflection as a process to be "mastered" by individuals for the purpose of solving problems and becoming competent professionals (Cinnamond & Zimpher, 1990).

All of these outcomes are interrelated and illustrate the impact of positivism and technicism on the discourse and practice of reform in teacher education. As with other recent efforts to reform education, the discourse of reflective teaching is

> infused with 'power' in Michel Foucault's sense; the implications are meant to seem inescapable. *If* we have the proper knowledge base, *if* we become more rigorous, *if* we pay more heed to content and less to method, *if* we underwrite merit and mastery, *if* we enlist more experts among ourselves, we will solve what are largely technical problems and will no longer be at risk. (Greene, 1989, p. 21)

The success of reflective teacher education cannot be measured by the number of individuals that become "competent reflectors." The bottom-line measure of the success in any program for teacher education will be found in its effects on the culture of teaching and ultimately in the ways in which classrooms and schools operate. This requires teacher educators to consider both the professional development of individual teachers as well as the larger community of teachers.

A significant limitation of reflective teacher education, as it is presently conceived, is its grounding in the idea that the individual learns to reflect on a particular experience individually (Cinnamond & Zimpher, 1990). The failure to acknowledge the truly interactive nature of reflection has led to conceptions of reflective teacher education that fail to sufficiently address the impact that social and institutional contexts have on the teachers' practice.

INDIVIDUALISM, COMMUNITY, AND TEACHERS' WORK

The primary emphasis in the research and practice of reflective teacher education has been on how *individuals* "make sense of the phenomena of experience that puzzle or perplex them" (Grimmett et al., 1990, p. 20). This emphasis has led to a conception of teaching that fails to address the importance of discourse (the most important item of socialization) and social interaction within the institutional context of schooling. As a result, the discussion of the historical processes that produced schools as institutions is muted and our ability to understand them is limited. As Berger and Luckmann (1966) point out, "Institutions . . . by the very fact of their existence, control human conduct by setting up predefined patterns of conduct, which channel it in one direction as against the many other directions that would theoretically be possible" (p. 55).

This controlling characteristic is inherent in institutions. Goodman (1989) has illustrated how our heritage, economic structures, and system of patriarchal and mass culture have contributed to the establishment of individualism as a national ideology, which affects our conceptions of the purposes of schools, teaching, and learning. Individualism is reflected in the "narrow utilitarian" orientation of the school curriculum (e.g., focus on skills mastery, fragmentation of subject matter, and knowledge viewed as existing outside the human mind); although this ideology is presented as a source of personal liberation, "in many ways it thwarts most individuals from genuine self-knowledge and authentic power over their lives" (Goodman, 1989, p. 103). As a result, individual advancement and commitment to the public good are perceived as oppositional.

Teacher education suffers from a similar imbalance between values of individuality and community. Research on teacher socialization demonstrates that interventions at the level of individual students, as many of the current reflective teacher education programs are conceived, are inadequate by themselves for altering teaching and teacher education (Zeichner & Gore, 1990).

Recent studies clearly point out that the process of becoming a teacher is more complex than simply acquiring cultural knowledge about teaching (e.g., Adler, 1984; Jordell, 1987; Ross, 1987; Zeichner & Tabachnick, 1985). A conception of teacher socialization has emerged that emphasizes the interplay between individuals and institutional cultures. This dialectical model provides a way of understanding the constraints of cultural and institutional structures while not overlooking the active role individuals play in the construction of their own professional identities (Ross, 1988a). Studies of teacher socialization have investigated how teachers come to hold particular theories of action, that is, sets of ideas and actions a person uses in dealing with problematic situations. These studies have illustrated the interactive relationships among a broad range of factors, including teachers' backgrounds (i.e., experiences, beliefs, and assumptions about teaching) as well as the contexts of the classroom and the school in which they teach. Although teachers' background experiences are of great importance at the preservice and induction stages of teaching, teaching experiences in particular classroom and school settings also shape the teachers' theories of action. Practice-generated theories become increasingly important as teachers become more experienced (Jordell, 1987).

Studies that have focused on institutional levels of analysis have shown that the various ideological and material conditions within teacher education institutions, schools, and society serve to establish limits on the range of options available to both teachers and teacher educators (Zeichner & Gore, 1990). The construct of social strategies, as developed by Lacey (1977), has been used to examine how teachers respond to the culture of schooling, particularly the pressures to conform regarding language, practice, and organizational norms. Social strategies are the means by which individuals respond to conflicts between the culture of the workplace and personal biography.

Three distinct social strategies are employed by preservice teachers in response to institutional cultures (Ross, 1988b). The first two are internalized adjustment and strategic compliance. Internalized adjustment represents a deep change in the individual: the teacher complies with the constraints and norms believing that "they are for the best" and makes a value commitment in addition to conforming his or her practice. Strategic compliance refers to situations in which individuals comply with norms and constraints of the situation but retain private reservations about them. The third strategy is strategic redefinition, which entails individuals without formal power attempting to change the constraints and norms of a particular situation by widening the range of acceptable behaviors in that setting.

The findings of teacher socialization research, such as the uses of social strategies, challenge the traditional conception of beginning teachers as passive recipients of the culture of teaching. The internalization of social norms is problematic; individuals' actions and institutional forces play a role in the development of professional identity. "Teachers influence and shape that into which they are being socialized at the same time that they are being shaped by a variety of forces at many levels" (Zeichner & Gore, 1990, p. 341). These forces include pupils, the ecology of the classroom, colleagues and institutional characteristics of the schools, and teachers' own personal biography. This dialectical model of teacher socialization connotes exchange, discourse, and change for both the individual and the social group. As such, this view provides a more holistic view of the process of becoming a teacher. One implication of this view for teacher education is that we need a conception of reflection that includes interaction between individuals and their particular institutional culture or community. For reflective teacher education to significantly affect teaching practice in the schools, it must move beyond educating reflective (individual) practitioners and be concerned with developing critical reflective communities of teachers. How do we begin to address these concerns and reformulate our ideas about reflective teaching?

What has been suggested as the limitations of Dewey's work (Cinnamond & Zimpher, 1990) probably results more from a misreading (or limited reading) of Dewey by teacher educators than from the nature of his theory of experience or his conception of reflection.[1] A closer reading of Dewey provides us with insights into how we might resolve the tensions between the values of individuality and community in teacher education.

As the above paragraphs illustrate, current conceptions of reflective teacher education are constrained by technical-mindedness and the ideology of individualism. In *Individualism Old and New* (1929), Dewey examined the effects of science, technology, and corporate industrialism on society, illustrating the urgent need to rethink traditional ideas about individualism. Older bases of community were destroyed as cooperative action was replaced by individual action, the work of the individual became a minor part of a larger whole of activities, and relations between people became increasingly impersonal. "The tragedy of the 'lost individual' is due to the fact that while individuals are now caught up into a vast complex of associations, there is no harmonious and coherent reflection of the import of these connections into the imaginative and emotional outlook on life" (p. 82). Dewey suggested that the new individualism must grow out of or take form in response to present realities—making them the means for realizing individually chosen ends.[2] "True integration is to be found in relevancy to the present, in active response to conditions as they present themselves, in the effort to make them over according to some consciously chosen possibility" (Dewey, 1929, p. 148).

Dewey's account is exemplified in recent research on the work of teaching that describes the processes of deskilling, reskilling, and intensification (Apple, 1986). The separation of conception and implementation in teachers' work has had a deskilling/reskilling effect. When jobs are deskilled, knowledge used by workers in carrying out their day-to-day work is replaced by new, more routinized techniques, which are required to perform the job (reskilling). For example, in an effort to improve science curriculum and teaching, the New York State Education Department has initiated centralized curriculum changes with extensive accountability mechanisms (e.g., minimum competency tests for students), which in effect "free" teachers from the responsibility for conceptualizing and evaluating the curricula they teach (see Ross, 1990). As a result, teachers are placed in the role of curriculum implementors instead of creators. As responsibility for creating one's own curriculum decreases, technical and management concerns become the foremost part of teachers' work. The State Education Department in New York is now focusing its efforts on improving public education through a proposal that creates a new relationship between the state and local practitioners:

> one in which the State asserts more vigorously its right to define *what* is to be learned, and local teachers, administrators, and boards of education have more freedom to decide *how* such learning is to occur. The State specifies more precisely the goals and desired learning outcomes, provides incentives and support, assesses progress, rewards success and applies sanctions to failure. (Sobol, 1990, pp. 7-8, emphasis in original)

In addition to affecting teachers' control of decisions about curriculum and teaching practices, this process also redefines the organizational structure of schools and changes the language and activities of teachers. For example, skills that teachers have developed as a result of education and job experience are broken into discrete units and redefined into specialized jobs (e.g., curriculum conceptualization is centralized and routinization of reskilled jobs is accompanied by intensification—that is, "more, quicker, faster").

The interaction or communication between the individual and society forms the basis of Dewey's interpretation of social experience, but it is not interaction between preexisting individuals and an artificial society. For society *is* individuals in relation to each other (Dewey, 1929).

> Only intellectual laziness leads us to conclude that since the form of thought and decision is individual, their content, their subject-matter, is also something purely personal . . . Association in the sense of connection and combination is a "law" of everything known to exist. Singular things act, but they act together. Nothing has been discovered which acts in entire iso-

lation. The action of everything is along with the action of other things. The "along with" is of such a kind that the behavior of each is modified by its connection with others. (Dewey, 1927, p. 22)

Working from a Deweyan perspective, the aim of teacher education is not limited to the development of reflective individuals that work within the schools as they presently exist, but the reconstruction of experience that will lead to new understandings of self-as-teacher and the discovery (restoration) of community among teachers and others working in schools. As mentioned in the opening essay of this volume, we must think about teaching as a universe of activity or culture in which cooperation is as important as personal initiative. The examination of interactions among individuals and cultural conditions should be the starting point for reflective teacher education. "The business of inquiry is with the ways in which specified constituents of human nature, native or already modified, interact with specified constituents of a given culture" (Dewey, 1939, p. 32).

As Greene (1989) points out, in addition to concerns about competent action, we must talk more readily about what teaching practice is for, about the conditions and purposes of teaching. If teaching is to be transformed, teacher educators must "work to alter the institutional, social and political contexts [of teaching] and the principles and practices of authority, legitimacy and control underlying them" (Zeichner & Gore, 1990, p. 343).

RECOVERING A DEWEYAN PERSPECTIVE OF REFLECTION

Working from Dewey's conception of reflection as a product of interactions among individuals and the contexts in which they practice enhances our ability to construct approaches to teacher education that are responsive to the interactive nature of teaching. An educative experience, in Dewey's terms, is one which leads to the "reconstruction or reorganization of experience, which adds to the meaning of experience, and which increases ability to direct the course of subsequent experience" (Dewey, 1916, p. 76). These kinds of experiences produce new understandings of self, situations, and the assumptions undergirding actions in those situations. Challenging the taken-for-granted facets of everyday experience is a key characteristic of reflective thinking. Habitual modes of activity and the assumptions that undergird them must be critically examined. The resulting "puzzlement and subsequent reflection about a practice situation or the presuppositions that guide action in it lead to a mode of knowing that could be described as dialectical" (Grimmett et al., 1990, p. 27). The source of knowledge for reflection is found in both the context of the action setting and in the practical application of personal knowledge. The function of reflective thought and the knowledge it produces is to *transform* practice, not simply to solve technical problems.

Dewey identifies two things as necessary for the attainment of reflective thought: *genuine interest* on the part of the individual and a *social framework* in which interest can be cultivated for both the individual and society (Axtelle & Burnett, 1970). Genuine interest is an activity, "a course of action, an occupation, or pursuit [that] absorbs the powers of an individual in a thoroughgoing way" (Dewey, 1913, p. 65). Interest requires the identification of self with an object or objects (e.g., subject matter, materials, conditions) in such a way that one's well-being is tied intrinsically to bringing about a specific state of affairs that will most likely produce satisfaction. Reconstruction of experience in teacher education includes attending to ways in which personal biography constitutes both the content and consequence of reflective thinking. Reconstruction of self-as-teacher focuses on helping teachers become more aware of how setting and personal history influence their practice by shaping their beliefs, values, feelings, and felt needs.

The second essential for the attainment of reflective thought and practice is a social framework in which interest can be cultivated. Dewey (1927) called for the improvement of the methods and conditions of debate, and discussion through the development of community and dialogue. Individual reflection is not enough; the development of a vital and democratic community of educators requires "face-to-face associations." Understanding and acting on this idea is essential if Dewey's recommendations for teaching and schooling are to be realized. Democratic community life—conjoint communicated experience—is the basis of individual intelligence and the improvement of conditions of teaching and schooling.

Promoting more reflective approaches to teaching and curriculum work in schools requires us to consider how teacher education might change both individual and cultural action. This demands methods that challenge and change (a) the language used to describe, explain, and justify actions; (b) the activities that constitute education as a form of social life; and (c) the patterns of social relationship that constitute education (Kemmis & McTaggart, 1988). A pedagogical knowledge base — whether generated from personal inquiry of teachers or discipline-based research — is not alone sufficient to accomplish these aims. What is required is a question-posing approach (Tom, 1987), such as action research, to stimulate reflection and guide thought and action about the commonplaces of schooling.

Collaborative action research aims to establish groups committed to changing themselves and their educational work. Action research as a form of collective self-reflective inquiry is "undertaken by participants in social situations in order to improve the rationality and justice of their own social or educational practices, as well as their understanding of these practices and the situation in which these practices are carried out" (Kemmis & McTaggart, 1988, p. 5). Critical self-reflection as part of a collaborative group is necessary to identify how language and practices become constrained or distorted by structural forces in schools. This type of action research aims to develop personal practical knowledge and theories of action that are essential for the transformation of practice in particular settings. Reflection as reconstruction of experience focuses on explicating the taken-for-granted assumptions and cultural constructions that constrain and frustrate practice. The purpose of reflection in this conception is the transformation of one's understanding of the cultural and institutional constraints that affect the practice of teaching. The action research process is then a social process involving a social analysis which locates individuals' language, practices, and relationships in a wider context (Kemmis & McTaggart, 1988).

For example, Cornett (1990) describes how he uses action projects to help teachers analyze the impact of their personal theories of action on what their students have an opportunity to learn. The focus is on teachers explicating and analyzing the systematic theories, beliefs, and assumptions they hold as a result of personal experiences. This includes both nonteaching activities (such as life as a student or parent) and practical experiences that occur as a result of teaching and curriculum work. The aim of this project is the development of self-as-teacher through the "increased insights into the complex and practical nature of teaching; the degree to which they are and should be reflective about practice; the role of the teacher in determining the curriculum and the impact of systematic analysis (action research) of teaching on teachers' views of themselves as professionals" (p. 188).

Descriptions of recent efforts to create critical, self-reflective communities of teachers based upon collaborative action research principles are available also in the literature. For example, Carson (1990) provides a description of educators working as the Collaborative Action Research in Peace Education group and their efforts to reflect on and learn from their practice. In focusing on the difficulties experienced in implementing peace education, Carson illustrates how the taken-for-granted aspects of practice in the everyday work of the group were called into question. "The difficulty we encountered in implementing peace education," Carson notes, "should not be seen as an irritation but as a positive experience awakening us to meaning and to the complexity of life" (p. 172). Carson's description and work by Sanger (1990) and Ross (in press) illustrate how collaborative action research groups provide both a supportive and critical climate for the reconstruction of experience through reflection in both preservice and inservice teacher education. As Sanger argues,

> Only by destabilizing their deeper structures of knowing can teachers gain insights into and control over meaningful changes in their practice . . . The quality and support of the group's joint focus on aspects of classroom life enable the individual to take up the risk and challenge of bringing about professional change. Their joint ventures lead to ownership of the research process, interpersonal epistemologies, the generation of both theoretical and practical knowledge and, often, the capacity to represent minority educational views to the wider institutional community. (1990, pp. 177-178)

CONCLUSION

In this chapter I have argued that current conceptions of reflective practice in teaching and teacher education rely too heavily on notions of reflective thought and practice as being individually developed. Research on teacher socialization highlights the tensions that exist between values of individualism and community in teachers' work. Teacher education will be more effective in transforming teaching practices through the recovery of a truly

Deweyan notion of reflection (one that focuses on the interaction between the individual and the social framework) and the use of strategies such as collaborative action research to stimulate reflection and to provide a framework for a question-posing approach to teacher education.

12

GAIL McCUTCHEON ⎯⎯⎯⎯⎯⎯⎯⎯⎯⎯⎯⎯⎯⎯⎯⎯⎯⎯

Facilitating Teacher Personal Theorizing

THE DEVELOPMENT OF THEORIES OF PRACTICE

This chapter discusses how teachers develop their theories of practice. Examples of such theories are presented and ways of facilitating teachers' theorizing and evolving understandings of practice are described. The word practice is rather telling here in that one of its meanings according to *Webster's New World Dictionary* is "to do repeatedly so as to become proficient" (as in practicing a musical instrument or gymnastic feat).

Indeed, while teaching, teachers develop theories of practice in just this way; through teaching ("practicing"), teachers keep working to enhance their proficiency and perfect their work further by increasing their expertise and their understanding of how students learn, how motivation and discipline occur, the appropriate nature and use of rewards, appropriate roles for teachers, relationships with parents, and other matters in order to achieve optimum conditions so that students have access to the curriculum.

A teacher's theory of action consists of sets of beliefs, images, and constructs about such matters as what constitutes an educated person, the nature of knowledge, the society and the psychology of student learning, motivation, and discipline. Because of differences among teachers, these theories vary from one teacher to the next. One difference is in their personal experiences before becoming teachers. Through such experiences, people make sense of the world, and the reservoir of these experiences is one source of teachers' theories of practice. Experiences while growing up, going to school, working, and interacting with people and the world shape our knowledge and attitudes. Because these experiences and the meanings individuals make of them differ, teachers' theories of practice differ. Theories of action also differ because of differences in the context of teaching. The context, like teachers' past experiences, also affords opportunities for making meaning. Contextual differences in the community's socioeconomic status, the discipline or field being taught, and other professionals' theories are some differences that may account for variations among teachers' theories of practice.

A pragmatic aim—to produce desired consequences—is inevitably a professional teacher's intention, for it is what he or she was hired to do and was presumed to be professionally skilled in accomplishing. However, although professional aims in education are pragmatic, they can be assumed to be neither dispassionate nor value free. To the contrary, educational decisions inherently include normative aspects, and professional teachers care passionately about their work and students' progress. Indeed, it is because of this feature of teaching and because of its importance to society that teachers work to improve their efforts. That is, professional teachers try to improve because they feel responsible to their students, families, and society, not to a mandate or law.

Practical knowledge is required to perform professional tasks, a kind of knowledge Argyris (1982) refers to as "theories of action." These theories are vital to success in teaching because educational problems are practical problems (Reid 1978). They cannot be solved merely by discovering new knowledge or inventing some solution. To be effective, solutions must be put into action in ways appropriate to the circumstances peculiar to a context. In Carr and Kemmis's words,

> All practical activities are guided by some theory . . . For teachers could not even begin to "practice" without some knowledge of the situation in which they are operating and some idea of what it is that needs to be done. In this sense anybody engaged in the "practice" of educating must already possess some "theory" of education which structures his activities and guides his decisions. (1983, p. 110)

Teachers do not operate on the basis of a single theory of practice, but rather on the basis of many (of which they may or may not be aware). However, whether or not teachers are conscious of all of their reasons for actions, all professional work is rational, according to Argyris, in that it is intentional. Teachers may not be fully aware of their reasoning, but it is in the nature of their work that teachers are always trying to accomplish something when they act professionally. As Argyris's research has shown, people rarely produce actions that do not make sense to themselves: they have intentions about what it is that they are trying to accomplish. The degree to which they are aware of their intentions varies, but so far we have found that their actions are intentionally rational. Their actions are explicitly or tacitly designed to achieve some intended consequences. (1982, p. 41)

Teachers select and enact every teaching practice rationally because they are engaged in intentional, purposive action to create optimum conditions for learning to occur.

Teachers develop these theories of practice partly on the basis of their experiences prior to teaching. They develop them while teaching as they observe a series of small experiments aimed at improving their work and as they find out what is particularly efficacious. Perhaps undergraduate education and practice teaching have less influence on these theories of practice than teachers' experiences do because of the degree of responsibility involved in teaching. Faced with the somewhat awesome responsibility of educating these students and motivated intrinsically to do so, teachers find themselves having to solve all sorts of problems. Clearly no one else (a cooperating teacher, a methods professor) can resolve them or is ultimately responsible for doing so. By observing students and lessons, scrutinizing written assignments, and listening to students' responses and discussions, teachers accumulate ideas about how students learn, how motivation works, how to work with parents, the place of policies and classroom materials, and how to organize their work and teaching. They do so by reflecting upon and interpreting their experiences.

Kolb's (1981) work in cognitive theory provides a generalized way to understand how teachers develop their theories of practice. His theory is remarkably like Dewey's theory of experience (1938), and emphasizes the dialectical nature of human transactions in experience. He portrays such learning in a four-stage cycle (see Figure 12.1). In explaining the model, Kolb states, "Immediate concrete experience is the basis for observation and reflection. An individual uses these observations to build an idea, generalization or "theory" from which new implications serve as guides in acting to create new experiences" (1981, p. 235).

Another way to consider teachers' theories of practice is to see them as images or metaphors. Elbaz (1983) defines images as "a brief descriptive and sometimes metaphoric statement" (p. 254). In her work, image has taken on the form of a linguistic

FIGURE 12.1
Kolb's Model of Cognitive Theory

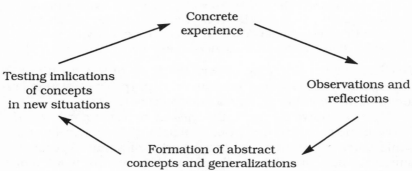

tool. Clandinin (1986) also works with this conceptualization of image and believes such images to be composed of a moral dimension, an emotional dimension, and a personal private and professional dimension.

> Because a teacher's world is essentially a world of action, teachers are not often in a situation when they must put terms on their actions. Talking about what they do is not necessarily a part of their life. Consequently, images were expressed in practice occasionally before they were expressed in words. (p. 149)

As we have seen, we can conceive of the sets of meanings teachers make of their practice as theories that resemble formal theories and as images. In both cases, teachers develop the sets of meanings out of experiences previous to teaching and experiences they have while teaching.

Carr (1980) believes that although some progress has been made about educators' views of the practice/theory relationship, "teachers continue to cling to an image of theory as incomprehensible jargon that has nothing to do with their everyday problems" (p. 60). This may be the case, but a growing body of literature (e.g., Grundy, 1987; Clark & Peterson, 1986; Oberg, 1987; Shulman, 1986) has started to explore the development and nature of teachers' planning and thinking, the complexity of teaching, and the development of teachers' theories of action. Clearly, teachers themselves theorize, although they may not recognize it as such, for in a large sense teachers' actions are their theories. This literature depicts teachers' struggles to understand and ponder their practice in efforts to improve and articulate it. Although Carr may be correct that teachers see theories as composed of "incomprehensible jargon" removed from their everyday problems, they clearly are themselves theorizing about their practice through reflection about practice and actions.

Simply put, teachers approach their work with different beliefs about particular matters. Theorists have used several different terms to discuss teachers' interrelated clusters of beliefs about their practice. Kelly (1955) argues that we construct the world through sets of constructed and opposing polarities. Several researchers (e.g., Nash, 1973; Oberg, 1987; Taylor, 1976) have used this theory as a starting point to understand teachers' "constructs." Hammersley (1977) writes of teachers' "perspectives" as ordered sets of beliefs from which teachers make sense of their situation. Clandinin (1986) and Elbaz (1983) think of these interrelated beliefs as "images." Schön (1983) examines theories professionals develop from their practice.

Just as theorists have used different terms with regard to the teachers' meanings, so they also have different languages for discussing processes used to develop them. Gadamer refers to "hermeneutic consciousness," Dewey to "deliberation," and Lewis to "introspection."

Gadamer (1976) points out that reflection is a powerful process in bringing to consciousness our tacit (and therefore unquestioned) assumptions and beliefs when he says, "The real power of hermeneutic consciousness is our ability to see what is questionable . . . Reflection on a given preunderstanding brings before me something that otherwise happens behind my back" (p. 38). Actions are in a sense behind our backs when we do not examine them but merely take them for granted. When we scrutinize them, bring them to consciousness and question them, we are able to understand and transform our actions so they are more consonant with beliefs about matters such as how students learn, what should be the nature and purposes of schooling, what students should learn, how humans organize knowledge, what to do about formulating the best relationships among people, and the like. This constitutes a form of deliberation in that it is reasoned practice and it is taken deliberately, not out of whim or habit.

Dewey (1922) describes deliberation as

an experiment in finding out what the various lines of possible action are really like. It is an experiment in making various combinations of selected elements of habits and impulses, to see what the resultant action would be like if it were entered upon. But the trial is in imagination, not in overt fact. The experiment is carried on by tentative rehearsals in thought which do not affect physical facts outside the body. Thought runs ahead and foresees outcomes, and thereby avoids having to await the instruction of actual failure and disaster. An act overtly tried out is irrevocable, its consequences cannot be blotted out. An act tried out in imagination is not final or fatal. It is retrievable. (p. 190)

Lewis (1955) terms it "introspection."

In introspection we try to look "inside ourselves" and see what is going on. But nearly everything that was going on a moment before is stopped by the very act of our turning to look at it. Unfortunately this does not mean that introspection finds nothing. On the contrary, it finds precisely what is left behind by the suspension of all our normal activities; and what is left behind is mainly mental images and physical sensations. The great error is to mistake this mere sediment or track or byproduct for the activities themselves. That is how men may come to believe that thought is only unspoken words, or the appreciation of poetry only a collection of mental pictures, when these in reality are what the thought or the appreciation, when interrupted, leave behind—like the swell at sea, working after the wind has dropped. (pp. 218-219)

Teachers' theories of action consist of the common elements underlying their practice. Their actions constitute their theories because actions constitute the medium of the expression of practice. Some of the tenets are tacit (not articulated in words), but some are stated. Some aspects of a teacher's theory are tacit because they are not consciously held, reflected, or deliberated upon. Perhaps teachers have difficulty expressing their theories in words because they are so used to expressing them in actions. Indeed, this may be the cause of the tacit dimension to teachers' theories; because they are unarticulated, teachers are unaware of them but can act on them. Teachers develop and refine their theories of action by acting and reflecting on those actions, although some teachers report they are influenced by workshops, graduate courses, and compelling literature.

COMMON THREADS IN TEACHERS' THEORIES OF PRACTICE

This section describes several teachers' theories of action and overviews some of their common elements. Elementary-, secondary-, and college-level teachers in graduate study provided the data base for this discussion and analysis. Their teaching experience ranged from ten to twenty-three years and occurred in rural, suburban, or city schools. Their theories should not be seen as common to all teachers, but it is interesting to explore these seasoned professionals' theories and the issues related to them. The common threads discussed include constructivist learning theory, regard for students, and roles of teachers' theories. (In order to provide anonymity, fictitious names have been used. Quotes that appear below have been drawn from field notes and other research documents.)

Constructivist Learning Theory

A common feature of these teachers' theories is that they believe students have to construct knowledge, not merely memorize it, in order to learn. Therefore, they plan lessons where active (not necessarily *activity*) learning occurs. These are not lecturers. Nor do they frequently use textbooks. Samuel, the coordinator of the library and learning center in his school, reasons it this way:

> Because of the information explosion, instruction needs to center more on the process of learning itself than on subject content. Students need to learn to locate information in order to become independent learners.

Judith, an elementary school teacher, concurs:

> I am becoming more and more convinced that the teaching of math is not the teaching of numbers. It involves instead the mastery of the concepts by methods other than rote and repetition. To this end, I have begun an extensive use of manipulatives in my math classes.

Lisa, an elementary teacher, states,

> The following are a number of factors that I feel influence how children learn:
>
> * Children learn by being actively involved in the learning process. Children need opportunities to discuss and manipulate ideas as well as practice what it is you want them to learn. Children learn to write by writing, not filling in blanks on a grammar work sheet.
>
> * Prior knowledge is a crucial factor in learning. We need to know what children already know or don't know before we begin instruction. We can improve children's learning by help-

ing children make connections between new and prior knowledge.

* Children learn by being in a learning environment that is conducive to risk taking and inquiry. We learn by making mis-
takes and being able to self-correct them.

* Learning can be enhanced by providing students with techniques that help them know what they know or don't know
and what to do about it when comprehension breaks
down . . . the ability of a learner to be aware of one's activities
and monitor that learning [is] metacognition.

* I feel that learning can be enhanced through an instructional
model that provides for modeling support and guided practice
before the teacher gradually releases the responsibility of the
learning over to students thereby enabling them to become
independent learners.

These are some of the factors I try to keep in mind while planning lessons. The materials and content for the lessons are
addressed in the lesson plans. The curriculum rationale for
this series of lessons is that both content and processes are
important components of the social studies program. We cannot
teach either as ends in themselves.

Sean, a secondary school science teacher, observes,

In biology, the kids have to see a point themselves, and the
best way is to have materials that provoke thinking and permit
them to draw conclusions. So when I'm teaching about genes
and human inheritance, I have them work in pairs to study
this on a worksheet. Then, after the students entered their
characteristics on the worksheet, I explained the second part of
tho activity. The students were to determine their mother's and
father's characteristics through interview and add these to their
worksheets. When I first attempted this exercise some years
ago, I encountered a problem that I had not planned for. Many
of our students live with only one of their natural parents, or in
some cases they live with no parental contact. It would therefore
not be possible for these students to determine their parent's
traits. I came up with a solution so that almost all students
would complete the same process. I have the students list their
own traits and then have them interview one parent only. Using
these two pieces of information, I have the students construct a
composite image of their other parent. This is an excellent learning process as the students develop a very clear understanding
of human inheritance while getting to play detective. For the few

students with no parental contact, the detective work is more difficult, but some educated guesses can be made and some interesting results have been formulated.

Additionally, the key to good discipline, according to these teachers, is having an interesting curriculum and activities which take into account constructivist learning theory. Claude, a secondary school drama teacher, suggests,

> When you have exciting things going on, like improvisational drama about problems the kids typically face (role playing), they get so involved that I never have discipline problems. When the biggest arguments are over who gets to play the different roles, I figure I don't have these problems, and it's because the kids are too excited about class to think about interrupting it.

Regard for Students

Unlike the significantly different examples of theories about learning, there was considerably less variation in teachers' theories of regard for students. Most of these teachers would agree with Mark, an elementary school teacher, who has (almost) unconditional positive regard for his students.

> There's something good in every one of them. It's different for different kids, and it isn't always academic. Sometimes it's just that you can count on a certain kid to be in a good mood. Another kid might be a shining leader or enthusiastic. But everyone has something good for him or for her. And some of these kids are very brave to be like they are, given their home life. While I teach I use their individual strengths. Given how it's going, I sort of know who to call on. Sometimes I have to call on the enthusiastic kid or the good mood kid just to uplift a discussion and get things moving.

Roles of Teachers' Theories of Action

Preactive Planning. While envisioning and otherwise planning lessons, the tenets of these teacher theories or images are criteria against which teachers plan courses of action. Those fitting with the theory are planned, and those not fitting are discarded or revised substantially. This is one reason for the failure of curriculum implementation strategies whereby teachers are to use curriculum materials as directed. When the materials call for acting on a learning theory, a form of classroom organization, or teaching content with which the teacher disagrees, teachers either transform the activities to make them consonant with their theories or do not teach those activities (see McCutcheon, 1988, for elaboration). So, for example, Health Objective #26 (whatever it is) might not be taught for a variety of reasons:

* It's not important because children have no control over that—parents do.

* That's not a health problem in this area where these kids live.

* We incorporated that when doing Objective #24.

* I don't have the materials needed to do it.

* That's something parents should teach their kids, not the school.

* Students have to be older to deal with that content, not fourth graders.

Interactive Planning. Another facet of the role of teachers' theories of action concerns the reshaping of plans while teaching and the seemingly extemporaneous actions teachers take. Since teachers' theories of action also underlie and guide these off-hand remarks to students, the reshaping of plans takes place because of unforeseen circumstances (e.g., the students need less help with directions than envisioned, necessary material is not available, time is too short, a fire drill interrupts the lesson at midpoint). Many of these extemporaneous actions occur in the blink of an eye, thousands are taken each day, and teachers simply do not have time to reason out the best strategy. They must, and do, act on the basis of their own theories, not out of simple, random reactions. If they hold students with positive regard, they will not simply fly off the handle to berate a one-time miscreant. As Cornett (1987) found in his intensive study of one teacher's theory of practice,

> It [positive regard for the students] permeates her teaching to the degree that it becomes a "non-negotiable" theory and serves as the anchor for her thinking about instruction. Whether she was lecturing, discussing reading materials, monitoring a simulation, or reading "senior announcements," *no* examples of her possible disavowal of this theory were observed. (p. 137)

Perhaps more important than the specific content of individual theories of action, these teachers have unearthed their theories of action, have seen their uses, and have reflected on them. Lisa demonstrates her understanding of the interplay between her theories of action and practices in the following chart:

TABLE 12.1
Lisa's Understanding of the Interplay Between Theories of Action
and Her Teaching Practices

Personal, Practical Theories of Planning (I believe . . .)	*Evidence of Theories of Practice* (I do . . .)
I believe that children learn being actively involved in the learning process.	Students have opportunities to practice the skills necessary to develop their research skills. The activities require the students to think and do.
I believe that an instructional model should provide students with an explanation of what you want the student to do and why, as well as provide a model of that behavior and guided practice to help students become independent learners.	The lessons provide a model of what it is the children are to do and guided practice.
I believe that learning strategies help students become independent learners and that both content and strategies are important components of the social program.	Students have opportunities to learn content about the Inuit people by participating in the development of a research question and gathering data to answer it.
It is important to build on student's prior knowledge of the topic.	The lesson begins by examining the needs of the student's own families and then comparing their needs to those of the Inuit people. The lesson also tapped on the student's prior knowledge of environments.
Learning is enhanced by providing students with techniques	Children are reminded to read over their work as they go and

TABLE 12.1 (continued)

Personal, Practical Theories of Planning (*I believe . . .*)	*Evidence of Theories of Practice* (*I do . . .*)
that help them monitor their own learning.	ask themselves "Does this make sense? How can I clarify this?"
There will always be external factors that operate as constraints when teaching. We must be careful these do not become excuses for not teaching.	The lessons were modified to take constraints of class size and materials into account.

Given the fact that teachers do theorize, and that they are seldom explicitly aware of the nature of that theorizing, what then can we do to facilitate the systematic recognition of this theorizing and its significance?

FACILITATING TEACHER THEORIZING

Bringing these theories to a conscious level seems to be an important goal for the education of experienced teachers. It is worthwhile for several reasons. For one, if teachers understand their own theories, they can examine them and reconstruct theories that seem unwarranted or that might promote what teachers perceive as deleterious, unintended consequences, such as a lack of equity or an overdependency on the teacher for learning. A second reason is to bring to light tacit (consciously unknown) dimensions of the theory. Yet a third reason concerns communicative competence, perhaps the most important reason. When teachers understand their own theories of practice, such understandings yield a self-confidence because teachers can articulate their beliefs to parents, administrators, student teachers, and one another. They can justify their practices articulately when they know them. In a sense they own their own practice because they understand it and so are able to communicate with others about it. Although teachers recognize that their theory is always growing because they fine-tune it while teaching, the self-confidence of understanding one's own practice and being in control of it is an important reason for facilitating this work.

I have developed in my graduate courses several assignments aimed at facilitating teacher thinking about their theories of action. Early assignments were aimed at reflecting on practice in a manner similar to creative writing. The directions for this activity were as follows:

> You have just won millions of dollars in a lottery. You tell your principal that you want to take off one year from teaching to do something you've always dreamed of doing. However, s/he says you may not because you're too good a teacher. Undaunted (and wealthy), you have a clone made of yourself. You are fortunate that human cloning has just become available! The clone arrives and looks just like you. But now you need to help the clone understand how you teach so you'll be able to get away with taking off a year, unbeknownst to your principal. Clearly you cannot teach your clone each little detail about how you teach. Reflect on your daily actions and conceive of your philosophy and understandings of the nature of teaching, students, subject matter and the "housekeeping chores" involved in maintaining your class. Explain this in a paper 18 to 25 pages in length.

This assignment met with some success. From this a second variation evolved so that students could then choose between the two creative writing options:

> Just outside your classroom a spaceship landed last night. You don't realize it, but the aliens are a small group of anthropologists from a planet studying behavior of intelligent life forms in raising their offspring. This particular group is studying the institution of schooling and was assigned to study your class. Their mission is to describe the general principles underlying what you do when you teach, how you treat students and content, and what you must believe about those matters. Write their report in 18 to 25 pages.

These assignments were successful in that they started teachers systematically thinking about their practices and the principles underlying them. The open-endedness was helpful to many. However, some teachers indicated that both versions of the assignment were too unwieldy, and they sought more structure, definition, and strategies for reflection. They complained that it was difficult to do the assignment in part because they couldn't really "see" themselves teaching and were unable to examine their work in the detail they desired. I suggested to several teachers that they audiotape or videotape some of their own lessons and keep relevant teaching materials and student work from those lessons for more detailed examination. The idea spread through the class and has become the method of data collection for the assignment because teachers were clearly able to examine their own practices closely when viewing or hearing these tapes and seemed to understand their own practices at deeper levels. This change from thinking about the assignment within a creative writing framework and the reported theories as images to an analysis and interpretation of data (videotapes and student work) and the theories as more akin to formal theories paralleled my own research.

Developing the assignment, assigning it, and collecting papers is but one part of facilitating such work. It is also necessary to make time to discuss the theories in order to understand them, and to make time so teachers can question each other, practice defending their theories, and understand how the theories work in practice. It is important to help students recognize that their theories of practice will continue to grow so they do not reify the theories they write for this assignment.

Students have written about the value of this approach and the evolving nature of their insights into their theorizing. Lois captures this in the following:

> When I began this assignment, I had no idea what my personal theories were concerning teaching. Now that I have reflected on what occurred during this lesson, I can truthfully say I am happy with the results. I was amazed that I came up with so many theories or beliefs. All of these theories center around my own personal values and beliefs and my own philosophy of life. However, I have never actually put these values, beliefs, or philosophy into such clear focus as I did for this assignment. I uncovered these theories at different times in the course of completing this assignment. Some of the theories were apparent when I began trying to decide how to approach this task. Some were clear when I began planning the lesson. Even during the lesson I remember thinking about some parts of theories that I wanted to jot down later. After each of the five classes were analyzed, I took a few minutes to reflect on what had happened. Many theories became apparent then. Later, when I listened to the audio tapes I had recorded during the lessons, I became aware of other theories. And, finally as I began writing this paper I focused on some theories I had somehow failed to notice previously.

Facilitating teacher theorizing must be linked to the professor's theory of practice. Facilitation involves (a) encouraging students to share in developing the agenda for class; (b) nurturing the view that systematic study of practice is important for professional growth; (c) engendering teacher self-respect as a result of introspection; and (d) promoting the acceptance of theories as tentative and requiring continual testing in the world of practice. The intent of the assignments is to provide insights for individual reflection. Class discussion provides a climate of support that serves to facilitate systematic teacher theorizing. Professors who see their role as one of imparting knowledge would probably be unlikely to adopt this approach.

13

THOMAS M. SKRTIC
LINDA P. WARE

Reflective Teaching and the Problem of School Organization

Teacher theorizing has become an increasingly important theme in the contemporary discourse on education reform and school renewal. Although the idea that teachers should think about teaching dates back to the progressive education movement, the revival of interest in teacher theorizing has been stimulated by Schön's (1983) concept of the reflective practitioner, and particularly his subsequent arguments (1987, 1988, 1989) for reflection-in-action as a means for teachers to enhance their understanding of instructional practices and to see themselves "as builders of repertoire rather than accumulators of procedures and methods" (1988, p. 26). The first purpose of this chapter is to address the question of the degree to which reflective teaching, or teacher theorizing, is a real possibility in schools as they are currently organized.

Of course, this question has been addressed before. For example, Dewey (1910/1987, 1928/1965), Freire (1970), and Schön (1983, 1988) himself have argued that traditional school organization works against teacher theorizing. In fact, Schön has been very clear about the fact that reflective professional practice will require a fundamentally different organizational form.

> To the extent that an institution seeks to accommodate to the reflection-in-action of its professional members, it must meet several extraordinary conditions. In contrast to the normal bureaucratic emphasis on uniform procedures, objective measures of performance, and center/periphery systems of control, a reflective institution must place a high priority on flexible procedures, differentiated responses, qualitative appreciation of complex processes, and decentralized responsibility for judgement and action. In contrast to the normal bureaucratic empha-

sis on technical rationality, a reflective institution must make a
place for attention to conflicting values and purpose. (Schön,
1983, p. 338)

Thus, for Schön, reflective teaching requires a reflective school
organization. The second purpose of this chapter is to introduce
such an organizational form for schools.

Before proceeding to the discussion of school organization,
however, it will be helpful to clarify what we mean by *reflection*,
and to note where our understanding differs from that of Schön.
Drawing on Dewey (1910/1987, 1910/1989), Bernstein (1983),
Rorty (1979), and Freire (1970), and thus ultimately on the
antifoundational theory of knowledge contained in philosophical
pragmatism, we understand reflection to be an intellectual act
that begins with a perceived problem which presupposes a set of
shifting and historically situated interests and which obtains in
social discourse. There is no difference of opinion on the matter
of a problem. Schön's conceptualization of reflection is premised
on the emergence of a problem, a violation of expectation. Reflective teaching, for him, is a process which is set in motion "when
people are presented with a surprise" (1989, p. 204), "a problematic situation that cannot be readily converted to a manageable problem" (1989, p. 201).

The difference of opinion occurs over the question of whether
reflection is an individual act premised on volition or a social
act grounded in political discourse. Although Schön's (1983,
1989) two principal examples of reflection-in-action—a jazz band
improvising and a group of teachers reframing a problem—are
social, he consistently characterizes reflection as a solitary act of
volition, one in which the only discourse that takes place is
between a practitioner and a problematic situation, a conversation in which "the situation talks back, the practitioner listens,
and as he appreciates what he hears, he reframes the situation
once again" (Schön, 1983, pp. 131-132). Our third purpose is to
argue, from an organizational perspective, that reflective teaching, in the sense of inventing and reinventing educational practices to solve unexpected problems, requires a reflective discourse within a community of interests.

Overall, our position is that teacher theorizing, or reflective
teaching, is not a real possibility in schools as they are currently
organized, managed, and governed; that there is an organiza-

tional form for schools in which it is a possibility; and, that, when it does occur, reflective teaching is a social phenomenon.

TWO DISCOURSES ON SCHOOL ORGANIZATION

Contemporary insights into school organization emanate from two primary sources: the prescriptive discourse of educational administration and the theoretical discourse of the multidisciplinary field of organization analysis. The rational-technical approach to industrial organization, with its interest in social efficiency, was applied to school organizations around the turn of the century (Callahan, 1962; Haber, 1964). It is dominated by practitioners in business and industry, who ultimately are concerned with controlling people who work in organizations (Pfeffer, 1982). Although in principle the theoretical discourse is concerned with understanding organizations and their effects on people and society (Pfeffer, 1982; Scott, 1981), historically it has tended to serve the interests of business and industry as well, because of the dominant influence of functionalism in the social disciplines (Burrell & Morgan, 1979). However, over the past thirty years, a number of substantive (Scott, 1981) and methodological (Morgan, 1983) developments have provided new perspectives and insights on organization, including school organization.

The following analysis is an abridged version of a more extended treatment of school organization presented in Skrtic (1987, 1988, 1991a, 1991b). The present version approaches school organization from a largely structural frame of reference, which is formed by combining configuration theory (Miller & Mintzberg, 1983; Mintzberg, 1979) and what we will call institutionalization theory (Meyer & Rowan, 1977, 1978; Meyer & Scott, 1983). Together, these theories provide a way to understand traditional school organization as a two-structure arrangement that is inherently nonadaptable to both the macrolevel of organization and the microlevel of the professional.[1]

SCHOOL ORGANIZATION AS A MIXED METAPHOR[2]

The central idea in configuration theory is that organizations structure themselves into somewhat naturally occurring configurations according to the nature of their work, their means of coordination, and a variety of situational factors. Applying this logic, Mintzberg constructs several idealized or metaphoric configurations of organization, three of which are relevant to the present discussion. The first two—the machine bureaucracy and the professional bureaucracy—are essential for understanding traditional school organization, and the third—the "adhocracy"—provides, in our view, a metaphor for understanding the conditions necessary for teacher theorizing.

Given the nature of their work, means of coordination, and situational conditions, school organizations structure themselves as professional bureaucracies (Mintzberg, 1979), even though in this century they have been managed and governed as machine bureaucracies (Callahan, 1962; Clark, 1985). According to the logic of institutionalization theory, school organizations deal with this contradiction by maintaining two structures—an inner material structure, the professional bureaucracy, which conforms to the technical demands of their work; and an outer normative structure, the machine bureaucracy, which conforms to the cultural demands of their institutionalized environments. The differences between the two configurations stem from the nature of their work, which influences the way they can distribute work among their workers and subsequently coordinate its completion. Organizations configure themselves as machine bureaucracies when their work is simple enough to be rationalized into a series of separate subtasks, each of which can be done by a separate worker. This type of work is coordinated by standardizing the work processes, which is accomplished through formalization, or the specification of precise rules for doing each subtask in the sequence.

Organizations that do work that is too complex to be rationalized, and thus too ambiguous to be standardized and formalized, configure themselves as professional bureaucracies. Here, division of labor is achieved through specialization, which distributes the clients among the workers, each of whom does all aspects of the work with his or her assigned client cohort. This type of work is coordinated by standardizing the skills of the worker, which is accomplished through professionalization, or intensive skill training and socialization.

Finally, an organization's division of labor and means of coordination shape the nature of the interdependency, or coupling, among its workers (March & Olsen, 1976; Thompson, 1967; Weick, 1976, 1982). Because machine bureaucracies coordinate their work through rationalization and formalization, their workers are tightly coupled, a situation in which, like links in a chain, each worker is highly dependent on every other worker. In a professional bureaucracy, however, specialization and professionalization create a loosely coupled form of interdependency, a situation in which each professional works closely with his or her clients and only loosely with other professionals. Here, the work is coordinated by each professional knowing roughly what everyone else is doing by way of their common training and socialization, rather than through direct communication or cooperative effort.

MANAGING PROFESSIONAL BUREAUCRACIES LIKE MACHINE BUREAUCRACIES

The logic of formalization in the machine bureaucracy is premised on minimizing discretion and separating theory from practice. The theory behind the work rests with the technocrats who rationalize, standardize, and formalize it. In principle, by applying the theory, they solve all of the problems associated with the work so that the workers do not have to think and thus can complete their work by simply following the rules. Professionalization, however, is premised on maximizing discretion and on uniting theory and practice in the professional because the ambiguity of complex work requires the worker to think: that is, in principle, teachers must know the theory behind their work and have enough discretion to be able to adapt the theory to their students' particular needs.

However, from the configuration perspective, professionalization circumscribes practice because it provides professionals with a finite repertoire of standard programs. In schools, the logic of specialization means that students whose needs fall outside the standard programs of their assigned teacher must be sent to a different teacher, one who presumably has the appropriate standard programs. Furthermore, over time professionalization ultimately results "in convergent thinking, in the deductive reasoning of the professional who sees the specific situation in terms of the general concept" (Mintzberg, 1979, p. 375). A fully open-ended process—one that seeks a truly creative solution to each unique need—requires innovation. But, in principle, professionals, including teachers, do not invent entirely new programs; they perfect the standard programs in their repertoires (Perrow, 1970; Simon, 1977; Weick, 1976). Instead of accommodating heterogeneity, they screen it out, either by forcing the client's needs into one of their standard programs, or by forcing the client out of the professional-client relationship altogether

(Mintzberg, 1979; Segal, 1974), which gives rise to the need for special, remedial, compensatory, and gifted education programs (Skrtic, 1987, 1988, 1991a, 1991b). The existence of these special needs programs minimizes the need for teachers to theorize or reflect on their practices because they remove problematic situations from the practice context. In effect, there are no problematic situations; when a potential problem arises, it is redefined as a social, cultural, or individual pathology, or as a problem of motivation, and relegated to one of the various special needs programs (Skrtic, 1988, 1991a, 1991b).

Moreover, given the prescriptive discourse of educational administration, schools are managed as if they were machine bureaucracies (Clark, 1985: Weick, 1982), even though the demands of work are complex. In principle, this drives the professional bureaucracy toward the machine bureaucracy configuration because it separates theory and practice and reduces professional discretion. In turn, this reduces further the degree to which teachers can personalize their standard programs, as well as the necessity to do so, which results in fewer students who can be retained in regular classrooms, thus reducing further the opportunity for theorizing (Skrtic, 1991a).

Fortunately, however, rationalization and formalization do not work completely in school organizations because, from the institutionalization perspective, the machine bureaucracy structure, where the rationalization and formulation are inscribed, is decoupled from the professional bureaucracy structure, where the work is done. That is, the outer machine bureaucracy structure of schools is a myth that permits school organizations to do their work according to the localized judgments of professionals while protecting their legitimacy by giving the public the appearance of the machine bureaucracy it expects. Although this protects the teacher's discretion somewhat and thus, depending on the will and capacity of individual teachers, potentially creates more occasions for theorizing, it also creates a situation in which professionals can practice with impunity from bureaucratic and legal modes of accountability (Lipsky, 1975; Weatherley & Lipsky, 1977). In any event, decoupling doesn't work completely either. No matter how contradictory they may be, rationalization and formalization require at least overt conformity to their precepts (Mintzberg, 1979; Dalton, 1959), which, more than would have been the case otherwise, circumscribes professional thought and discretion. Ultimately, this forces more students out of the regular classroom and into the special needs programs and minimizes the necessity, occasion, and capacity for theorizing and reflection (Skrtic, 1991a).

Bureaucracies and Change

From the configuration perspective, because both the machine bureaucracy and the professional bureaucracy are premised on the principle of standardization, they are inherently nonadaptable structures. Although change is fiercely resisted in both configurations, it can be forced on a machine bureaucracy through a rational-technical process of rerationalizing the work and reformalizing worker behavior. However, when a professional bureaucracy is required to change, it cannot respond by making rational-technical adjustments in its work because its coordination rests within each professional, not in its work processes. Nevertheless, because schools are managed and governed as if they were machine bureaucracies, attempts to change them typically follow the rational-technical approach (House, 1979), which assumes that changes in, or additions to, the existing rationalization and formalization will result in changes in the way the work gets done. But, because the existing rationalization and formalization are decoupled from the actual work, rational-technical reforms are largely absorbed into the mythical machine bureaucracy structure, where they serve the purpose of signaling the public that a change has occurred when, in fact, it has not. Nevertheless, although such reforms fail to bring about the desired changes (Cuban, 1979; Elmore & McLaughlin, 1988), they do extend the existing rationalization and formalization which, because they require at least overt conformity, drive the organization further toward the machine bureaucracy configuration (Wise, 1988; Skrtic, 1987, 1991a). This, of course, circumscribes professional discretion even further, which ultimately forces even more students out of regular classrooms and into the special needs programs and minimizes still further the necessity, occasion, and capacity for theorizing and reflection.

For example, the rational-technical nature of Public Law 94-142, the Education for All Handicapped Act (EHA), has had precisely this effect. By extending existing rationalization and formalization, it has reduced professional thought and discretion and thus intensified professionalization and reduced personalization, which has resulted in consistently larger numbers of students identified as handicapped (Skrtic, 1987, 1991a). Moreover, because there is a legal limit on the number of students that can be identified as handicapped, as well as a political limit on the amount of school failure society will tolerate, the EHA, in conjunction with other rational-technical reforms associated with the excellence movement (Meier, 1984; Wise, 1988), helped to create the new "at-risk" category of student casualties (Cuban, 1983, 1989; Skrtic, 1991a, 1991b).

Decoupled Subunits

Even though schools are nonadaptable structures, their status as public organizations means that they must respond to environmental demands for change. As noted, from the institutionalization perspective, schools deal with this problem by using their outer machine bureaucracy structure to signal the environment that a change has occurred. Another important way in which schools relieve pressure for change is by creating decoupled subunits, which is possible because the loosely coupled interdependency within the organization creates a situation in which the various units (classrooms and programs) are decoupled from one another. As such, schools can respond to pressure for change by simply adding on, and subsequently decoupling from the basic operation, separate programs or specialists to deal with the change demand, which buffers the organization from the change demand by making any substantial reorganization of activity unnecessary (Meyer & Rowan, 1977; Zucker, 1981).

Here again, special education provides empirical support for the theory. The segregated special classroom emerged during the progressive era to absorb students whose needs fell outside the available standard programs in school organizations (Lazerson, 1983; Sarason & Doris, 1979). In organizational terms, these special classrooms preserved the legitimacy of traditional school organizations and their conventional programs by signaling compliance with the public demand to serve a broader range of students. Structurally, special education is an organizational artifact that functions as a legitimizing device. It is a barrier to teacher theorizing because it absorbs problematic situations, thus eliminating them as a potential source of innovation (Skrtic, 1991a, 1991b).

The Adhocracy Configuration

The professional bureaucracy is nonadaptable because it is premised on the principle of standardization, which configures it as a performance organization for perfecting standard programs, not a problem-solving organization for inventing new ones. However, the adhocracy configuration is premised on the principle of innovation rather than standardization; it is a problem-solving organization configured to invent new programs. Adhocracies emerge in dynamic environments where innovation and adaptation are necessary for survival. As such, they configure themselves as the inverse of the bureaucratic form (Burns & Stalker, 1966; Woodward, 1965). The difference between the adhocracy and the professional bureaucracy is that, faced with a problem, the adhocracy "engages in creative effort to find a novel solution; the professional bureaucracy pigeonholes it into a known contingency to which it can apply a standard program. One engages in divergent thinking aimed at innovation; the other in convergent thinking aimed at perfection" (Mintzberg, 1979, p. 436).

Perhaps the best-known example of this configuration is the National Aeronautics and Space Administration (NASA) during its Apollo Program in the 1960s. At that time, NASA configured itself as an adhocracy because there were no standard programs for putting an astronaut on the moon, which meant that it had to invent and reinvent its programs on an ad hoc basis, on the way to the moon, as it were. Like a professional bureaucracy, it used professional workers, but instead of using *specialization* to distribute its work and *professionalization* to coordinate it, NASA used *collaboration* and *mutual adjustment*, respectively.

Under such an arrangement, division of labor is achieved by deploying professionals from various specializations on multidisciplinary project teams, a situation in which team members work collaboratively on the team's project and assume joint responsibility for its completion. Under mutual adjustment, coordination is achieved through informal communication among team members as they invent and reinvent novel problem solutions on an ad hoc basis, a process that requires them to adapt, adjust, and revise their conventional theories and practices relative to those of their colleagues and the teams' progress on the tasks at hand (Chandler & Sayles, 1971; Mintzberg, 1979). Together, the structural contingencies of collaboration and mutual adjustment give rise to a *discursive coupling* arrangement that is premised on reflective thought and thus on the unification of theory and practice in the team of workers (see Burns & Stalker, 1966). Under these organizational contingencies, division of labor and coordination of work are achieved through a presumed community of interest among the professionals relative to the organization's progress toward its mission, rather than through an ideological identification with a professional culture or a formalized relationship with an organization (Burns & Stalker, 1966; Chandler & Sayles, 1971; Romzek & Dubnick, 1987).

In terms of accountability, the advantage of the adhocracy over a decentralized professional bureaucracy—which is what reflective teaching and teacher theorizing imply—is that it does not simply substitute a "romantic decentralist," or professional, mode of accountability for the traditional "hyperrationalist," or legal-bureaucratic, mode (Timar & Kirp, 1988, p. 130). Ultimately, it replaces the legal-bureaucratic mode of accountability with a professional-political mode in which work is controlled by experts who, although they act with discretion, are subject to sanctions which emerge within a political discourse among professionals and client constituencies (see Burns & Stalker, 1966; Skrtic, 1991a).

Finally, although student diversity in the traditional bureaucratic school organization represents a liability, in an adhocratic school organization diversity is an asset, an enduring uncertainty, an occasion to reflect and thus, ultimately, a valuable source of innovation. In the adhocratic form, the moral argument for educational equity coincides completely with the technical capacity of its structural contingencies to provide it. Moreover, in the adhocratic school organization, teacher theorizing requires the student diversity that only educational equity can provide (Skrtic, 1991a, 1991b).

ADHOCRACY AND DEMOCRACY

The idea of creating the conditions for reflection in public schools was introduced earlier in the century by pragmatist philosophers and progressive reformers who were concerned that democracy was being distorted by bureaucracy. As Weber (1922/1978) explained, democracy and bureaucracy grow coincidentally because democratic government requires the development of the bureaucratic administrative form. With time, however, bureaucracy becomes more autonomous and independent of public control while, at the same time, democracy declines because, although it is intended to be dynamic, the bureaucratic form on which it depends resists change. As more of life comes under the control of its standard problem solutions and impersonal encounters, bureaucracy diminishes the need to solve problems and to engage in discourse, which stunts the growth of reflective thought and ultimately undercuts the ability of the public to govern itself (also see Dewey, 1927/1988).

Dewey (1927/1988) framed the pragmatists' concern over the course of democracy as a twofold problem: a bewildered public which, because it could not express its interests, was unfit for participation in democracy; and inadequate methods and conditions for reflective discourse, which were needed if the public was ever to develop a sense of itself as a community of interests. The solution for the pragmatist philosophers and progressive reformers was to restore democracy through a cultural transformation. The vehicle for transformation was a system of public education (Dewey, 1897, 1916/1980, 1930/1988) reconceptualized in terms of progressive education, which Dewey (1899/1976) described as a pedagogy that promotes reflective thought by engaging students' minds with problems, rather than filling their heads with "facts." But it was here that the progressive reformers realized the inherent contradiction of progressive education as a means of cultural transformation: its conceptual circularity. That is, the cultural transformation of the public, and the structural transformation of the school organizations that were required to achieve it, presupposed each other, "for education inevitably involves institutions as well as the ideas to be communicated, and unshackling students . . . must therefore await the unshackling of their teachers" (Kloppenberg, 1986, p. 377).

Although the problem of an unreflective public has worsened since the pragmatist philosophers and progressive reformers politicized it, the prospects for reflective discourse have improved considerably. Developments at the margins of the social disciplines and the field of education are providing new insights into the nature of and need for an expanded political discourse in society and in public education (Bernstein, 1983; Giroux, 1988; Greene, 1978). Moreover, three decades of unsuccessful planned change have forced education into a healthy confrontation with uncertainty, a confrontation that has given new relevancy to ideas such as teacher theorizing and reflective teaching. However, today as during the progressive era, the possibility of reflective teaching and cultural transformation through education turns on the conditions necessary for actualizing and sustaining reflective discourse. The adhocratic form, we believe, provides the structural conditions in which collaborative problem solving through reflective discourse within a community of interests can emerge and be sustained in public education. Given such conditions in public education, and the fact that democracy *is* collaborative problem solving through reflective discourse within a community of interests, we may yet be able to save ourselves, our children, and our democracy from bureaucracy.

14

JOHN C. DARESH _____

Reflections on Practice:
Implications for Administrator Preparation

Throughout the chapters of this book, authors have spoken about the inherent values of reflective practice in the world of classroom teachers. Attention has been directed toward both preservice and inservice applications for those who work directly with pupils in classrooms. A prevailing view presented not only here but in the literature at large has been that the professional teacher should be encouraged to move beyond issues related to "how" to carry out instruction to some of the reasons "why" teaching certain things to certain students in certain ways might be valid.

The importance of reflective practice as it may be related to the activities of a classroom teacher is clearly being established as a centerpiece of an emerging image of professionalism in schools. There is little doubt that, because the teaching-learning process is the central feature of any school, attention to the role and behavior of the teacher must be seen as the primary focus of any discussion related to the improvement of practice. However, the importance of other actors in the framework of the school is also sufficiently accepted that discussions about the value of reflection and personal theorizing must not ignore these other parties. As a result, attention in this chapter is being directed specifically toward the role of the school administrator and how it may be changed drastically in the future if increased attention is paid to the development of more thoughtful and reflective behavior.

In particular, this chapter addresses the ways in which an increased attention to the utilization of reflective practices may serve as the basis for some needed improvements in the quality of programs designed to prepare future educational leaders. The chapter begins with a description of traditional assumptions and practices that have been associated with preservice preparation activities. Next, these practices are contrasted with prevailing assumptions related to approaches that might take on a perspective more consistent with a view supportive of encouraging more reflective behavior on the part of aspiring administrators. Here, a model for administrator preservice professional development is suggested in the expectation that more emphasis on developing reflective skills will significantly improve the field of administrator preparation. Finally, the chapter concludes with a presentation of some of the ways in which leadership preparation programs might be clearly modified in the future.

TRADITIONAL APPROACHES TO PREPARING ADMINISTRATORS

The formal role of the educational administrator is a relatively recent inclusion in the framework of American schools. With the exception of large, urban school districts, the majority of American schools operated without the existence of full-time professional administrators until about one hundred years ago. As circumstances dictated, the prevailing pattern in most places across the nation called for the relatively small groups of teachers constituting the faculties of the majority of schools to engage in self-governing and self-regulating decision patterns and arrangements.

As the size and complexity of schools and school districts grew through the latter part of the nineteenth century, it was no longer possible for the daily management of school systems to be viewed as a type of part-time job taken up by one of the regular classroom teachers. There was a decided shift away from the practice of making use of a head teacher to engage in administrative tasks. Instead, there was a formal identification of a full-time, professional school administrator who was made responsible for coordinating, directing, managing, and leading the activities of the individual school or the large school district. Along with this creation of the formal role of the educational administrator came the belief that some form of specialized training was needed to prepare people to take on this new role. As a result, educational administration programs were created. The institution traditionally charged with the duty of carrying out the preservice preparation of school administrators has been the university, and training has been viewed as a postbaccalaureate experience. During the 1930s, it became generally accepted that school administrators would need to complete a graduate degree at a university as the first step in a preservice preparation program that would culminate in the receipt of a license or certificate offered by a state education agency. This image of the university as the "preparing agency" for school administrators took root; today, more than five hundred institutions provide preservice programs for aspiring school administrators across the United States.

The purpose here is not to present a detailed review of the history of educational administration programs at universities across the country. However, it is important to note a number of characteristics related to most preservice preparation programs. First, these activities are largely an American invention and tradition. No other nation, including Canada, has formalized the process of administrator preparation to the same extent that we have in this country. Second, an inherent assumption in the majority of programs designed to prepare future school administrators has been that people will be able to learn how to carry out their roles by enrolling in university courses which deal with effective management practices. Third, it has also been widely held that effective management techniques in schools are closely related to effective management practices followed in any field. Finally, the most consistent view of the activities used to prepare people to become school administrators is that they do not appear to be successful in reaching their objectives. Criticism has come from many quarters, but the most visible signs of discontent have come from the National Commission on Excellence in Educational Administration (1987).

Academic Preparation in Universities

The traditional approach followed in the preparation of individuals who would serve as educational administrators has been relatively simple, at least from the perspective of the institutions that have provided the preparation programs. After a few years of teaching experience, a person would enroll in a graduate education program at a local university. In addition to receiving a master's degree, the aspiring administrator would, with careful planning (so as not to take "too many" courses), complete the requirements for an entry-level administrative certificate. In many cases, the graduate degree would be in the field of educational administration, although it has also been common for people to pursue degrees in elementary or secondary education, curriculum and instruction, social studies education, or any one of many other academic fields while also taking the proper courses prescribed by the state department of education or the university as the requirements for receiving an endorsement as a school administrator. This approach has normally been a comfortable one for students to follow because the "hurdles" to a career in school administration are clear and well defined: Take X number of university courses, file an application, pay a fee, and become certified (if not always qualified) to run a school. Then, go look for a job—maybe. Universities have tended to like this model, too. Whenever competency and certification for a job can be satisfied by people enrolling in courses, it keeps lecture halls filled and professors employed.

Depending on one's point of view, happily or unhappily it was recognized long ago in many states that something beyond the completion of campus-based graduate courses in school administration was needed to help people as they prepared to take on principalships and superintendencies. Getting a lot of A's and B's on a university transcript did not really prepare a person to serve as a school administrator. Furthermore, as Charles Achilles (1987) notes, most academic programs designed to prepare future school administrators contain a number of shortcomings. Such programs are limited largely because they rely on structured courses which are not:

1. taken in any particular sequence
2. differentiated for differing degree levels (M.A. or Ph.D./Ed.D.) or levels of administration (principalship or superintendency)
3. designed with some type of unifying conceptual framework
4. developed with an underlying reliance on learning theory (or perhaps any overarching theory base), particularly adult learning theory
5. closely aligned with desired outcomes, or coordinated with the work administrators do—or should do
6. typically related to rigorous evaluation, either singly or for their contribution to a total administrator preparation program

Field-Based Learning

In recent years, there has been a growing recognition that the preparation of school administrators cannot be achieved solely through a reliance on university-based courses. Instead, learning to be a school leader requires that individuals go out into the "real world" of schools to acquire the skills that will be needed to perform their future jobs effectively. As a result, there has been an increasing effort to include some type of field-based learning experiences as part of programs designed to prepare future educational administrators. In 1986, Gousha, LoPresti, and Jones conducted a survey of universities involved with educational administration programs across the nation and discovered that, because of state education agency requirements for certification, internships, planned field experiences, and other forms of practica were required in twenty-five states. This represents an increase of fifteen cases over the past fifteen years. This number continues to grow, and it is likely that field-based learning programs will soon become a universal requirement for administrator certification in the United States, assuming that administrator certification continues to be a fact of life.

The move toward more practice-related administrator preparation has been endorsed by the majority of reformers. The National Commission on Excellence in Educational Administration (1987), Goodlad (1984), Cornett (1983), Achilles (1987), and Baltzell and Dentler (1983) are among the crowd who have provided a clear and consistent call for administrator preparation programs to stop teaching about administration and instead direct greater attention toward helping people to learn how to administer schools. A suggestion to this effect offered by the Southern Regional Education Board (SERB) is fairly representative: "Colleges need to develop programs solidly grounded in theory, but which also include some practicality. Internships, offered in full cooperation with local school districts, are one solution."

Field-based learning, or "learning at Nellie's elbow," as the British might call it, is based on several fundamental assumptions (Daresh, 1988):

1. It provides people with an opportunity to test their commitment to a career before actually following that career path.
2. Individuals can gain insights into a school, its goals, and how they may be achieved.
3. Students are able to apply knowledge and skills gained through college courses in a practical setting.

4. People can progressively develop competencies through participation in a range of practical experiences.
5. Aspiring educational leaders are able to evaluate progress and identify areas where further personal and professional development is needed.

Although these assumptions are reasonable expectations for the value to be derived from a program that requires people to "learn by doing," they are rarely fully achieved. The typical administrative internship does not allow a person to become so deeply involved with the life of a particular school that he or she can have any serious impact on the nature of the organization's goals. Furthermore, it is not likely that aspiring administrators will change their minds about their career selection when they take one field-based course at the conclusion of their preservice program.

Despite the relatively persistent emphasis on the need for field-based learning programs to prepare administrators, some limitations derive from this form of learning, in large part when it is not combined with other models or dimensions of learning such as strong academic preparation at universities. In the field of teacher education, many authorities have questioned some fundamental assumptions about the value of student teaching as a valid learning device. From Dewey (1938) to the observations of Berliner (1984), Cruickshank and Armaline (1986), and Zeichner (1985), numerous cautions have been offered that field-based learning experiences may actually be viewed as "miseducative," and that they create cognitive and behavioral traps which often close avenues to conceptual and social changes that may be warranted (Daresh & Pape, 1987). Field-based programs too often only serve to prepare people for working in the past or present conditions of schools, not for what they might become in the future. The field experience for preparing future educational leaders cannot be viewed in the same way as the apprenticeship utilized in the training of plumbers and electricians, who are prepared for the future by being taught the time-honored techniques that have worked well in the past. Field-based learning experiences may be extremely powerful ways for people to learn about their craft. On the other hand, too great a reliance on the practicum would be as unwise as attempts to prepare people for leadership roles "by the book"—only through academic preparation found on a university campus.

AN EXPANDED VIEW OF ADMINISTRATOR PREPARATION

We know that there are limitations on the traditional practices used in the preservice preparation of school administrators. Academic preparation does not provide the "whole picture" by itself, and the picture provided by field-based learning may be distorted. Further, we have an increasing knowledge base that suggests that beginning administrators need to know more about themselves than simply how to carry out required administrative tasks if they are to succeed in their jobs (Duke, 1984; Daresh, 1986a; Weindling & Earley, 1987; Wright, 1989). As a result, a different vision of administrator preparation is in order. This expanded view must build upon the strengths of academic preparation and field-based learning, but it must also include reliance on the individual aspiring administrator taking greater control over personal learning by engaging in systematic personal and professional formation as he or she advances toward a career in educational leadership. This concept of formation is grounded largely in the concepts of reflection and personal theorizing that have been explored throughout this book.

Personal and professional formation consists of those activities consciously directed toward assisting aspiring administrators to synthesize learnings acquired through other sources, and also to develop a personalized appreciation of what it means to be an educational leader. It is a concept borrowed directly from the field of religious education, where there has been a long history of working with future religious leaders to develop a clear understanding of personal commitment to religious dogma. This ongoing process is referred to as "spiritual formation." We make use of this term as part of the preservice preparation of educational leaders because a major problem faced by the novice is the lack of understanding concerning what leadership, authority, power, and control mean on a very individualized level. Personal and professional formation may be seen as a way to address this problem while also providing a person with a way of constructing a personalized moral and ethical stance that may be utilized in framing responses to a wide variety of future administrative problems.

At least three specific elements may be viewed as components of personal and professional formation. These are mentoring, personal reflection, and personal platform development.

Mentoring

Mentoring is an accepted practice that has been endorsed as a part of the developmental process in many professions. As Schein (1978) notes, the concept has long been used in business organizations. Mentoring is a crucial component of experiential learning programs. Mentors are needed to help neophytes in a field find their way and make sense out of what is happening around them in an organization, and also what may be going on in their personal lives. There is considerable potential to be found in applying the concept of mentoring to the personal and professional formation of school administrators.

Mentors are different from role models or field supervisors who may work with aspiring administrators during other formal field-based learning activities such as internships or planned field experiences. Kram (1985), for example, notes that other terms that might be used to describe developmental relationships in work settings might include *sponsorship, coaching, role modeling, counseling,* and *friendship.* Shapiro, Haseltine, and Rowe (1978) suggest that there is a type of continuum of advisory relationships that facilitate access to positions of managerial leadership. On one end is a "peer pal" relationship, and on the other end is the "mentor" relationship, or the type envisioned as an important part of personal and professional formation (Merriam, 1983):

> *Peer pal*—Someone at the same level as yourself with whom you share information, strategies, and mutual support for mutual benefit
>
> *Guide*—Can explain the system, but is not usually in the position to champion a protégé
>
> *Sponsor*—Less powerful than a patron in promoting and shaping the career of a protégé
>
> *Patron*—An influential person who uses his or her power to help a person advance in his or her career
>
> *Mentor*—An intense paternalistic relationship in which an individual assumes the roles of both teacher and professional advocate (p. 164)

The types of developmental relationships described focus on the business-related concept of finding ways to foster career advancement, which, in the world of private industry, is typically defined as moving upward in the promotion hierarchy toward some tangible goal as a senior regional manager, vice president, or even company president. The type of mentoring envisioned as part of the personal and professional formation of future school administrators deals more with the concept of finding individuals who will assist other individuals in finding ways to survive and ultimately succeed in the field.

Among the responsibilities and characteristics seen as ideal for mentors in a professional development program for school administrators are the following (Daresh & Playko, 1992):

1. Experience as a practicing administrator, and recognition of effective performance in that role
2. Demonstration of positive leadership qualities
3. Ability to "ask the right questions" of the protégé with whom they are working, and not just give the "right answer" all the time
4. Acceptance of "other ways of doing things" and avoidance of the tendency to tell protégés that the only way to do something is "the way I've always done it"
5. Expression of the sincere desire to see protégés go beyond their present levels of performance, even when that may mean going beyond the mentor's own abilities
6. Ability to model the values of continuous self-improvement, learning, and reflection
7. Awareness of the political and social realities of life in at least one school system
8. Comfort with the task of working with the developmental needs of adult learners
9. Above all other qualities, the ability to listen to others, help others clarify their perceptions, and "cause" others to reflect on the experiences they have

Mentoring as part of the personal and professional formation of school administrators is a critical responsibility. Consequently, a person who would serve as a mentor must possess a deep desire to work in this capacity. An ideal arrangement for mentoring would involve the careful matching of protégés with mentors. There would be a one-to-one matching based on analyses of career goals, interpersonal styles, learning needs, and many other variables that might be explored prior to placing administrative candidates with mentors.

Mentoring relationships have important positive effects on the career development of both protégés and mentors. Daresh and Playko (1990) interviewed a group of mentors who worked with aspiring administrators as part of an experimental program supported by the Danforth Foundation and found that the participating administrators indicated that they had derived a number of important benefits from their work in the project:

1. They were able to understand their own professional roles and values and methods of operating as the result of having aspiring administrators constantly seeking clarification of their practices and ways of approaching problems.
2. They experienced a sense of renewed commitment to their work, and to the potential of their positions to bring about positive change in their schools and districts.
3. They achieved a sense of satisfaction because their work with aspiring administrators enabled them to refine their own interpersonal communication skills and abilities.

Personal Reflection

A second important element in personal and professional formation is related to the development of skills supportive of personal reflection to guide administrative performance. Reflection about one's professional performance in a role is a rather simple concept to define. As Posner (1985) observes concerning the use of reflectivity in student teaching, people would benefit greatly from their experiences if they had the opportunity to prepare for and think about their actions before they carried them out. The basic idea is simply stated: a reflective practitioner would be the person who realizes that, before he or she tries to solve problems, it is critical to think about the nature of the "right" problem to be solved.

In the professional development of educators, there has been a consistent call for adding reflection as a component for teacher candidates. In an analysis of one of the drawbacks to student teaching practices, Beyer (1984) observes that teaching candidates often learn negative behaviors in the field because they are prone to engage in "uncritical acceptance" of what they see, hear, and experience. The same danger, of course, exists in training programs for administrators, who may see wholly unacceptable or even unethical practices being rewarded "in reality." Reflection, particularly if directed by a sensitive mentor, is a way to encourage the aspiring administrator to make critical judgments about the appropriateness of activities and behaviors witnessed out in the field. Again, as Beyer (1984) states, "Experiences which promote uncritical replication of observed practice are antithetical to the purposes of education itself. Promoting activities . . . which generate such perspective is, thus, contradictory to some fundamental purposes of education as this is often understood" (p. 37).

Developing reflective skill is one important way to question the value of practices and assumptions seen out in the field, and this is a critical part of developing a personalized professional identity. Questions that may be used to guide the process of personal reflection and help a person to focus on what leadership is all about might include any or all of the following:

What have I seen out in the field?

How does what I have seen fit my personal view of what life as an administrator will be?

Why is what I have seen important?

What have I learned?

What do I want to know more about?

How can I describe what I have seen?

In what ways can I verify my description of what I have seen?

What is the meaning of my experience?

How does the description and my personal meaning relate to my personalized vision of what "should" be?

What else can be learned?

What is the overall significance of what I have done and seen?

Now that I have done something, so what?

If beginning administrators proceed through practical, on-the-job experiences that are followed by a period of reflecting on the answers to questions such as these, they should develop a much deeper understanding of administration. Personalized reflection may also result in a person making a deliberate decision to leave administration or not even go into it in the first place. That, too, would be a desirable outcome in that it might reduce the number of people who pursue careers in administration out of "accident" or some false sense of purpose rather than as a result of a conscious and deliberate plan and design.

One way to integrate personal reflection would be through an expectation that candidates for future administrative positions would keep a diary, or reflective log, in which they would regularly record their personal descriptions of reality and their responses to some of the questions that were listed earlier. Writing these observations down in a formal way develops skills at articulating important personal beliefs that may be of use in the future.

Educational Platform Development

Another important part of professional development for future administrators involves the preparation of a formal statement of one's own educational philosophy, beliefs, and values. Sergiovanni and Starratt (1988) refer to this activity as the development of a personalized educational platform. In their view, professional educators should be encouraged periodically to review personal stances about important educational issues. In doing this, people would state the ideas that they espouse, much as a political candidate makes statements. The major difference would be that the educational platform should be designed to communicate a person's attitudes, values, and beliefs about education, even if these statements run contrary to the sentiments of the majority of people "out in the public."

Sergiovanni and Starratt suggest that an educational platform might include personalized responses to questions that come from the following ten major issues:

1. The aims of education
2. Major achievements of students
3. The social significance of student learning
4. The image of the learner
5. The value of the curriculum
6. The image of the teacher
7. The preferred kind of pedagogy
8. The primary language of discourse to be used in the learning situation
9. The preferred kind of school climate

Clearly, there are no absolutely "correct" or "incorrect" answers to any of these issues; however, the process of spending time to think through, and actually write out, personal interpretations of each of these items would have a number of advantages, particularly for people moving into new professional roles. Preparing a platform statement enables individuals to recognize their strongest beliefs (and perhaps unwanted biases as well) about significant issues in professional education. Some of the responses to the ten areas will come about much more quickly than will others. These areas will serve as place holders for concepts that probably involve the strongest allegiance to certain values, which may be viewed as "core" or "non-negotiable" values for an individual. A second benefit is that it may alert individuals to probably conflicts that are likely to lie ahead. In addition to individual platforms, all organizations also subscribe to, at least implicitly, strong statements of public values, usually stated as part of institutional philosophies and mission statements. When people enjoy a deep understanding of their educational platforms, they may tell in advance where sources of conflict are to be found in relationships with organizations. Understanding the exact sources of probable value disputes should assist most individuals in finding more effective ways of dealing with life in institutions.

Every aspiring, beginning, or continuing administrator should periodically articulate a personal educational platform. Furthermore, there is also considerable value in sharing this platform statement with others, a mentor or other colleagues. This sharing process should take place with considerable regularity and frequency. This process is helpful in enabling others to gain insights into one's behavior and, perhaps even more importantly, in causing an individual to be as clear as possible about the nature of personal values and beliefs. A platform is something which is never really completed. Rather, platform preparation and personal theorizing in general must be viewed as a dynamic and ongoing activity carried out by every thoughtful individual in the field of school administration.

There are other features of professional development which could legitimately be included as part of the process of personal and professional formation. For example, understanding interpersonal style differences among the various individuals who constitute an organization is quite important. Also, there is great value in the individual aspiring administrator formally developing a statement of an action plan that will be followed in relation to a personalized philosophy, theory, or platform. However, the areas of mentoring, reflection, and platform development represent the most essential parts of an administrator preparation program that goes well beyond the traditional issues of learning about administration through academic preparation and skill development through field-based learning.

PUTTING IT ALL TOGETHER

Discussions of recommended changes in administrator preparation programs necessitate some additional considerations of what the changes might ultimately mean, and how changes in preservice preparation might be translated into continuing revisions of what educational administration is all about in practice.

In terms of outcomes to be derived by encouraging greater attention to be placed on personal and professional formation, as described in this chapter, perhaps the greatest single benefit is likely to be the fact that future administrators might be better prepared to engage in more proactive behavior as professionals. A consistent and generally well-deserved criticism of many educational administrators in the past has been that they do not lead. Instead, they tend to wait to react to crisis situations that are encountered on the job. To some extent, reacting is a part of the role of school administrators. It is not always possible to anticipate what problems are likely to be encountered. On the other hand, when administrators of schools sit back and wait to encounter the next problem, they may easily fall into a pattern of behavior that causes considerable frustration on the part of their professional colleagues. Consider, for example, the number of times when classroom teachers and other educational personnel feel as if the decisions made by the "person in charge" are solely a response to an immediate problem—sort of a "squeaky wheel" approach to fixing organizational problems. It is nearly impossible to feel positive about working in a setting where each crisis will be met by the creation of a spontaneous policy as a way to minimize personal strain on the leader. A much more desirable situation would be the creation of an organizational climate where there is a general sense of "the way we do things around here." A big part of that climate comes from leadership which is consistent, fair, and predictable.

Another desirable outcome from settings where leadership is forged in a more proactive way, with greater emphasis on formation than on training, would be the creation of organizations where leaders are not threatened by those with whom they work. There is little doubt in our mind that the future will see increasing emphasis on the importance of emergent leadership patterns in schools that include individuals who work well beyond the confines of the administrator's office. Also, the empowerment of professional educators is rapidly moving beyond the phase of serving as a buzzword. The educational administrator of the future must be much more comfortable about working in a world marked by collegial relationships with teachers and other educators. That level of comfort must be developed in the earliest stages of administrative development. Greater emphasis on formation may help in that process.

The second issue to be considered deals with sustaining personal and professional formation once an individual has moved out into an administrative position. How can reflection and personal theorizing be maintained out in the "real world"? This is a difficult issue because there is a constant press by experienced colleagues to behave in ways that might be contrary to the vision we have shared here.

Mentoring is one way that might serve as the basis for keeping the process of formation alive and well. Earlier in this chapter, mentoring was described primarily in terms of preservice preparation. Here, the suggestion is that mentors may be identified to work with experienced colleagues throughout their careers. In this way, the importance of collegial professional relationships might be made even more apparent as people go through what has traditionally been a very isolated and lonely experience. The literature is filled with descriptions of the loneliness of the administrator's role. Ongoing mentoring and collegial support might be ways of reducing this sense of separation on the job.

Another strategy that might be used to maintain the force of personal and professional formation might be the development of formal strategies that require individuals to stay tuned to their senses through constant reflective activities. Two interesting models are now found around the nation which may serve as the basis for ongoing administrator professional development. The first is found in the work of the Silver Center for Reflective Practice at Hofstra University. Here, the vision of principal inservice started by the late Paula Silver with her Apex Center at the University of Illinois (Silver, 1986) is kept alive in a program where practicing principals are encouraged to maintain case records and analyses of issues and problems encountered on the job, for future sharing with colleagues. Another model worth considering because of its importance to personal and professional formation is the Peer-Assisted Leadership Program (PAL) developed at the Far West Laboratory (Barnett, 1987). Here, principals engage in structured, reflective interviewing activities and shadowing of each other while on the job. In both programs, the goal is to help individuals to break out of traditional, reactive patterns of thought and behavior so that they might become more sensitive to their own ways of behaving and solving complex professional problems.

At present, educational administration is undergoing considerable revision as a field of practice and study. The great number of reform reports appearing on the topic of leadership must be seen in conjunction with almost daily popular attacks in the media regarding the ineffectiveness and inefficiency of school administrators across the country. There is considerable reason to believe that a good deal of present criticism is an overreaction to shortcomings seen in school practice. Nevertheless, there is a clear need to think about ways to improve leadership development in schools.

SUMMARY

In this chapter, a vision of a different approach to the preparation of school administrators was presented. This view included an approach that would place greater emphasis on the development of personal theorizing and reflection rough the process of what was described as personal and professional formation. It was noted that traditional approaches to administrator preparation were based on the belief that people need to learn about their work through learning in structured academic settings, coupled with some additional skill acquisition through field-based learning activities.

The primary value shared throughout this chapter was that educational leadership will continue to be an important feature of good schools. At the same time, leadership is becoming an increasingly complex issue to be achieved in most settings, and it can no longer be viewed as something which is bestowed on a few chosen, special school administrators who, once annointed, never need to be concerned with practice again. Instead, leadership of schools will continue to be important, but those who are in leadership roles need to be prepared to deal with the fluid and dynamic nature of their duties in the future. Personal and professional formation, as part of the preservice preparation process, may be an important way to achieve some recognition of true professional responsibility.

IV

REFLECTIONS ON TEACHER
PERSONAL THEORIZING

15

LANDON E. BEYER _____

The Personal and the Social in Education

The idea that theoretical inquiry by teachers has an important, even vital, role within the domain of schooling, although not a new one, has hardly been a central conviction within educational discourse until recently. This, of course, reflects the status of teaching as a profession—including, importantly, the gender, social class, and racial boundaries within which it has developed—and the ways in which teaching has been conceptualized and understood. Those involved in setting educational policies, preparing aspiring teachers, administering schools, and working within the academy have been influential in diminishing the role of the teacher in a way that has generally denied her or him a voice in the articulation of educational theory.

It has been a commonplace, within the dominant traditions of schooling and teaching, to consider the teacher as a kind of technician. The dominant activity of the teacher conceived in these terms involves the transmission of knowledge, values, and ideas, sanctioned by"experts" working outside the classroom. This conception has been enhanced by the view that the teacher must adopt those methodologies, personality traits, and (now, especially, classroom management) strategies that have largely occupied the course of study for prospective teachers. Within this conception, teaching is largely a kind of application process, based upon a model of technical rationality ("for result X, apply strategies 1 and 2 in situation Y"). Appropriate preparation for such activities consists in acquiring various "tricks of the trade," a variety of technical and procedural approaches to instruction, and becoming socialized into professional expectations. The movement to introduce "competency-based" teaching and teacher education practices reflects these tendencies. More recently, the attempt to locate the appropriate "knowledge base for teaching," although somewhat more sophisticated, has tended to reflect the same conception of teaching as an essentially applicative process. Similarly, there have been many recommendations to make teacher preparation an exclusively graduate-level, "professional" enterprise, to be undertaken after the completion of an undergraduate liberal education in the "academic" disciplines. This too results in a picture of teaching as applying intrinsically valuable knowledge acquired prior to teacher preparation, with the aid of methodological strategies and pedagogical principles that are the special focus of that preparation (Holmes Group, 1986).

In these and similar characterizations of teaching and professionalism, teachers *apply* the ideas, perspectives, and theoretical frameworks of others acquired through liberal learning. This process of application is to be enhanced by professional education—a process, we should note, that many have thought should be based on studies arising from the behavioral sciences. Together, the knowledge sanctioned by liberal learning and the principles and strategies acquired through professional study are to combine to increase student achievement and the status of teaching. Such a perspective does not recognize a significant role for teacher theorizing. Indeed, it seems to harken back to the nineteenth-century image of the normal school program, albeit in a more sophisticated form, which was one important source of the picture of teacher as applicative technician and manager rather than theoretical inquirer.

Further complicating the possible value of teacher theorizing is the fact that there are a variety of meanings to the term *theory* and an equally wide array of theoretical discourses to which we might refer in discussing the ways in which teachers might engage in theorizing. Yet, in spite of this array of theoretical possibilities, we have tended to uncritically and narrowly adopt a rather positivistic view of theorizing within the domain of education. In this view, theories result from accumulated observations, objectively validated and carefully controlled, with conclusions based on some mathematical or logical calculus. To ensure objectivity, the contexts within which observations are carried out (including both the individual circumstances of the observer and the larger social, political, economic, and ideological contexts within which he or she observes) must be excluded. The search has been for a neutral language in which to express precise, quantitative, objective, and verifiable observations that will provide a foundation for certain knowledge (for critiques of this emphasis in education, see the chapter by Lynda Stone, this volume; Beyer, 1988; for criticisms of the philosophical traditions involved, see Bernstein, 1983; Rorty, 1979, 1989). This positivistic emphasis within much educational theory may explain, at least in part, the comparative lack of emphasis historically placed on teacher theorizing. For, if theorizing is to be as controlled and contextually dislocated as the positivists have insisted, there will be precious little opportunity for teacher theorizing, given the rather demanding, dense, and variable contexts within which teachers work—contexts that cannot be shunted aside in favor of some notion of objectivity.

Yet, numerous writers have exposed the questionable assumptions on which this view of theory rests, and have suggested alternative possibilities for theorizing that are more compatible with the activities of teaching. The most often cited work in this connection appears to be that of Donald Schön (1983, 1987), who bases much of his analysis in professions other than teaching. Shulman (1987) and others involved in empirical research on teaching have also identified aspects of pedagogy that are resistant to the kind of positivistic thinking that has until recently dominated in education. He argues that teaching is a reasoned activity requiring a depth of knowledge that undergoes constant change even as it becomes an object or reflection. Clandinin (1986) has also been insightful in helping develop an understanding of teaching in which reflection and theorizing are central activities, and subject to dialectical transformations. Such observations and analyses have challenged the notion of teaching as an applied, technical domain. They have enhanced the vitality of theorizing within education and respected the value of the practitioner's theoretical insights as crucial elements of professionalism (Beyer, Feinberg, Pagano, and Whitson, 1989).

My purpose in this chapter to raise some additional questions about the contexts and directions of educational theorizing and to suggest ways in which a commitment to teacher theorizing, practical intelligence or wisdom, and the contextual elements of reflection might be extended. Foremost among my concerns is the danger that reflection, debates over values and priorities, and critique—especially within the current social and ideological climate—will tend toward moral relativism. There are at least three possible sources for this relativism. First, critiques of positivism have been persuasive in their suggestion that there are no forms of knowledge that are foundational or transcendental. It seems, then, that judgments of value must be "relative" (to the context in which they are made and/or to the people who make them). If this is the case, we might *express* different values or priorities within education, but it appears that we can't properly *disagree* about them. We are left, then, with a view of value judgments and disputes based on emotivism, where such judgments are seen as merely the expression of personal preferences (MacIntyre, 1984). Second, there has been a tendency within education to think about "values" as needing "clarification" rather than debate and justification. Partly because of the dominance of a powerful hidden curriculum (see Apple, 1975), we have devalued conflict in schools as we have emphasized either a benign consensus or an equally pallid tolerance of divergent expressions of value. Applied to teaching, this can result in thinking about theorizing—especially "teacher *personal* theorizing"—as an exclusively autobiographical, individual, even isolated activity, the results of which can only be judged by their consistency with the practices that constitute teaching. We may, in other words, think about theorizing as an excessively private matter. Yet as Pagano (1990) has recently commented, "Even when we talk to ourselves, we're talking to someone else" (p. xviii). Teacher theorizing is unavoidably embedded within personal histories, interpretive communities, social contexts, and historical traditions, as well as within the immediate environment of the classroom or other settings in which it is carried out. Third, in considering the values that ought to infuse teaching and schooling in general, we have tended to adopt an uncritical view of schools as furthering the interests of the social status quo—however that may be defined at a particular historical moment. Viewing schools as responding to the "needs" of powerful sectors of U.S. society, we have assumed all too often that our activities must be governed by whatever set of priorities—ranging from partially socialized factory workers to high-tech employees and citizens who, armed with computer literacy and a spirit of internationalism, can recapture our competitive economic and military edge—these sectors have identified. This is true, of course, even when these priorities are misleading or when they are used to cover up more deep-seated problems or issues.

These issues are to some extent overlapping. The emergence of emotivism is closely linked to the kind of culture and society in which we live, for example, just as a retreat to relativism is related to our tendency to regard as unproblematic the role of schools in furthering certain aspects of the social status quo.

Although the issues just raised cannot be comprehensively dealt with in a chapter of this length, we can begin to raise an alternative perspective on theorizing in general, and the possibilities for teacher theorizing in particular, with which they can be addressed. One important part of this alternative is an awareness of the contexts within which educational theories are articulated, the ends that these contexts have served, and the possibilities for alternative conceptions of educational and social values.

Such an awareness requires a relational perspective on schooling according to which the personal and the political are continuous rather than dichotomous, and the development of a moral imagination with which alternative futures may be not only depicted but acted upon. As will be developed more thoroughly below, the emphases on positivistic theories within education that can perhaps be most clearly seen in behavioral psychology, and on normative assumptions in theories that place primary value on responding to the "needs" of powerful social institutions and groups, have resulted in educational theory being dominated by an individualist, accommodation-oriented perspective.

THE CONTEXTS OF EDUCATIONAL THEORIZING[1]

In education, as in other domains, what we are able to observe and what sense we make of our observations are centrally affected by the theoretical framework which we employ—either consciously or tacitly—as a part of our observations. It may be most useful to think about theoretical frameworks as providing sets of lenses through which we are enabled to discern certain features of our experienced environment. At the same time, these lenses affect what we cannot see as well. The more or less continuous adoption of one sort of theoretical lens, and the forms of language and presumptions that attend and become embedded in it, can result in the reification of a particular way of seeing in which its own assumptions remain hidden even as it resists other theoretical possibilities. If we are to understand the prospects for teacher theorizing, we must be clear about the forms of language and preconceptions that have been dominant within educational theorizing and the contexts of schooling. For these have not only helped fabricate current realities of theorizing and schooling, but also stand as important obstacles to other ways of theorizing, alternative ways of seeing and ultimately acting.

Like all complicated institutions and activities, the field of education has been the scene of disputes among schools of thought that are quite divergent. It would be a mistake to depict the field as if it were an unbroken line of homogeneous thought and practice within which the major issues and problems have been settled. Continued debate over complex issues makes education the lively enterprise that it is. On the other hand, there are historical and contemporary traditions within the field that have been dominant within the contexts of schooling and that therefore have had a significant impact on the kind and quality of theorizing that transpires there. In outlining some of these traditions, I do not mean to imply that other points of view have not been important or persuasive, but only that the ideas discussed here have been influential in shaping the situation faced today, as we rethink the role of theory and the identity of teachers. Indeed, it is tempting to say that those ideas found most appropriate for the activities of schooling and teaching have often been less than the most educationally justifiable.

From the beginning of the common school movement in the United States until roughly the second decade of this century, the teacher was the central figure and feature of the public schools. The formal curriculum largely resulted from local community interests and controls, without the kind of standardization that is so prevalent today. A primary goal of the early school was a cultivated socialization for students who, especially in the case of the urban poor, were often seen as unruly, tending toward delinquency, and in need of "moral uplift" (Nasaw, 1979).

The subsequent fascination with curriculum issues—and the types of theorizing that accompanied them—cannot be understood apart from broader social, economic, and political shifts and the culture of schooling they helped recreate. One such shift concerned the high regard in which science, technology, and industrial development were placed. As hinted at in the earlier discussion concerning the influence of positivism, a growing faith in science, many thought, would lead to the remediation of a host of social and political problems. The hope offered by science, and the scientific method, was the hope for predictability, objectivity, and certainty of outcome in a variety of institutions and processes—ones that lay well outside the scientific laboratory. Within this context, if a field could claim to be utilizing scientific procedures, bounded by scientific standards and promising scientifically verifiable outcomes, it might be assured of both prestige and broad public support. Modeled after a picture of the natural sciences,[2] a claim to legitimacy for its pursuits rested importantly on the utilization of a presumably systematic, quantitative, neutral methodology and the articulation of hypotheses, objective observations, and the disinterested evaluation of data.

Perhaps the clearest example of this emphasis on science within education occurred with the emergence of educational psychology and its commitment to behaviorism. A behavioral approach to educational psychology promised just the sort of precision and predictability that would catapult education into a modern science, away from older, more conceptually fuzzy ideas such as those associated with "mental discipline" or the liberal arts. The faith in science embraced by one of the founders of educational psychology, Edward L. Thorndike, is rather obvious:

> We should regard nothing as outside the scope of science, and every regularity or law that science can discover in the consequence of events is a step towards the only freedom that is of use to men and an aid to the good life . . . The world needs, not only the vision and valuation of great sages, and the practical psychology of men of affairs, but also scientific method to test the worth of the prophets' dreams. (cited in Marvin, 1937, pp. 196-197)

Thorndike and his followers sought the development of systematic procedures for reinforcing approved behaviors and diminishing undesirable ones. Through such a system, the general control of human behavior, including those aspects associated with learning, could become a reality.

Another reality that has affected educational theorizing concerns the perspectives and ideologies associated with the growing industrialization of the United States. As older crafts and small businesses were displaced by larger corporate structures, the control of the processes of production became tighter and to some extent more impersonal. As factories expanded in size and number under the control of a central corporate body, it became increasingly important for owners and managers to not only efficiently organize work on the shop floor, but also to guard against the formation of workers' unions that might undermine their power. One of the most effective weapons to be employed in this search for efficiency and control was provided by a commitment to scientific management. As discussed by its founder, Frederick Winslow Taylor (1911), scientific management pronounced that

> the principal object of management should be to secure the maximum prosperity for the employer, coupled with the maximum prosperity for each employee . . . maximum prosperity for each employee means not only higher wages than are usually received by men of his class, but, of more importance still, it also means the development of each man to his state of maximum efficiency. (p. 9)

To ensure maximum productivity, the workplace must be made predictable, manageable, and efficient. The activities of each worker are to be segmented, broken down into smaller and smaller component parts, and rationalized, with each worker responsible for a smaller and smaller portion of the total process of production. The manager, in turn, organizes production through the centralization of decision making, and the processes of classification, analysis, and differentiation of tasks guarantee certainty of outcome and increased profits.

For the founders of the modern curriculum field, these emphases on standardization, centralization, and efficiency were to play a signal role—and one that has continued since that time. The outcomes of the curriculum, like the outcomes of work on the shop floor, had to be measurable and predictable, with the activities themselves efficiently organized and planned. This led to the precise prespecification of educational objectives, preferably in behavioral terms, again reflecting the ideals of educational psychology. At the same time, the curriculum had to be matched to the likely destiny of students—a destiny itself strongly shaped by the growing industrialization of the United States. The development of a differentiated curriculum was one consequence of this concern for efficiency and predestination. As Herbert M. Kliebard (1975) has documented, the

> extrapolation of the principles of scientific management to the area of curriculum made the child the object on which the bureaucratic machinery of the school operates. He became the raw material from which the school-factory must fashion a product drawn to the specifications of social convention. What was at first simply a direct application of general management principles to the management of schools became the central metaphor on which modern curriculum theory rests. (p. 56)

If education could be attuned to the values of efficiency, productivity, and scientific management, individual students would be given a differentiated curriculum through which they would acquire not only the correct forms of knowledge, given their likely economic and social trajectories, but also the habits, values, and social outlook necessary to maintain political stability and to further the interests of the powerful.

Concerns about the growing numbers of immigrant groups in the decades just before and after World War I also had an effect on the nature of educational theorizing (see Franklin, 1986). These were especially pronounced in urban areas of the United States, where concerns about the decline of "community values" were often heard. This concern was most often translated into a commitment to altering the customs, beliefs, values, and forms of language of the foreign-born so that they would embody the "correct" values and standards. Through a process of acculturation in schools, a kind of cultural homogeneity could be promoted that might help sustain the interests of those in privileged positions. As Michael W. Apple (1979) has argued,

> The crusade to eliminate diversity was heightened . . . as the population increased. Something had to be done about the rapid growth in the numbers upon numbers of "different" children to be acculturated. The answer was bureaucratization—the seemingly commonsensical consolidation of schools and standardization of procedures and curriculum, both of which would promote economy and efficiency. (pp. 66-67)

Combining these emphases on allegedly scientific procedures, the search for efficient curriculum policies and practices that would further industrialization as they rationalized the workplace, and the acculturation of students who are "different" through bureaucratization, we may begin to see a picture of schooling and teaching that was to have a lasting impact on educational theorizing. First, the search for value-free, certain knowledge through the adoption of positivistic approaches to theory is related to a reliance on behavioral science that continues to be strong. The assumption is that human behavior can be controlled or manipulated through the enactment of reinforcement strategies, for example, in devising behavior modification techniques, so as to ensure the desired outcomes. It is now thought that the behavioral sciences can ensure achievement in schools, as we increasingly model cognitive capacity on a view of the human mind that has a strong affinity with computerization, human capital assumptions, and theories of artificial intelligence (Noble, 1988). Such a commitment to certainty and fundamental knowledge continually leads educators to search for the answer to enigmas and dilemmas that will resolve them "once and for all."

Second, an individualistic perspective on educational issues has been fostered that continues to dominate educational thinking. The basic "unit of analysis" is the student, the textbook, the teacher, the classroom, and so on (Apple & Beyer, 1988). Although it is important to remain sensitive to the individual predicaments of students and teachers, this perspective overlooks the ways in which larger structures and commitments continue to shape educational institutions and the individual actions of those who work there. In the process of incorporating such a theoretical lens, we tend to see only atomistic individuals, isolating educational problems as if they pertain only to the student or the teacher or the family (Bellah, Madsen, Sullivan, Swidler, & Tipton, 1985). Lost is a relational perspective that integrates educational and allied domains.

Third, instead of a site for intellectual curiosity, inquiry, and exploration, school becomes a workplace where students work toward prespecified ends, through a process bounded by concerns for efficiency, predictability, and acculturation. The "factory model" of curriculum making emphasizes a means-end rationality in which the articulation of technical procedures is highlighted at the expense of an ethical consideration of the ends to be attained. The teacher is cast as a manager of activities and procedures who must efficiently adjust them so that the proper outcomes can be efficiently attained.

Fourth, this approach to teaching transforms multifaceted normative questions—such as what knowledge is of most worth, what values ought to underlie social relations in the classroom, and what forms of literacy ought to be emphasized—into technically and procedurally resolvable problems. In a general way, value debates tend to give way to "how to" questions: how to motivate my students, how to raise reading test scores significantly, how to maintain order through the adoption of often quite reductive classroom management techniques, and the like. Technical and procedural outlines for instruction tend therefore to supplant political and moral conversations, as we attempt to ameliorate problems that have much deeper and more profound origins and consequences.

The tendency for procedural certainty, atomistic individualism, technical rationality, and amelioration to be highlighted in schools has resulted in corresponding theoretical emphases. Moreover, the dominant traditions, values, and culture of teacher education have furthered the technization of teaching and the search for stability that remain hallmarks of teaching as it continues to be conceived. As teacher preparation programs emphasize field-based experiences aimed at replicating current practices, efficiently organizing and managing classrooms, and responding to fears about personal and professional survival, and as these emphases discount more inquiry-oriented and reflective approaches (Liston & Zeichner, 1991), the culture of teacher preparation becomes dynamically intertwined with the dominant culture of the classroom.

The chapters in this book offer insightful alternatives to these tendencies because they offer different conceptions of theorizing and educational cultures. In the following section I want to suggest additional possibilities for such redirections as we value teacher theorizing within the historical and current conditions of schooling.

TEACHERS AND CRITICAL, CONTEXTUAL THEORIZING

The dominant orientations to teaching and teacher preparation have served to hide the political and social commitments that have shaped teaching and curricula. This has been accomplished partly through the veneer of allegedly "value-free" inquiry and knowledge that was the promise of positivism. In addition, this "hiddenness" of the political quality of education has been enhanced by the segmentation of conception and action, theory and practice, which are deeply embedded in school life. As teaching becomes more technicized and deskilled, with less and less autonomy for teachers, it becomes more difficult for a theoretical community to be seen as indispensable for the activities of teaching.

In pointing to these shortcomings, I want to make clear that I am not suggesting that there is some inherent limitation in teachers' capacities that leads them to "fall into line" with prevailing traditions and values. Instead, I am suggesting that the way teachers are often prepared—the ways in which we treat questions of knowledge and social structure, and those dealing with normative issues and political interests within teacher preparation—plus the culture that tends to dominate in public

educational institutions in the United States, together constitute a powerful set of professional and institutional values that
shape teachers' ways of thinking in particular ways. Nor is this
traceable exclusively to developing states of mind in prospective
teachers that are reinforced by compatible expectations in
schools. For just as ideological presuppositions built into school
practice extend ways of thinking acquired in teacher preparation,
so the very material and physical contexts of schooling reinforce
ways of acting that are consistent with these dominant presuppositions. The fact that elementary school classrooms often contain thirty or more children with quite diverse backgrounds,
needs, and interests leads teachers to make decisions almost
constantly, with little time for anything but immediate, amelio-
rative action. Again, the fact that teaching tends to be associated
with atomistic individualism, accomplished typically without
benefit of collegial exchange and cooperative planning and without support for alternative practices and directions, leads to a
sort of reification, where "what is" (the descriptive question)
becomes a substitute for "what ought to be" (the normative question). And the fact that the evaluation of teaching tends to be
along bureaucratic and technical lines—Are Ms. Allen's second
graders scoring at or above the norm in reading? Is Ms. Brown
keeping her pupils "on task?" Why aren't the fourth-grade teachers better able to control their students during recess? and the
like—diminishes the likelihood of risk taking among teachers.
It is not that teachers are generally lacking in personal qualities
or intellectual capabilities, but that the context within which
they work reinforces the parameters, often acquired earlier,
within which theorizing and reflecting on practice take place.

Efforts to highlight the importance of teacher theorizing, then,
must be reflexive—that is, they must include among their theoretical considerations the effects of the teacher's environment
(both material and ideological) on his or her opportunities for
theorizing, and the kind of theorizing that is likely to occur given
this environment. Changing these opportunities, altering the
forms of theorizing that will be seen as appropriate, will almost
certainly necessitate an alteration of the culture within which
theory is created—better yet, these things must be dialectically
related, as theoretical insights invite changed physical and ideological circumstances, and vice versa.

Therefore, central to the conception of teacher theorizing
advocated here is an emphasis on praxis. This refers to a com-

mitment to critical reflection—for example, on the origins of what we regard as social and educational common sense, whose interests it serves, what alternatives exist or can be created, and how this is related to our own moral and political positions. Rather than accept uncritically notions of what is "provided" or "beyond question," teacher theorizing must include the deceptively simple questions of "why?" and "to what end?" and "what are the alternatives?" In addition to critiques and criticisms of "what is," teacher theorizing must help create alternative perspectives and divergent practices within schools that can bring to life "what ought to be." Praxis also includes a sensitivity to the dynamics of power within educational institutions and within the array of social, political, economic, and ideological constraints in which schools are embedded. As detailed in Beyer and Apple (1988),

> this involves not only the justifiable concern for reflective action, but thought and action combined and enlivened by a sense of power and politics. It involves both conscious understanding of and action in schools on solving our daily problems . . . But it also requires critically reflective practices that alter the material and ideological conditions that cause the problems we are facing as educators in the first place. (p. 4)

Combined with a relational perspective on schooling, this commitment to praxis entails a view of the school's social relations, values, and habits of mind and heart that recognizes how these "internal" dynamics of schools are consistent with the dynamics of power in society.

A central concern in fostering a commitment to praxis is understanding current realities (in classrooms and other settings) without reifying them, just as the development of alternative ways of thinking, seeing, and theorizing must not lead to romanticizing their plausibility within the current context. To deny the authenticity of current realities or to suppose that they can be overcome simply with the development of "better theorizing" is to engage in a form of idealism antithetical to praxis; similarly, to focus only on the current predicaments of schooling without struggling to develop other theories and strategies for intervention is to regard the current reality as the only viable one. Neither course of action is tenable. Praxis entails a familiarity with current reality without being overcome by it, and a commitment to a reflection on alternatives that is based in part in concrete action. This requires that we see reflection and action as mutually reinforcing, and that we walk a sort of intellectual and ideological tightrope, giving in neither to cynicism about "what is" nor to idealism about how to create "what might yet be."

What is understandably but regrettably missing from much current theorizing about schooling and teaching is a critical theory that can contextualize schools as it enhances teacher empowerment. Because of the dominant traditions in schooling and teacher preparation, and the related nature of the workplace of teaching, the connections between school practice and the interrelated contexts within which it takes place and which provide a substantial part of its meaning tend to be obscured if not invisible. That is, the emphases on proceduralism, amelioration, and so on isolate school phenomena; in an attempt to be "scientific" or "professional" or simply to "fit in," we have defined our jobs in predominantly apolitical, nonideological terms, isolating in the process the school, our classroom, and our students. Even the efforts of teachers who struggle to alleviate some of the more immediately constraining influences on classroom life—which must be recognized and applauded—often remain unconnected to ideas, involvements, and actions that are not especially visible within the immediate confines of educational institutions, as perceived through the theoretical, ideological, and material frames of reference sanctioned by the dominant culture of schooling.

Part of the problem here is that we typically posit two separate "spheres" or areas of influence, the "school" and the "wider society"; then, even within a good deal of literature that wants to make the latter a subject of discussion and critique, connections or bridges must be built that connect these spheres, allowing us to discuss possible overlaps or linkages between them. What is needed, though, is a more integrated, synthetic vision of education, one that is of a piece with some social, political, and ideological set of commitments, even if these differ from those which now exist. Instead of conceptualizing schooling, the day-to-day life of teachers, and society as essentially separable or isolatable, we do better to see these things as coextensive. This entails thinking carefully and imaginatively about why things happen as they do in schools, and what alternatives we might build together.

Central to this view of teaching is the development of a historical consciousness. Rather than regard schools, educational policies and practices, and teacher preparation as natural, commonsensical, or unchangeable, we must recognize the various groups that have vied for control of schooling and the values, interests, and perspectives schools have served (Kliebard, 1986). This does several things. It undermines the essentially false assumption that schools were designed "for the benefit of all," and that their workings are disconnected from more general social, political, and ideological realities. The meaning of teaching as it has been filtered through the gender, class, and racial categories that have shaped the nature of schooling must become a subject of analysis for practicing teachers, just as the dominant traditions of teaching and curriculum discussed above must be made available to teachers. But, understanding the genesis of present circumstances is of more than simple historical interest. For, in seeing the constructed nature of schooling and teaching, and the interests that have dominated in them, we make at least potentially possible its reconstruction along alternative lines. Examining both historical continuities and discontinuities, we may together conceive of an alternative future. Seeing the world of schooling as something other than divinely inspired or "naturally generated," we may help make possible different educational and social worlds.

This approach to teacher theorizing emphasizes the relationship between the hidden and overt curriculum, forms of evaluation, pedagogical approaches, and social relations within the classroom and the dynamics of social power. Not only must certain forms of knowledge be excluded from the classroom because of a finite amount of time, for example, but particular forms of knowledge (either some group's knowledge that lacks social status, or an approach to a subject matter that resists "official" interpretations of events and people, alternative ways of thinking about a subject matter, nonmainstream interpretations of significant events, and so on) are rejected for political and ideological reasons. Thus, a central question becomes how to take a moral stand on the issue of "which knowledge is of most worth," while considering the politics of this process of deliberation. As critical theorizing among teachers necessitates the replacement of proceduralism and technical rationality by normative discourse and moral action, we must encourage teacher theorizing that uncovers the moral dimensions of day-to-day classroom life, connecting it to social and political contexts that may lie, at least materially, beyond the classroom door.

An important element of teacher theorizing must be related to developing options, alternatives, and possibilities that foster autonomous, creative, independent, and critical inquirers. For example, instead of relying on prepackaged curricula at the elementary level, these must become the object of pedagogical and ideological critique by teachers. Questions such as What are the visions of the student and the teacher contained in these materials? How much autonomy do they require or permit? What sort of social relations do they support or require? What sort of people will be judged to be "successful" as a result of undergoing this curriculum? and What sort of world am I helping to build through this process? must be actively engaged—through, for example, action research projects (see the chapters by Ross and by Cornett, Chase, Miller, Schrock, Bennett, Goins, and Hammond, this volume). Instead of the technical procedures associated with much curriculum development, teacher theorizing must include the development of their own pedagogical and moral platforms, which, together with more concrete subject matter and social interaction preferences, can result in their own curricular materials and activities (Barone, 1988).

CONCLUSIONS

There is much that needs to be praised about the revitalized emphases on teacher theorizing that are represented in this volume. As we reclaim the theoretical inquiry that undergirds all practice and counteract the image of the teacher as a skilled technician who applies the knowledge and values that have been ordained as worthy by external "experts" whose motivations are often less than praiseworthy, we revitalize the profession. At the same time, we undermine the dominant traditions of schooling and teacher preparation documented earlier in this chapter. Acknowledging the theoretical work undertaken by teachers who are truly professionals helps alter the status of teaching and the possibilities for schooling.

Having said that, it is also important to keep in mind that what counts as legitimate theorizing, and as appropriate activities for teaching, will depend both upon the culture within which it is practiced and the material and ideological contours of daily life in schools. Given the dominant values and preoccupations of schools and teacher preparation programs, we cannot be naive about the power of theory, on its own, to substantively alter current realities of schooling. Creating space for the kinds of critical inquiry that have been advanced here will no doubt require, and be propelled by, alterations in the workplace of teaching that allow for the sort of collegiality, autonomy, and familiarity with a contextualized perspective on schooling that are the prerequisites of critical theory. The establishment of an altered theoretical terrain and the reform of the teacher's workplace will be accomplished through a dialectical interaction between these things, and by altered forms of teacher preparation.

The forms of theorizing advocated here will in some important ways remain intimately personal, of course. Especially at a time when the responsibility of the person who writes and theorizes is being challenged by some, we must be clear about the obligations we acquire as creators of our own perspectives and understandings through the adoption of new theoretical lenses. At the same time, we must be careful that a commitment to teacher personal theorizing does not fall victim to the same tendency toward atomistic individualism that has dominated discourse in schooling, and to the proclivity toward relativism that has become influential in modern social life. Nor can we any longer assume that the ends of education as they have been advanced by the more powerful interests of U.S. society are pedagogically appropriate, as we place schooling within its appropriate social and political contexts.

In the end, it is a question not only of *who* does the theorizing that attends schooling but, equally important, of the assumptions and preconceptions that guide it. More important still, the choice of theoretical lenses must be governed by an essentially moral consideration of the kind of world to which it can lead for all of us.

16

WILLIAM H. SCHUBERT _____

Personal Theorizing About
Teacher Personal Theorizing

We moved two months ago, and it vividly occurred to me that
moving inspires an interpretation of one's life. Looking at the
stored-away artifacts of one's past causes one to remember and
recreate one's past, to consider how it contributed to one's present, and to imaginatively project possibilities it might bring for
one's future. For me, as an educator for almost twenty-five years
(one who had been reflecting on how to write this chapter), I was
at least subconsciously aware of the educational dimensions of
my life in the parade of artifacts that passed my vision as we
packed, moved, unpacked, and reorganized our belongings. I am
convinced that this chapter began in earnest in an almost empty
room in the place from which we moved when one of the movers
appeared from a large walk-in closet where he had been wrestling
a file cabinet. In his hand he carried a blue notebook that had
somehow fallen out of the back of a file drawer and was lodged,
apparently for some years, between the file and the wall. "Do
you want this?" he queried. Indeed, I did; it was my student
teaching log from 1966! "What did I think about teaching then?"
I wondered, "How did I interpret my experience?" For the next few
days I took what opportunity emerged to read my words of over
two decades ago.

The accounts I read in that journal jogged my nearly lost
memories of students and episodes of my early teaching experience. I wondered what became of those lives I had once touched
ever so briefly. Who have they been and who are they becoming
as they now approach the age of forty? As I continued the process of moving, unpacking, and organizing over the next days
and weeks, I thought more of those lives I had visited as a student teacher at Laketon Elementary School near Manchester
College in rural Indiana. I thought, too, of all the others in a
decade of work with elementary school children. Earlier than

student teaching I remembered "cadet teaching" as a high school senior in Charles Hampel's sixth-grade classroom in Butler, Indiana. And, of course, I reflected on all of the students in the Chicago suburb of Downers Grove. I thought of the concluding words of that blue student teaching journal, "More than ever before I realize that my life is for education." Each year of teaching (including the past fifteen years with undergraduate and graduate students), each interaction with a student or a class, helps me reconstruct my personal meaning of "a life for education."

This process of reflective reconstruction is what John Dewey referred to as the essential definition of education itself. In *Democracy and Education* (Dewey, 1916) he concluded that education is "that reconstruction or reorganization of experience which adds to the meaning of experience, and which increases ability to direct the course of subsequent experience" (p. 76). My own growing image of what it means to be an educator is a central dimension of my more pervasive reconstruction of my life's experience. As a schoolteacher I became increasingly convinced that reflections on my experience in search of an increased sense of direction were my research, my scholarly work, my inservice education. Although I wrote about those reflections, my growing theory of experience as an educator, much that was most important was too complex and too saturated with the hurry of the moment to be rendered in written form. I am reminded of a public television production of a story about a young man who fancied himself a writer of great unwritten novels. Similarly, despite my interludes of writing, I considered my teaching a time of theorizing, a time of doing unwritten "research" on teaching. I thought that the most fundamental "research" of this kind occurred when I asked questions about curriculum, when I wondered about what is worthwhile to know and experience—for my students and for myself—and when we wondered together about these questions.

I will say more about this later, but now I want to stress that the intervening years have continued to convince me that such reflection as I experienced, and as I am sure other teachers experience, is fully worthy of the label *research*, or *scholarship*, or *theory*. To be certain, it invokes a new image of these terms, but I want to argue here that it is a necessary and neglected image. It is necessary to overcome the elitist assumption that only those who have been sanctioned by the credentials, peer review, and promotions of academe are worthy of the title *scholar, researcher,* or *theorist.* A more populist notion has been neglected, avoided — even prevented. Perhaps it is not an exaggeration to say that the diminished significance of teacher reflection on the part of holders of academic capital is an instance of ideological hegemony by the privileged of the scholarly class. Just as in the socioeconomic class analysis of schooling, in educational institutions themselves the values supported are those that help keep the dominant in dominant positions.

Whether the above is a conscious conspiracy or not is not the main point. Theory, research, and scholarship are today commodities legitimately produced by those in universities and research agencies. Teachers and other nonuniversity educators are outsiders — at best deemed receivers of "translations" of research, scholarship, and theory. Perhaps even more important than the hierarchical inequity of this state of affairs, as salient as it is, is what is lost in terms of insight and understanding. By not recognizing teachers as researchers, theorists, and scholars, we decontextualize the complexity of what theory could be. This is not to argue that theory of the prescriptive and descriptive varieties done by researchers and scholars should be discarded as unworthy. I am suggesting that teachers and other educators (such as parents) are continuously building implicit theories that need to be recognized. Notice that I said "are continuously building."

To acknowledge teachers as already theory builders does not represent a mere call for mini-research projects, simple versions of what "real" researchers do. It does not call merely for a notion of university-school collaboration in which university consultants, well-meaning though they may be, teach teachers strategies of research which they employ in their classrooms. This is to perpetuate the controlling balance of power in the university. Good teachers, I am suggesting, are already theory builders, creators of perspectives, belief systems, and personal constructs — in essence of complex networks of values and ideas that are modified with each subsequent experience, which is the design of natural reflection, and which guides and inspires their action as educators (see Schubert, 1982). Not only do I suggest that this process is worthy of inclusion under the label of *research,* but I wonder if it might be worthy of a more important label, because research as usually conceived may not be able to capture what perceptive teachers' reflections grasp in their unwritten-ness.

Herein resides the challenge of this book as I read it. How is it possible for those traditionally accepted as researchers to form collaborative relationships with teachers to illuminate insight from their implicit private perspectives (theories)? This, I ascertain, is the call of this book: to find and *interpret* the public potential in private reflection. In other words, how can insight and understanding about teaching be culled from the private reflections of teachers without distorting either the experiential repertoires and guiding constructs of those teachers or the extracted dimensions? The essays in this book push the boundaries of inquiry toward this end in different and creative ways. Even the end itself is problematic, shimmering in uncertainty. Does it lie more in written renditions, variations on current conceptions of qualitative research, or does it reside more fully in new forms of communication—perhaps oral networks of communication that are obviously more the forte of teachers (though we researchers forever seem to constrain them in our favorite mode—written exposition)?

In the pages remaining, I wish to explore some possibilities for research that investigate this central problem. I feel that I must continue in an autobiographical fashion, because my reflection on the nature of interpretive inquiry into the personal theorizing of teachers lies at the center of my work over the years. Besides, I agree with Sartre that any writing that has meaning is, in fact, autobiographic.

POSSIBILITIES FOR INTERPRETATION

Returning for a moment to that dilapidated student teaching journal noted earlier, I recall an account of constructing a sociogram, required of all student teachers in my group. I noted that my sociogram of students in my sixth-grade classroom was viewed as exceptionally complex—I seemed to add more and more layers of interaction on my map with additional questions. I was struggling with the great complexity, with the impossibility, of a complete picture. I knew that so much more was in my growing image of these students than could be adequately represented in a sociogram; moreover, my journal could not do them justice either. And even my emerging perspective, though greater than sociogram or journal, barely scratched the surface of what was there—or of what I might be able to perceive in a classroom ten or twenty years hence. Whether it could be rendered in writing in any full sense or not, my teaching career convinced me that the interpretation of teaching was essential to my work. It informed and guided what I decided, how I acted, and how I interacted. Therefore, inspired by my master's work in the philosophy of education, I read Dewey and other philosophers to enhance my ability to reflect on my teaching—to reconstruct my image of who I was and how to help my students grow.

When I entered doctoral studies, I continued this quest and still thank my advisor, J. Harlan Shores at the University of Illinois-Urbana, for allowing and enabling me to make the further study of this process become the organizing center of my coursework and dissertation. If that was the beginning of my legitimated inquiry (that which could be written) into the curriculum of teacher personal theorizing, its continuation is apparent in my next fifteen years of scholarly endeavor. Thus, each of the research thrusts that have interested me in the past and that I hope will be part of my future have roots in the theorizing I experienced as a teacher. I will begin with "teacher lore" because it is closest to the central thrust of this book; then I will return to it as one of several possibilities for further inquiry supported by this book.

TEACHER LORE

As a teacher I felt that I developed insights worth sharing with fellow teachers, with teacher education students, and even with researchers. I relished the opportunity to be assigned student teachers. Overall, however, there were very few avenues to meaningful sharing. The right configuration of degrees and titles was not yet in place to warrant widespread publishing or consulting or even teaching at the undergraduate level, although I managed to do some of each of these. Nonetheless, the situation driven home most fully was that the teacher's voices are effectually silenced.

In doctoral work in the area of curriculum studies I was struck by the prominent omission of teachers, not to mention their voices, in curriculum literature. It seemed that the literature acknowledged everyone from central office officials in school districts, principals, school board members, policymakers at the state and national levels, and superintendents, to professors, accreditors, researchers, and leaders in private-sector business and industry. They were all deemed capable of deciding what was valuable to teach, but ironically teachers were less often considered as capable. Teachers were implementors, those who were to carry out directives from higher authorities. I resented this, and, like most teachers, I knew better. Teachers make curriculum choices every moment of their daily work; they shape the curriculum actually experienced by students. My doctoral dissertation was designed to illustrate this by showing that teachers' everyday reflections elicit actions that, in fact, are the curriculum (Schubert, 1975).

When I think about my life as a teacher, as noted earlier, I see teachers as builders of personal theory about what teaching situations are like, what is worth teaching and learning, what it means to grow as a human being, and what it means to contribute to one's society and world. To take the idea of moving, with which I opened this chapter, a step further as an analogy, I see movement itself as the seedbed of theory. Again, I refer to theory as George Kelly (1955) did when he called it "personal constructs." As we move in the world, we derive meaning through transacting with that which we encounter. Such meaning becomes the continuously revised structures that enable us to interpret our lives and empower us to engage in the world. So, teachers interacting with the world of their classroom *are*, in fact, curriculum theory—an *embodied* theory of teaching and what is (and ought to be) taught. Their action, the kind of person they are, is their practice (a major portion of the curriculum that actually influences the lives of students). Therefore, as we try to resolve the age-old problem of the relation of theory and practice in education, we might do well to consider that a most important and much neglected dimension of it is integrated in the lives of teachers.

What I am doing in this chapter, as the title says, is engaging in personal theorizing about teacher personal theorizing. Indeed, this is not a difficult task in one salient sense, because I am a teacher. Thus, I am not writing about some phenomenon under inquiry, something other; rather, I am writing *of* that which I am at the university and when consulting, that which I have been in elementary and junior high schools, and that which I hope to continue to be by extending myself as teacher in new directions. As a teacher my personal theorizing about teaching is intricately interwoven and embedded within me. As I engage in experiences and reflect on them, I reconstruct my theory. Thus, my theory is in a state of continuous revision. It is revised by all of the ways of knowing, the personal versions of epistemological bases, that are part of my way of dealing with the world: direct experience, intuition, empirical investigation, reflection, revelation, and so on. The action that I live, my impact on and transactions with the world, is my practice. Thus, I see one resolution of the perennial bifurcation of theory and practice as embedded in the teacher. The teacher's orientation, an ongoing reconstruction of guiding ideas, may be seen as theory. This image of theory is a kind of deep structure of the person. The person, the teacher, does more than reflect—he or she moves in the world. That movement and its effects constitute the teacher practice. Theorizing for me is the combined process of acting in the world and reflecting on it in ways that redesign assumptions that guide further action. One quite obvious way to study the perennial theory-practice problem in education, a way to integrate the dualistically separated images of theory and practice, is to focus on the theorizing of teachers. This points to the need to study what I have labeled "teacher lore."

Teacher lore has two quite different meanings for me. The first pertains to a project that I have directed since 1985 at the University of Illinois at Chicago, called the Teacher Lore Project. The second use of the term *teacher lore* designates a very broad array of work that enhances understanding of teachers' perspectives and how they develop. The range of the latter is indeed great. I discuss it at some length in a chapter in *The Stories Lives Tell* (Witherell & Noddings, 1991). The larger notion of teacher lore must include, for instance, aspects of research on teachers' *thought processes* that have emerged as a result of inquiry into teachers' *implicit theories* as summarized by Clark and Peterson (1986). Similarly, a genre of work by Michael Connelly and others emerged from the practical curriculum philosophy of Joseph Schwab (1970) under the label *personal-practical knowledge* and has recently been brought together by Connelly and Clandinin (1988). An array of case studies of teachers surely should be part of teacher lore (e.g., Ayers, 1989; Bullough, 1989; Epstein, 1981), and so should the range of insightful renditions of teaching—from the first-person accounts of John Holt (1964, 1981), Herb Kohl (1968, 1978), and Jonathan Kozol (1967, 1975) from the 1960s onward to the recent writings of master teachers such as Eliot Wigginton (1986), Mike Rose (1989), and Vivian Paley (1984). In phenomenological investigation one finds another entry point into the larger notion of teacher lore (see van Manen, 1986, and cases in the journal he founded in 1982, *Phenomenology and Pedagogy*). From a critical perspective we find

Paulo Freire's (1970) perspective derived from teaching Brazilian peasants, as well as analyses and accounts of teachers by Apple and Weis (1983) and Giroux and McLaren (1989). In addition, teacher lore may be found in portrayals of and perspectives on teachers in literature on supervision, teacher education, the several subject matter areas, evaluation, and work which has stemmed from Donald Schön's emphasis on reflective practitioners in many professional fields (Schön, 1983). Teacher lore is clearly related to the Deweyan tradition of inquiry and progressive teaching consistent with the philosophy of John Dewey; thus, historical inquiry is clearly relevant to understanding teacher lore. There is a rich history of biographies and autobiographs of teachers that needs to be examined for insight into the character of their theorizing. Moreover, teacher lore is not limited to factual accounts; some of the most vivid and insightful sources of insight into teaching are available in the arts and literature, a vast untapped source (Willis & Schubert, 1991).

The other dimension of "teacher lore," the Teacher Lore Project, was a response to a perceived gap (Grand Canyon even) in the literature. With a small group of graduate students, mostly former teachers, we wondered at the lack of credibility given teachers in research on teachers and teaching. It occurred to us that although an increasing amount of research now focuses on teachers, it usually is *about* them, rather than *of* and *by* them (Schubert & Schubert, 1981). We wanted to know what teachers learned from their experience, what the fruits of their reflection on experience have been. What, unencumbered by lenses we researchers often use to examine them, have they concluded? What do teachers perceive as giving meaning and direction to their lives as teachers? What do they want to tell us about their work, both the mundane and the ideal? What conclusions, what stories? The results of the study since 1986 have resulted in several articles and chapters, seven dissertations, and a set of brief articles in the Summer 1990 issue of *Kappa Delta Pi Record*, by myself and the five former students who produced dissertations on different aspects of teacher lore, thus defining much of the Teacher Lore Project (see Hulsebosch, 1988; Jagla, 1989; Koerner, 1989; Melnick, 1988; Millies, 1989; Schubert & Ayers, 1992). We have looked at teachers' relationships with parents, teachers' imagination and intuition, teachers' images of their work, teachers' use of out-of-school experiences in their students' lives, and teachers' pedagogical personalities, assumptions, and repertoires.

Both the general idea of teacher lore and the more specific mission of the Teacher Lore Project are extended by this book. The organizing center of teacher personal theorizing, as designed by Ross, Cornett, and McCutcheon (this volume), captures for me the essence of what has been missed in the study of teachers and teaching. This book represents direct and indirect explorations into this dimension of teachers' lives. That personal theorizing is embedded in a life is indelibly portrayed by Bill Ayers as he relates experiences with autobiography, biography, and co-biography with teachers. Lynda Stone broadens the perspective on personal theorizing in philosophical and cultural contexts by illustrating four images of meaning, two from modern/epistemological and two from postmodern/postepistemological origins. Teacher personal theorizing in selected subject areas is reported by Audrey Kleinsasser (language arts) and Sharon Pape (mathematics and reading) in the section on studies; however, both probe to deeper strata of the theorizing experience, going considerably beyond the more popular cognitive psychology assumptions that assert thinking to be domain specific. They move more deeply to situate theorizing in the culture of educative circumstances and in the constructs of meaning continuously being reformulated by teachers. By applying Levi-Strauss's term *bricolage* to teaching, Walter Parker and Janet McDaniel highlight the centrality of masterful improvisation in the complexity of teaching's dailyness. The richness of theorizing, of juggling countless variables and possibilities at once and simultaneously relating them to an evolving value system or philosophy of teaching, is the everyday experience of teaching. This complexity of theorizing is portrayed vividly by Ken Tobin and colleagues in secondary and elementary science teaching, by Stephen J. Thornton in social studies teaching at the elementary school level, and by Jeff Cornett and associates across a variety of contexts and levels.

Implications from such a picture of teachers as personal theorizers are indeed far-reaching. Wayne Ross suggests ways to prepare teachers for theorizing in the beginning years, Tom Skrtic and Linda Ware look at structures and practices that act as barriers to reflective practice, Gail McCutcheon points to alternatives for encouraging reflective practice and John Daresh speaks to implications for administration. All of the topics in the implications section of the book rest, I believe, on two central assumptions. The first is that teachers, like all human beings, are natural theorizers. They want to ask important questions about their life and work. They want to inquire about their students, their students' life circumstances, and what would be of value for them to experience. They want to understand better what it means for their students to grow into better, more fulfilled human beings, and what it means for them to contribute to society and to the world. At the same time another assumption, one as depressing as the first is uplifting, reigns strongly evident; teachers' natural propensity to inquire and theorize about these central human matters is inhibited and squelched by the press of rules, regulations, and institutional and societal structures that they face daily. This oppression severs the holistic character of their desire to create with students a sense of purpose, to develop experiences that help the purpose evolve, and to design some reflective assessment of the growth experienced. State bureaucrats make artificial purposes and bestow them on teachers with the expectation that they will implement them; then evaluation corporations are called upon to define *real* progress. It is not surprising that the circumstances of this second assumption are beginning to overwhelm and spoil the freshness of the first assumption. Yet at the same time we can find creative suggestions in the implications section of this book, ones that have the potential to overcome the dismal effects of the second assumption and restore opportunity for teachers to improve teaching through personal theorizing.

POSSIBILITIES

My own personal theorizing about the personal theorizing of teachers again brings me back to my days of elementary school teaching, how I built on that work as a doctoral student and beginning teacher educator, and how that continuum of experience is a central basis for the work I do in curriculum and teaching today—the scholarship, the teaching, and the service to schools and other educative settings. In the following, therefore, I relate five dimensions of inquiry that I see as next phases of my own work and as prospective areas of exploration revealed by this book: history and philosophy, teacher lore, nonschool curricula, student lore, and teacher education.

History and Philosophy
(Toward Curriculum Theorizing)

As an elementary school teacher I continuously challenged my assumptions on the basis of my experience with children. It was not enough to merely plan and replan lessons with a different twist. I needed to consider new ranges of possibilities—and especially the why of them. Philosophers (Dewey, Whitehead, Russell, Bergson, and numerous others) became companions in my search for guiding assumptions. Through history, too, progressive educators came alive and entered my discourse, as did curriculum scholars of the past and present. In fact, I soon became convinced that a good teacher must be a curriculum theorizer. Doctoral work with J. Harlan Shores reinforced my conviction that my inclination to reconstruct assumptions through philosophy and history coalesced in curriculum theory.

I became convinced that to be a good teacher one must be in the continuous process of reconstructing assumptions. Assumptions are the basis for decision and action, and teachers' daily decision and action are laced with curriculum questions: What knowledge and experiences are most worthwhile for these students? How might experiences be designed to help students develop increased meaning and direction in their lives? What are the best ways to help learners participate in the creation of their lives? How can I better understand the consequences of my life with these young learners for personal growth, societal improvement, and the betterment of the world?

Of course, it is not the case that all (or most) teachers ask these questions directly as historical and/or philosophical forms of inquiry. I knew that my method of asking them was unusual; nevertheless, the best teachers I encountered have what Zumwalt (1989) has nicely called a "curricular vision of teaching." Some reflect on fundamental curriculum questions through the arts, some through parenting—a host of avenues exist. The central point is that they are curriculum theorizers. They are not content to mindlessly accept state mandates, textbooks, or school district curriculum guides as answers to the great questions of how humanity recreates itself—and the important questions of teaching must foundationally be about this very matter.

To develop a theoretical conceptualization of how teachers' imagination is sparked by the reconstruction of their assumptions was the topic of my doctoral dissertation (Schubert, 1975), and that interest has been an impetus for much of my work since then. The serious study of what it *means* (as Lynda Stone points out) to be a reflective teacher is potentially one of the most profound philosophical problems that can be faced. It has been faced before, by great philosophers (from Plato to Dewey), by an array of notable artists and literary figures (see Willis & Schubert, 1991), and by good teachers and parents from time immemorial. The study of teacher personal theorizing needs to focus more fully on these sources of curriculum theorizing.

Teacher Lore (Revisited)

The idea of "teacher lore," discussed at some length earlier, needs to be revisited continuously. It needs to be expanded and refined. The good teachers with whom we have spoken in the Teacher Lore Project concur that they have knowledge (perspectives, insights, ideas, repertoires) worth sharing. As an elementary teacher, I felt the same way, and as a college teacher I still do; however, there are more outlets for the college teacher to publish and share such knowledge (though there are fewer rewards for such writing than for more detached scholarly discourse). Yet, by comparison, teachers have fewer outlets for communicating what they have learned. Some of the teacher networks of communication in England that stemmed from Lawrence Stenhouse's "teacher-as-researcher" movement provide a very important precedent for what the extension of teacher lore could become if practiced by teachers interviewing other teachers in action-research-oriented programs of inservice education (Stenhouse, 1975, 1980; Rudduck & Hopkins, 1985). I have been working with variations on this approach in several Chicago area schools.

Nonschool Curricula

As an elementary teacher my curriculum theorizing was enhanced as I came to know my students better. As I knew more about their lives outside of school I felt in a better position to design with them experiences that fit their needs and interests. In fact, I often recall wishing that a few days could be set aside each year just to have individual conversations (informal interviews) with my students. Although that luxury was not afforded in any formal way, I developed strategies whereby I could have individual conferences with students during class time, while others were involved in independent study or small-group projects.

Now, much later, my work as a teacher educator and interviews from the Teacher Lore Project convince me that good teaching, teaching that transforms, is based on knowledge of the nonschool settings that have had an impact on the outlooks of students' lives: homes, families, peer groups, nonschool organizations (from church and sports to street gangs), mass media, jobs or vocations, hobbies or avocations (Schubert, 1981). All of these nonschool educative circumstances have a profound impact on the outlook of students. Although only some of them can be said to have formal curricula (e.g., scouting organizations), all embody implicit dimensions of curriculum (e.g., implicit purposes, selections of learning experiences, organizational patterns, evaluation approaches). Whereas the latter set of dimensions is drawn from the work of Ralph Tyler (1949), nonschool curricula can be said to be equally susceptible to analysis by curricular commonplaces developed by Joseph Schwab (teacher, learner, subject matter, milieu; Schwab, 1973). Or one could analyze nonschool curricula by the categories Eisner (1985) applies to all schools: the explicit (intended), implicit (covert or hidden), and the null (omitted or neglected) curricula. These and other conceptions of the curriculum that are usually applied to the school curriculum can, I contend, help teachers in theorizing about the nonschool curriculum. As I have argued elsewhere (Schubert, 1986, pp. 107-110), a more holistic or ecological view is needed that situates the school curriculum in the larger context of the array of "curricula" that contribute to the emerging outlooks of young people. To teach is to want to have an impact on the outlook of students, and a teacher is in a much better position to know the what, how, and why of influencing students if she or he is aware of other impacts on the students' emerging outlooks. Thus, we need to address more fully than before the issue of how to provide greater insight into the nonschool dimensions of students' lives.

Student Lore

Work with teachers in the Teacher Lore Project has increasingly convinced me that one of the greatest unsung areas of teacher personal theorizing focuses on students. This includes nonschool curricula, noted above, and a host of other aspects of student life—most principally, how they interact with and experience school. As an elementary school teacher, I constantly wondered how the students experienced—what they thought of—what we did together. In a very broad sense, I wanted to know what the experienced curriculum was for them—as distinguished from the intended or the implemented curriculum (i.e., the planned and taught curriculum). Today, I have the same kinds of wonderings about how my graduate and undergraduate students respond to or experience the curriculum of my college classes.

I think the term *student lore* captures the need here. We need to know more about the ongoing flow of the consequences of teaching in the lives of students. If a primary curriculum question is "What is worthwhile to know and experience?" then we must ask what students have, in fact, come to know and experience (Weston, 1992). Beyond this, we hope that students participate in their own learning, which means that they deal with the means and ends of that endeavor. In doing so they become increasingly their own curriculum directors, so to speak. The organizing center of their lives becomes developing curricula that help them reconstruct those lives. Reconstruction of this sort means engaging in the difficult questions of what it means to live a better life and to contribute more fully to the world.

We know very little about the ways in which students think about these matters. We know very little about that which they deem valuable. We need better studies of what teacher theorizing reveals about this, and we need a new breed of investigation into what students themselves make of their life in the world. What do they consider worthwhile? What are its consequences? How much of what they perceive as valuable is attributable to teaching in schools? Teaching in homes, from peers, from nonschool organizations, from elsewhere? What might knowledge of what students deem worthwhile teach teachers about what should be provided for (with) students? How can we come to know more about such matters?

Teacher Education

Surely, using more creative strategies for researchers is one way to learn more about teachers' guiding assumptions, teacher lore, nonschool curricula, and student lore. However, the investigation of teacher personal theorizing must not rely on researchers alone. It must engage teachers as partners and it must expand greatly the notion of investigation (or research) itself. Does research, for instance, have to be written? Clearly, good teachers investigate their situations all the time. They ask important questions and find important answers. They refine their assumptions, generate knowledge from reflecting on what it means to be a teacher, come to understand nonschool curricula in the lives of their students, and attempt to know more about how classroom life and the curriculum implicit in it alter the outlooks of their students. Nevertheless, this serious inquiry is seldom considered significant enough to merit the label of *research*. Similarly, it is not even acknowledged as teacher education. Ironically, it *is* the way teachers are educated every day.

If researchers and teacher educators are serious when they voice the words *partnership, collaboration,* and the like, they will need to respect the integrity and the sophistication of personal theorizing by teachers as a valuable and necessary (albeit vastly neglected) form of both research and teacher education. Those who want to use "research" to educate teachers must figure out ways to tap the experiential insights and understandings of teachers as a new and important kind of research. Those who purport to educate teachers, especially through inservice education, must acknowledge the serious self-educative study that good teachers do as the principal inservice education of professionals. Moreover, researchers from universities and research agencies must become prepared to accept the insights of teachers and use different criteria for judging their worth than the criteria usually used to judge research studies. The different epistemologies, or ways of knowing, at work in teacher personal theorizing require revised ways to judge the credibility and worth of ideas developed in the course of such theorizing. Good teachers model an ongoing, self-directed teacher education. They should be studied and assisted (see Tobin & Lamaster and Cornett et al. in this volume).

CONCLUDING STATEMENT

I feel that I have traveled a considerable distance in this chapter, a personal distance in my own life as an educator as well as a distance through educational literature and ideas that extend from ancient times into hoped futures. I tried to make the medium, my own personal theorizing, consistent with my message that personal theorizing of teachers should be given increased stature among communities of educational researchers and theorists. Books such as this one go far to give greater credibility to teacher insights derived from everyday theorizing ("everyday" meant as something done daily, not something pedestrian). I have tried to point out that my own sense of hope for education (theory, research, and practice) is consonant with the ideals of this book. In this spirit I advocate that educators (from schools, universities, and other walks of life, such as homes) devote greater attention to the understanding of guiding assumptions, to teachers and students as curriculum theorizers, to discovering more about what teachers and students learn when they reflect carefully on their experience, and to creating the kind of inservice education that values and recognizes the centrality of such work. I know these concerns will be central to my own theorizing in the years ahead.

DOCUMENTATION

CHAPTER 1. TEACHER PERSONAL THEORIZING AND
RESEARCH ON CURRICULUM AND TEACHING

Notes

1. The brief overview of research programs that follows is meant to provide a context for the discussion of teacher personal theorizing and is not intended to be an exhaustive review or analysis of paradigms in the study of teaching. A more complete examination of these issues can be found in Shulman (1986).

2. Initially, the focus was on pupil mediation of teaching (Anderson, 1984). More recent efforts have been made to study both teachers' and students' cognitional knowledge as well as their actions (Peterson, 1988). The most recent synthesis of pupil mediation research is found in Wittrock (1986).

3. An important exception to this fact is Walter Doyle (1983), who has successfully studied cognitive and social mediation of teaching together.

4. See Wirth's (1989) account of Dewey's work at the University of Chicago Laboratory School for examples of teachers' involvement in research investigations.

5. The roles that social and institutional structures play in shaping the language and activity of teaching are more fully discussed in the chapter by Ross in this volume.

References

Alexander, T. M. (1987). *John Dewey's theory of art, experience, and nature: The horizons of feeling.* Albany, NY: State University of New York Press.

Anderson, L. (1984). The environment of instruction: The function of seatwork in a commercially developed curriculum. In G. Duffy, L. Roehler, & J. Mason (Eds.), *Comprehension instruction: Perspectives and suggestions.* New York: Longman.

Anderson, L., Evertson, C., & Brophy, J. (1979). Children's preconceptions and content-area textbooks. In G. Duffy, L. Roehler, & J. Mason (Eds.), *Comprehension instruction: Perspectives and suggestions.* New York: Longman.

Brophy, J. E. (1983). Classroom organization and management. *Elementary School Journal, 83,* 265-286.

Brophy, J. E., & Good, T. L. (1986). Teacher behavior and student achievement. In M. C. Wittrock (Ed.), *Handbook of research on teaching* (3rd ed., pp. 328-375). New York: Macmillan.

Carr, W., & Kemmis, S. (1986). *Becoming critical: Education, knowledge, and action research.* London: Falmer Press.

Cazden, C. (1986). Classroom discourse. In M. C. Wittrock (Ed.), *Handbook of research on teaching* (3rd ed., pp. 432-463). New York: Macmillan.

Cazden, C. B., John, V. P., & Hymes, D. (Eds.). (1972). *Functions of language in the classroom.* New York: Teachers College Press.

Clark, C. M., & Peterson, P. L. (1986). Teachers' thought processes. In M. C. Wittrock (Ed.), *Handbook of research on teaching* (3rd ed., pp. 255-296). New York: Macmillan.

Cochran-Smith, M., & Lytle, S. L. (1990). Research on teaching and teacher research: Issues that divide. *Educational Researcher, 19*(2), 2-11.

Coladarci, T., & Gage, N. L. (1984). Effects of minimal intervention on teacher behavior and student achievement. *American Educational Research Journal, 21,* 539-555.

Connelly, E. M., & Clandinin, D. J. (1988). *Teachers as curriculum planners: Narratives of experience.* New York: Teachers College Press.

Delamont, S., & Atkinson, P. (1980). The two traditions in educational ethnography: Sociology and anthropology compared. *British Journal of Sociology of Education, 1,* 139-152.

Dewey, J. (1900/1976). Psychology and social practice. In J. A. Boydston (Ed.), *John Dewey: The Middle Works, 1899-1924, Vol. 1: 1899-1901* (pp. 131-150). Carbondale, IL: Southern Illinois University Press.

———. (1902). *The child and the curriculum.* Chicago: University of Chicago Press.

———. (1904/1964). The relation of theory to practice in education. In

R. D. Archambault (Ed.), *John Dewey on Education: Selected essays* (pp. 313-338). Chicago: University of Chicago Press.

————. (1916). *Democracy and education.* New York: Free Press.

————. (1933). *How we think.* Lexington, MA: Heath.

Doyle, W. (1977). Learning in the classroom environment: An ecological analysis. *Journal of Teacher Education, 28,* 51-55.

————. (1983). Academic work. *Review of Educational Research, 53,* 159-199.

Dunkin, M. J., & Biddle, B. J. (1974). *The study of teaching.* New York: Holt, Rinehart, & Winston.

Elbaz, R. (1981). The teacher's "practical knowledge": Report of a case study. *Curriculum Inquiry, 7,* 43-71.

Erickson, F. (1973). What makes school ethnography ethnographic? *Council of Anthropology and Education Newsletter, 2,* 10-19.

————. (1986). Qualitative methods in research on teaching. In M. C. Wittrock (Ed.), *Handbook of research on teaching* (3rd ed., pp. 119-161). New York: Macmillan.

Evertson, C. M. (1985). Training teachers in classroom management: An experimental study in secondary school classrooms. *Journal of Educational Research, 79,* 51-58.

Fay, B. (1975). *Social theory and political practice.* London: George Allen & Unwin.

Feiman-Nemser, S., & Floden, R. E. (1986). The cultures of teaching. In M. C. Wittrock (Ed.), *Handbook of research on teaching* (3rd ed., pp. 505-526). New York: Macmillan.

Gage, N. L. (1978). *The scientific basis for the art of teaching.* New York: Teachers College Press.

Gage, N. L., & Needels, M. C. (1989). Process-product research on teaching: A review of criticisms. *The Elementary School Journal, 89,* 253-300.

Geertz, C. (1973). *The interpretation of cultures.* New York: Basic Books.

Good, T. L. (1979). Teacher effectiveness in the elementary school: What we know about it now. *Journal of Teacher Education, 30,* 52-64.

Good, T. L., & Brophy, J. E. (1986). School effects. In M. C. Wittrock (Ed.), *Handbook of research on teaching* (3rd ed., pp. 570-602). New York: Macmillan.

Green, J. L. (1983). Teaching and learning: A linguistic perspective. *Elementary School Journal, 83,* 353-391.

Hamilton, S. F. (1983). The social side of schooling: Ecological studies of classrooms and schools. *Elementary School Journal, 83,* 313-334.

House, E., Lapan, S., & Mathison, S. (1989). Teacher inference. *Cambridge Journal of Education, 19*(1), 53-58.

Howe, K. R. (1990, April). *Getting over the quantitative-qualitative debate.* Invited address at the American Educational Research Association annual meeting, Boston.

Parker, W. C. (1987). Teachers' mediation in social studies. *Theory and Research in Social Education, 15*(1), 1-22.

Peshkin, A. (1978). *Growing up American: Schooling and the survival of community.* Chicago: University of Chicago Press.

———. (1986). *God's choice: The total world of a fundamentalist Christian school.* Chicago: University of Chicago Press.

Peterson, P. L. (1988). Teachers' and students' cognitional knowledge for classroom teaching and learning. *Educational Researcher, 17*(5), 5-14.

Peterson, P. L., & Clark, C. M. (1978). Teachers' reports of their cognitive processes during teaching. American Educational Research Journal, 15, 555-565.

Reid, W. A. (1978). *Thinking about the curriculum.* London: Routledge & Kegan Paul.

Reid, W. A., & Walker, D. F. (Eds.) (1975). *Case studies in curriculum change.* London: Routledge & Kegan Paul.

Rosenshine, B., & Stevens, R. (1986). Teaching functions. In M. C. Wittrock (Ed.), *Handbook of research on teaching* (3rd ed., pp. 376-391). New York: Macmillan.

Sanders, D., & McCutcheon, G. (1986). The development of practical theories of teaching. *Journal of Curriculum and Supervision, 2*(1), 50-67.

Scheffler, I. (1974). *Four pragmatists: A critical introduction to Peirce, James, Mead, and Dewey.* New York: Routledge & Kegan Paul.

Schwab, J. J. (1969). The practical: A language for curriculum. *School Review, 77,* 1-23.

———. (1971). The practical: Arts of the eclectic. *School Review, 80,* 461-489.

————— . (1973). The practical 3: Translation into curriculum. *School Review, 81*, 501-522.

Shavelson, R. J. (1976). Teachers' decision making. In N. L. Gage (Ed.), *The psychology of teaching methods* (Yearbook of the National Society for the Study of Education). Chicago: University of Chicago Press.

Shulman, L. S. (1986). Paradigms and research programs in the study of teaching: A contemporary perspective. In M. C. Wittrock (Ed.), *Handbook of research on teaching* (3rd ed., pp. 3-36). New York: Macmillan.

Tom, A. R. (1984). *Teaching as a moral craft.* New York: Longman.

Walker, D. F. (1971). A naturalistic model for curriculum development. *School Review, 80*, 51-65.

————— . (1990). *Fundamentals of curriculum.* San Diego: Harcourt Brace Jovanovich.

Wirth, A. (1989). *John Dewey as educator: His design for work in education (1894-1904).* Lanham, MD: University Press of America.

Wittrock, M. C. (Ed.). (1986). *Handbook of research on teaching* (3rd ed.). New York: Macmillan.

Yinger, R. J. (1979). Routines in teacher planning. *Theory Into Practice, 18*, 163-169.

CHAPTER 2. PHILOSOPHY, MEANING CONSTRUCTS
AND TEACHER THEORIZING

Notes

The author wishes to thank the editors for their invitation and support for this chapter and especially Wayne Ross for his helpful critique and patience. Thanks too to the anonymous reviewers who pushed for its closer ties to the other chapters in the volume. In this revision, the philosophic ideas are more accessible and useful.

1. Donald Schön's (1983) term has significant utility for teacher theorizing reforms; see also the review essay by Hugh Munby and Thomas Russell (1989).

2. Philip Phenix (1964) uses "realms of meaning" to name forms of experience that are somewhat related to organized bodies of knowledge.

3. Consider one or more constructs that might encapsulate the multidimensional lives of "space travelers."

4. One obvious example is the process-product research that Ross (this volume) writes about.

5. This statement in no way refers to usages in the present volume.

6. Many readers will want to identify neo-Marxist critical theory with conversationalist meaning. This philosophic tradition, as well as some forms of phenomenology, is a precursory, modernist root of the meaning construct described here.

7. Ethical and all other theories must be seen as embedded in socially constructed meanings. Theories are themselves ethical.

References

Apple, M. (1979). *Ideology and curriculum.* Boston: Routledge & Kegan Paul.

Bernstein, R. (1983). *Beyond objectivism and relativism: Science, hermeneutics and praxis.* Philadelphia: University of Pennsylvania Press.

————— . (1986). Introduction. In *Philosophical profiles* (pp. 1-20). Philadelphia: University of Pennsylvania Press.

Brodkey, L. (1987). Postmodern pedagogy for progressive educators. *Journal of Education, 169*(3), 138-143.

Bruner, J. (1985). Narrative and paradigmatic modes of thought. In E. Eisner (Ed.), *Learning and teaching the ways of knowing* (pp. 97-115). Eighty-fourth yearbook of the National Society for the Study of Education. Chicago: University of Chicago Press.

Carr, W., & Kemmis, S. (1986). *Becoming critical: Education, knowledge, and action research.* London: Falmer.

Cherryholmes, C. (1988). *Power and criticism.* New York: Teachers College Press.

Cronbach, L., & Meehl, P. (1955). Construct validity in psychological tests. *Psychological Bulletin, 52,* 281-302.

Connelly, F. M., & Clandinin, D. J. (1985). Personal practical knowledge and the modes of knowing: Relevance for teaching and learning. In E. Eisner (Ed.), *Learning and teaching the ways of knowing* (pp. 174-198). Eighty-fourth yearbook of the National Society for the Study of Education. Chicago: University of Chicago Press.

————— . (1988). *Teachers as curriculum planners.* New York: Teachers College Press.

Dewey, J. (1929/1960). *The quest for certainty.* New York: G. P. Putnam's Sons.

Eagleton, T. (1983). *Literary theory: An introduction.* Oxford: Basil Blackwell.

Elbow, P. (1986). *Embracing contraries.* New York: Oxford University Press.

Fenstermacher, G. (1986). Philosophy of research on teaching: Three aspects. In M. Wittrock (Ed.), *Handbook of research on teaching* (3rd ed.) (pp. 37-49). New York: Macmillan.

Goodman, N. (1978). *Ways of worldmaking.* Indianapolis: Hackett.

Grimmett, P. (1988). The nature of reflection and Schön's conception in perspective. In P. Grimmett & G. Erickson (Eds.), *Reflection in teacher education* (pp. 5-15). Vancouver and New York: Pacific Educational Press and Teachers College Press.

Harding, S. (1986). *The science question in feminism.* Ithaca: Cornell University Press.

Lather, P. (1989). Postmodernism and the politics of enlightenment. *Educational Foundations, 3*(3), 7-28.

Lyotard, J. (1988). The postmodern condition. In K. Baynes, J. Bohman, & T. McCarthy (Eds.), *After philosophy* (pp. 73-94). Cambridge: MIT Press.

McCarthy, T. (1988). General introduction. In K. Baynes, J. Bohman, and T. McCarthy (Eds.), *After philosophy* (pp. 1-18). Cambridge: MIT Press.

Munby, H., & Russell, T. (1989). Educating the reflective teacher: An essay review of two books by Donald Schön. *Journal of Curriculum Studies, 21*(1), 71-80.

Pai, Y. (1990). *Cultural foundations of education.* Columbus: Merrill.

Phenix, P. (1964). *Realms of meaning.* New York: McGraw-Hill.

Quine, W., & Ulian, J. (1970). *The web of belief.* New York: Random House.

Richert, A. (1987a). *Reflex to reflection: Facilitating reflection in novice teachers.* Paper presented at the American Educational Research Association, Washington, DC.

———. (1987b). *Reflex to reflection: Facilitating reflection in novice teachers.* Unpublished doctoral dissertation, Stanford University.

Rorty, R. (1979). *Philosophy and the mirror of nature.* Princeton: Princeton University Press.

————. (1982a). Introduction: Pragmatism and philosophy. In *Consequences of pragmatism* (pp. xiii-xlvii). Minneapolis: University of Minnesota Press.

————. (1982b). Philosophy in America today. In *Consequences of pragmatism* (pp. 211-230). Minneapolis: University of Minnesota Press.

————. (1989a). *Contingency, irony and solidarity.* New York: Cambridge University Press.

————. (1989b). *Philosophy, literature and inter-cultural comparison: Heidegger, Kundera and Dickens.* Paper presented at the Sixth East-West Philosophers Conference, Honolulu.

Schön, D. (1983). *The reflective practitioner.* New York: Basic Books.

Shaver, J., O. L. Davis, & S. Helburn (1980). An interpretive report on the status of precollege social studies education based on three NSF-funded studies. In *What are the needs in precollege science, mathematics, and social science education? Views from the field.* Washington, DC: U.S. Government Printing Office.

Stone, L. (1989). Toward a transformational theory of teaching. In J. Giarelli (Ed.), *Philosophy of Education, 1988* (pp. 186-195). Normal, IL: Philosophy of Education Society.

————. (1990). *Contingency in teaching: A suggestive framework.* Paper presented at the annual meeting of the American Educational Research Association, Boston.

————. (1991a). The essentialist tension in reflective teacher education. In L. Valli (Ed.), *Reflective teacher education: Cases and critiques.* New York: State University of New York Press.

————. (1991b). *Postmodern social construction: Initiating dissonance.* Paper presented at the annual meeting of the American Educational Research Association, Chicago.

Taylor, C. (1985a). Language and human nature. In *Human agency and language* (pp. 215-247). Cambridge: Cambridge University Press.

————. (1985b). Theories of meaning. In *Human agency and language* (pp. 248-292). Cambridge: Cambridge University Press.

————. (1988). Overcoming epistemology. In K. Baynes, J. Bohman, and T. McCarthy (Eds.), *After philosophy?* (pp. 464-488). Cambridge: MIT press.

Van Manen, M. (1977). Linking ways of knowing with ways of being practical. *Curriculum Inquiry, 6*(3), 205-228.

Weiss, I. (1987). *Report of the 1983-1986 national survey of science and mathematics education.* Research Triangle Park, NC: Research Triangle Institute.

Young, R. (1990). *A critical theory of education.* New York: Teachers College Press.

Zeichner, K., & D. Liston (1987). Teaching student teachers to reflect. *Harvard Educational Review, 57*(1), 23-48.

CHAPTER 3. TEACHERS' STORIES:
AUTOBIOGRAPHY AND INQUIRY

References

Abbs, P. (1974). *Autobiography in education.* London: Heinemann.

————— . (1981). Education and the living image: Reflections on imagery, fantasy, and the art of recognition. *Teachers College Record, 82,* 475-496.

Allport, G. W. (1942). *The use of personal documents in psychological science.* New York: Social Science Research Council.

Ashton-Warner, S. (1958). *Spinster.* New York: Touchstone.

————— . (1963). *Teacher.* New York: Touchstone.

Berger, P. L. (1963). *Invitation to sociology.* Garden City, NJ: Anchor Books.

Bruner, J. (1983). *In search of mind.* New York: Harper Colophon.

Denton, D. E. (1974). That mode of being called teaching. In D. E. Denton (Ed.), Existentialism and phenomenology in education (pp. 99-118). New York: Teachers College Press.

Freire, P. (1970). *The pedagogy of the oppressed.* New York. Continuum.

Grumet, M. (1978). Supervision and situation: A methodology of self-report for teacher education. *Journal of Curriculum Theorizing, 1*(1) 191-257.

Kohl, H. (1967). *36 Children.* New York: The New American Library.

————— . (1984). *Growing minds: On becoming a teacher.* New York: Harper Colophon.

Lortie, D. C. (1975). *Schoolteacher: A sociological study.* Chicago: University of Chicago Press.

Mandel, B. J. (1980). Full of life now. In James Olney (Ed.), *Autobiography: Essays critical and theoretical.* Princeton: Princeton University Press.

Noddings, N. (1984). *Caring: A feminine approach to ethics and moral education.* Berkeley: University of California Press.

Paley, V. G. (1979). *White teacher.* Cambridge: Harvard University Press.

Pratt, C. (1948). *I learn from children: An adventure in progressive education.* New York: Simon and Schuster.

Rose, M. (1989). *Lives on the boundary.* New York: The Free Press.

Wigginton, E. (1985). *Sometimes a shining moment: The Foxfire experience.* Garden Grove, NY: Anchor/Doubleday.

CHAPTER 4. LEARNING HOW TO TEACH LANGUAGE ARTS:
A CULTURAL MODEL

Note

In part, the research discussed in this chapter was supported by a dissertation grant awarded in May 1988 by the school Division of the American Association of Publishers, New York, New York. The analyses presented here are those of the writer and do not represent the AAP. All names are pseudonyms.

References

Berliner, D. C. (1986). In pursuit of the expert pedagogue. *Educational Researcher, 15*(7), 1-23.

————. (1987). Ways of thinking about students and classrooms by more and less experienced teachers. In J. Calderhead (Ed.), *Exploring teachers' thinking* (pp. 60-83). Salisbury, England: Cassell.

Bullough, R. V., Jr. (1989). *First-year teacher: A case study.* New York: Teachers College Press.

Clandinin, D. J. (1986). *Classroom practice: Teachers' images in action.* London: Falmer Press.

Clark, C. M. (1979). *Choice of a model for research on teacher thinking.* (Research Series No. 20). Institute for Research on Teaching, Michigan State University, East Lansing.

Clark, C. M., & Peterson, P. L. (1986). Teachers' thought processes. In

M. C. Wittrock (Ed.), *Handbook of research on teaching* (3rd ed., pp. 255-296). New York: Macmillan.

Clift, R. (1988). *Learning to teach English—maybe.* Paper presented at the Annual Meeting of the American Educational Research Association, New Orleans.

Connelly, F. M., & Clandinin, J. (1984). Personal practical knowledge at Bay Street School: Ritual, personal philosophy and image. In R. Halkes & J. K. Olson (Eds.), *Teacher thinking: A new perspective on persisting problems in education* (pp. 103-111). Lisse, The Netherlands: Swets & Zeitlinger.

Corbin, J., & Strauss, A. (1990). Grounded theory research: Procedures, canons, and evaluative criteria. *Qualitative Sociology, 13*(1), 3-21.

Cornett, J. (1987). *Teacher personal practical theories and their influence upon teacher curricular and instructional actions: A case study of a secondary social studies teacher.* Unpublished doctoral dissertation, Ohio State University, Columbus.

Elbaz, F. (1983). *Teacher thinking: A study of practical knowledge.* New York: Nichols.

Erickson, F. (1986). Qualitative research methods in research on teaching. In M. C. Wittrock (Ed.), *Handbook of research on teaching* (3rd ed., pp. 297-314). New York: Macmillan.

Feiman-Nemser, S., & Floden, R. (1986). The cultures of teaching. In M. C. Wittrock (Ed.), *Handbook of research on teaching* (3rd ed., pp. 505-526). New York: Macmillan.

Geertz, C. (1973). Thick description: Toward an interpretive theory of culture. In C. Geertz, *The interpretation of cultures* (pp. 3-30). New York: Basic Books.

Glaser, B., & Strauss, A. (1965). *The discovery of grounded theory.* Chicago: Aldine.

Goodlad, J. I. (1990a). Better teachers for our nation's schools. *Phi Delta Kappan, 72*(3), 185-194.

———. (1990b). *Teachers for our nation's school.* San Francisco: Jossey-Bass.

Goodlad, J. I., Soder, R., & Sirotnik, K. A. (Eds.). (1990). *The moral dimensions of teaching.* San Francisco: Jossey-Bass.

Holmes Group. (1986). *Tomorrow's teachers: A report of the Holmes Group.* East Lansing, MI: Author.

Hunt, F. K. (1988). *The identification of critical elements of the class-within-a-class alternative service delivery model and the development of a teacher training package based on the critical elements identified.* Unpublished doctoral dissertation, University of Kansas, Lawrence.

Kleinsasser, A. M. (1988). *The reflection-in-action of novice language arts teachers: An inquiry into an epistemology of practice.* Unpublished doctoral dissertation, University of Kansas, Lawrence.

———— . (June, 1989). *Compared to teaching English, teaching math must be a piece of cake.* Paper presented at the 18th Wyoming Conference on English, the University of Wyoming, Laramie.

Lortie, D. (1975). *Schoolteacher: A sociological study.* Chicago: University of Chicago Press.

Shulman, L. (1986). Paradigms and research paradigms in the study of teaching. In M. C. Wittrock (Ed.), *Handbook of research on teaching* (3rd ed., pp. 3-36). New York: Macmillan.

Veenman, S. (1984). Perceived problems of beginning teachers. *Review of Educational Research, 54,* 143-178.

Waller, W. (1932). *The sociology of teaching.* New York: Wiley.

Weinstein, C. (1988). Preservice teachers' expectations about the first year of teaching. *Teaching & Teacher Education, 4*(1), 31-40.

———— . (March, 1989). *Prospective elementary teachers' beliefs about teaching.* Paper presented at the annual meeting of the American Educational Research Association, San Francisco.

CHAPTER 5. PERSONAL THEORIZING OF AN INTERN TEACHER

Note

1. Eighteen other student teachers were also interviewed in depth. Five of these were observed teaching after the initial interview and reinterviewed following observation. However, the principal interpretative device was the case study.

Data were collected for nine weeks of winter 1988 through biweekly observations, field notes, structured and conversational interviews, examination of texts and materials in use, student teachers' reflective professional journal entries, and school personnel with whom Nicole worked. Interviews were audiotaped and transcribed for analysis. Some tapes were quoted without being transcribed.

Data were analyzed inductively through a constant comparative method (Glaser & Strauss, 1967, pp. 101-115). Participants were given typed copies of the interview transcripts. Interpretations were reviewed by Nicole and other participants. A dialectical view of the relationship between thought and action, that is, one in which practice interacts with thought and illuminates theory, undergirded this work.

References

Calderhead, J. (Ed.). (1988). *Teachers' professional learning.* Philadelphia: Falmer Press.

Carr, W., & Kemmis, S. (1983). *Becoming critical: Knowing through action research.* Victoria, Australia: Deakin University Press.

Deal, T. E., & Chatman, R. M. (1989). Learning the ropes alone: Socializing new teachers. *Action in Teacher Education, 11*(1), 21-29.

Dewey, J. (1933). *How we think: A restatement of the relation of reflective thinking to the educative process.* Chicago: Henry Regency.

Glaser, B. G., & Strauss, A. L. (1967). *Discovery of grounded theory.* Chicago: Aldine.

Kelly, F. J., Brown, B. M., & Foxx, C. L. (1984). Dialectics of social adaptation and individual constructivism. *Genetic Psychology Monographs, 110,* 257-287.

Kelly, G. (1955). *The psychology of personal constructs.* New York: Norton.

———. (1963). *A theory of personality.* New York: Norton.

Knefflekamp, L. L. (1974). *Developmental instruction: Fostering intellectual and personal growth of college students.* Unpublished doctoral dissertation, University of Minnesota, Minneapolis.

McCutcheon, G. (1982). What in the world is curriculum theory? *Theory Into Practice, 21,* 18-22.

Pape, S. L. (1988). *Student teacher thinking: The development and content of practical theories.* Unpublished doctoral dissertation, Ohio State university, Columbus.

Perry, W. G. (1968). *Forms of intellectual and ethical development in the college years.* New York: Holt, Reinhart & Winston.

———. (1981). Cognitive and ethical growth: The making of meaning. In A. Chickering (Ed.), *The modern American college.* San Francisco: Jossey-Bass.

Piaget, J. (1970). *Genetic epistemology.* New York: Columbia University Press.

Sergiovanni, T. J., & Starrett, R. J. (1983). *Supervision: Human perspectives.* New York: McGraw-Hill.

CHAPTER 6. HOW DO ELEMENTARY TEACHERS DECIDE
WHAT TO TEACH IN SOCIAL STUDIES?

Note

The research reported in this chapter was partially supported by a grant from the General University Research Fund of the University of Delaware; however, the author is solely responsible for the views expressed. R. Neill Wenger is gratefully acknowledged for his assistance in the collection and analysis of the data.

References

Brophy, J. (1990). Teaching social studies for understanding and higher-order applications. *Elementary School Journal, 90,* 351-417.

Eisner, E. W. (1985). *The educational imagination: On the design and evaluation of school programs* (2nd ed.). New York: Macmillan.

Goodlad, J. I. (1984). *A place called school.* New York: McGraw-Hill.

Hertzberg, H. W. (1981). *Social studies reform, 1880-1980.* Boulder, CO: Social Science Education Consortium.

James, L. B., & Crape, L. M. (1968). *Geography for today's children.* New York: Appleton-Century-Crofts.

Joint Committee on Geographic Education, National Council for Geographic Education and Association of American Geographers. (1984). *Guidelines for geographic education: Elementary and secondary schools.* Washington, DC: Association of American Geographers; and Macomb, IL: National Council for Geographic Education.

Kaltsounis, T. (1986). *States and regions.* Morristown, NJ: Silver Burdett.

Lengel, J. G., & Superka, D. P. (1982). Curriculum patterns. In I. Morrissett (Ed.), *Social studies in the 1980s: A report of Project SPAN.* Alexandria, VA: Association for Supervision and Curriculum Development.

Levstik, L. S. (1989). *Subverting reform in the social studies: A fourth grade case study.* Paper presented at the annual meeting of the American Educational Research Association, San Francisco.

McCutcheon, G. (1981). Elementary school teachers' planning for social studies and other subjects. *Theory and Research in Social Education, 9*(1), 45-66.

McKee, S. J. (1988). Impediments to implementing critical thinking. *Social Education, 52,* 444-446.

Noddings, N. (1990). Feminist critiques in the professions. In C. B. Cazden (Ed.), *Review of research in education* (pp. 393-424). Washington, DC: American Educational Research Association.

Shaver, J. P., Davis, O. L., Jr., & Helburn, S. W. (1980). An interpretive report on the status of precollege social studies education based on three NSF-funded studies. In *What are the needs in precollege science, mathematics, and social science education? Views from the field.* Washington, DC: U.S. Government Printing Office.

Shulman, L. S. (1987). Knowledge and teaching: Foundation of the new reform. *Harvard Educational Review, 57,* 1-22.

Stanley, W. B. (1991). Teacher competence for social studies, In J. P. Shaver (Ed.), *Handbook of research on social studies teaching and learning* (pp. 249-262). New York: Macmillan.

Stodolsky, S. S. (1988). *The subject matters: Classroom activity in math and social studies.* Chicago: University of Chicago Press.

Stodolsky, S. S., & Glaessner, B. (1988). *Students' views about learning math and social studies.* Paper presented at the annual meeting of the American Educational Research Association, New Orleans.

Thornton, S. J. (1991). Teacher as curricular-instructional gatekeeper in social studies. In J. P. Shaver (Ed.), *Handbook of research on social studies teaching and learning* (pp. 237-248). New York: Macmillan.

Thornton, S. J. & Wenger, R. N. (1990). Geography curriculum and instruction in three fourth-grade classrooms. *Elementary School Journal, 90,* 515-531.

White, J. J. (1985). What works for teachers: A review of ethnographic research studies as they inform issues of social studies curriculum and instruction. In W. B. Stanley (Ed.), *Review of research in social studies education, 1976-1983* (pp. 215-307). Washington, DC: National Council for the Social Studies; and Boulder, CO: ERIC Clearinghouse for Social Studies/Social Science Education and Social Science Education Consortium.

——— . (1989). *The construction of substantial knowledge in social studies lessons.* Paper presented at the annual meeting of the American Educational Research Association, San Francisco.

CHAPTER 7. BRICOLAGE: TEACHERS DO IT DAILY

References

Apple, M. (1982). *Education and power.* Boston: Routledge & Kegan Paul.

Baron, J. B., & Sternberg, R. J. (1987). *Teaching thinking skills: Theory and practice.* New York: W. H. Freeman.

Berry, J. W., & Irvine, S. H. (1986). Bricolage: Savages do it daily. In R. J. Sternberg & R. K. Wagner (Eds.), *Practical intelligence: Nature and origins of competence in the everyday world* (pp. 271-306). Cambridge, England: Cambridge University Press.

Carson, T. R. (1986). Closing the gap between research and practice: Conversation as a mode of doing research. *Phenomenology + Pedagogy, 4,* 73-85.

Connelly, F. M., & Ben-Peretz, M. (1980). Teachers' roles in the using and doing of research and curriculum development. *Journal of Curriculum Studies, 12,* 95-107.

deBono, E. (1975). *CoRT Thinking.* London: Direct Educational Services.

deBono, E., & Howitt-Gleeson, M. (1979). *Learn to think!* London: Direct Educational Services.

Elbaz, F. (1983). *Teacher thinking: A study of practical knowledge.* London: Croom Helm.

Gadamer, H. G. (1985). *Truth and method.* New York: Crossroad.

Gage, N. L. (1963). Paradigms for research in teaching. In N. L. Gage (Ed.), *Handbook of research on teaching.* Chicago: Rand McNally.

Gardner, H. (1983). *Frames of mind.* New York: Basic Books.

Glaser, B. (1978). *Theoretical sensitivity.* Mill Valley, CA: Sociology Press.

Glaser, B., & Strauss, A. (1967). *Discovery of grounded theory.* Chicago: Aldine.

Goodlad, J. I. (1984). *A place called school.* New York: McGraw-Hill.

Hall, G. E., Wallace, R. C., Jr., & Dossett, W. A. (1973). *A developmental conceptualization of the adoption process within educational institutions.* Austin, TX: Research and Development Center for Teacher Education.

Jackson, P. W., & Kieslar, S. B. (1977). Fundamental research in education. *Educational Researcher, 6,* 13-18.

Levi-Strauss, C. (1962). *The savage mind.* London: Weidenfeld & Nicholson.

McDaniel, J. E. (1987). *The Interdisciplinary Block critical thinking program: Interim report* (Technical Report No. 2, unpublished manuscript). Seattle: Center for the Study of Civic Intelligence, University of Washington.

Olson, J. K. (1982). Classroom knowledge and curriculum change. In J. K. Olson (Ed.), *Innovations in the science curriculum.* London: Croom Helm.

Palmer, R. E. (1969). *Hermeneutics.* Evanston, IL: Northwestern University Press.

Parker, W. C. (1986). Dorothy's and Mary's mediation of a curriculum invention. *Phenomenology + Pedagogy, 4,* 20-31.

————. (1987). Teachers' mediation in social studies. *Theory and Research in Social Education, 15,* 1-22.

Parker, W. C. (1989). New directions in teacher education: Which direction? In J. A. Braun (Ed.), *Reforming teacher education* (pp. 161-148). New York: Garland.

Paul, R. W. (1987). Dialogical thinking. In J. B. Baron & R. J. Sternberg (Eds.), *Teaching thinking skills: Theory and practice* (pp. 127-148). New York: W. H. Freeman.

Perkins, D. N., Allen, R., & Hafner, J. (1983). Difficulties in everyday reasoning. In W. Maxwell (Ed.), *Thinking: The expanding frontier* (pp. 177-189). Philadelphia: Franklin Institute.

Purkey, S. C., & Smith, M. S. (1983). Effective schools: A review. *The Elementary School Journal, 83,* 427-452.

Reid, W. A. (1987). Institutions and practices: Professional education reports and the language of reform. *Educational Researcher, 16,* 10-15.

Rogoff, B., & Lave, J. (Eds.) (1984). *Everyday cognition: Its development in social context.* Cambridge, MA: Harvard University Press.

Schön, D. A. (1983). *The reflective practitioner.* New York: Basic Books.

Shavelson, R. J. (1973). What is the basic teaching skill? *Journal of Teacher Education, 14,* 144-151.

Shulman, L. (1987). Knowledge and teaching: Foundations of the New Reform. *Harvard Educational Review, 57,* 1-22.

Shweder, R. A., & Bourne, E. J. (1984). Does the concept of the person vary cross-culturally? In R. A. Shweder and R. A. LeVine (Eds.), *Culture theory: Essays on mind, self, and emotion.* London: Cambridge University Press.

Sirotnik, K. A. (1987, August). *The school as the center of change.* Paper presented at the Southwestern Bell Invitational Conference, "Restructuring Schooling for Quality Education," Trinity University, San Antonio, Texas.

Sternberg, R. J., & Wagner, R. K. (Eds.). (1986). *Practical intelligence: Nature and origins of competence in the everyday world.* Cambridge, England: Cambridge University Press.

Vygotsky, L. S. (1978). *Mind in society.* Cambridge, MA: Harvard University Press.

Westbury, I. (1984, April). *The invention of curricula.* Paper presented at the annual meeting of the American Educational Research Association, New Orleans.

Yin, R. K. (1984). *Case study research.* Beverly Hills, CA: Sage.

CHAPTER 8. AN INTERPRETATION OF HIGH SCHOOL SCIENCE
TEACHING BASED ON METAPHORS AND
BELIEFS FOR SPECIFIC ROLES

References

Erickson, F. (1986). Qualitative methods in research on teaching. In M. C. Wittrock (Ed.), *Handbook of research on teaching* (3rd ed.). New York: Macmillan.

Gallagher, J. J. (1989). *Research on secondary school science teachers' practices, knowledge and beliefs: A basis for restructuring.* Paper presented at the annual meeting of the American Association for the Advancement of Science, San Francisco.

National Commission on Excellence in Education. (1983). *A nation at risk: The imperative for educational reform.* Washington, DC: U.S. Government Printing Office.

Pope, M. L., & Gilbert, J. K. (1983). Explanation and metaphor: Some empirical questions in science education. *European Journal of Science Education, 5,* 249-261.

Tobin, K. (1987). Forces which shape the implemented curriculum in high school science and mathematics. *Journal of Teaching and Teacher Education, 4*(3), 287-298.

Tobin, K., & Espinet, M. (1989). Impediments to change: An application of peer coaching in high school science. *Journal of Research in Science Teaching, 26*(2), 105-120.

————. (in press). Teachers helping teachers to improve high school mathematics teaching. *School Science and Mathematics.*

Tobin, K., Kahle, J. B., & Fraser, B. J. (in press). *Windows into science classrooms: Problems associated with high level cognitive learning in science.* London: Falmer Press.

CHAPTER 9. INSIGHTS FROM THE ANALYSIS OF OUR OWN
THEORIZING: THE VIEWPOINTS OF SEVEN TEACHERS

Notes

1. Gail McCutcheon defines curriculum in this manner.

2. We believe that ongoing, systematic reflection is an integral part of our professional responsibility. Although we initially viewed this activity as taking time and energy away from "teaching," we realize that it should not be seen as an "extra activity" but rather as an expectation for the entire teaching profession.

3. Cornett and Miller express their appreciation for the support of Wichita State University, Dean Maurine Fry, and the Wichita Public Schools in this effort.

4. Bennett reviewed the following sources: "Helping Students Develop Strategies for Effective Learning," by C. E. Weinstein et al., 1989, *Educational Leadership, 46*(4), 17-19; "Putting Learning Strategies to Work," by S. J. Derry, 1989, *Educational Leadership, 46*(4), 4-10; "Knowing Is Not Thinking," by E. Janko, March 1989, *Phi Delta Kappan,* 543-544; "Memory, Imagination, and Learning: Connected by the Story," by K. Egan, February 1989, *Phi Delta Kappan,* 455-459; "Who Is Accountable for Thoughtfulness?" by R. Brown, September 1987, *Phi Delta Kappan,* 49-52; "Reflections on Measuring Thinking, While Listening to Mozart's Jupiter Symphony," by S. Wassermann, January 1989, *Phi Delta Kappan,* 365-370; and "Using Knowledge of How Students Think About Mathematics," by P. Peterson, E. Fennema, & T. Carpenter, 1989, *Educational Leadership, 46*(4), 42-46.

5. The alternative certification program (STEP) at the University of Central Florida consists of four phases. Cornett, Goins, and Hammond interacted in the fourth phase.

References

Calderhead, J. (1987). Introduction. In J. Calderhead (Ed.), *Explaining teachers' thinking* (pp. 1-19). London: Cassell.

Carr, W., & Kemmis, S. (1986). *Becoming critical: Education, knowledge, and action research.* London: Falmer Press.

Clark, C., & Peterson, P. (1986). Teachers' thought processes. In M. C. Wittrock (Ed.), *Handbook of research on teaching* (3rd ed., 255-296). New York: Macmillan.

Cornett, J. W. (1987). *Teacher personal practical theories and their influence upon teacher curricular and instructional actions: A case study of a secondary social studies teacher.* Unpublished doctoral dissertation, Ohio State University, Columbus.

———. (1990). Utilizing action research in graduate curriculum courses. *Theory Into Practice, 29*(3), 185-195.

Cornett, J. W., & Chase, S. (1989). *Determining the impact of participation in a case study of teacher thinking: The teacher's perspective one year later.* Paper presented at the College and University Faculty Assembly, National Council for the Social Studies Annual Conference, St. Louis, MO.

Cornett, J. W., Chase, S., & Miller, P. (1990). *Researcher and participant views of ethics: Is trust enough?* Paper presented at annual meeting of the American Educational Research Association, Boston, MA.

Dewey, J. (1933). *How we think.* Lexington, MA: Heath.

Garnett, P. J., & Tobin, K. (1988). Teaching for understanding: Exemplary practice in high school chemistry. *Journal of Research in Science Teaching, 26*(1), 1-14.

Kleinsasser, A. (1988). *The reflection-in-action of novice language arts teachers: An inquiry into an epistemology of practice.* Unpublished doctoral dissertation, University of Kansas, Lawrence.

McCutcheon, G. (1989). Teacher deliberation. In M. Apple and L. Beyer (Eds.), *Curriculum: Problems, politics, possibilities.* Albany: SUNY Press.

Miller, J. L., & Martens, M. L. (1990). *Dilemmas of hierarchy and imposition in collaborative inquiry.* Paper presented at the annual meeting of the American Educational Research Association, Boston, MA.

Oberg, A., & McCutcheon, G. (1987). Teachers' experience doing action research. *Peabody Journal of Education, 64*(2), 116-127.

Pape, S. (1988). *Student teacher thinking: The development and content of practical theories.* Unpublished doctoral dissertation, Ohio State University, Columbus.

Parker, W. C. (1987). Teachers' mediation in social studies. *Theory and Research in Social Education, 15*(1), 1-22.

Reid, W. A. (1979). Practical reasoning and curriculum theory: In search of a new paradigm. *Curriculum Inquiry, 9*(3), 187-207.

Ross, E. W., & Hannay, L. M. (1986). Toward a critical theory of reflective inquiry. *Journal of Teacher Education, 37*(5), 9-15.

Schubert, W. H. (1986). *Curriculum: Perspective, paradigm, and possibility.* New York: Macmillan.

Schwab, J. J. (1970). *The practical: A language for curriculum.* Washington, DC: National Education Association.

Walker, D. F. (1971). A naturalistic model for curriculum development. *School Review, 80,* 51-65.

CHAPTER 10. THE COGNITIVE REQUISITES FOR IMPROVING THE
PERFORMANCE OF ELEMENTARY MATHEMATICS
AND SCIENCE TEACHING

References

Erickson, F. (1986). Qualitative methods in research on teaching. In M. C. Wittrock (Ed.), *Handbook of research on teaching* (3rd ed.). New York: Macmillan.

Jakubowski, E., & Tobin, K. (1989). *The structural components for enhancing the teaching of mathematics and science.* Tallahassee, FL: Florida State University.

Murnane, R. J., & Raizen, S. A. (Eds.). (1988). *Improving indicators of the quality of science and mathematics education in grades K-12.* Washington, DC: National Academy Press.

National Commission on Excellence in Education. (1983). *A nation at risk: The imperative for educational reform.* Washington, DC: U.S. Government Printing Office.

Office of Technology Assessment (OTA). (1988, June). *Elementary & secondary education for science and engineering* (OTA-TM-SET-41). Washington, DC: U.S. Government Printing Office.

Tobin, K. (1990). Changing metaphors and beliefs: A master switch for teaching. *Theory into Practice, 29*(2), 122-127.

Tobin, K., Kahle, J. B., & Fraser, B. J. (Eds.). (1990). *Opening windows into science classrooms: Teaching for high level cognitive learning.* London: Falmer Press.

Tobin, K., & Ulerick, S. L. (1989, March). *An interpretation of high school science teaching based on metaphors and beliefs for specific roles.* Paper presented at the annual meeting of the American Educational Research Association, San Francisco.

Weiss, I. R. (1987, November). *Report of the 1983-86 national survey of science & mathematics education.* Research Triangle Park, NC: Research Triangle Institute.

CHAPTER 11. TEACHER PERSONAL THEORIZING AND
REFLECTIVE PRACTICE IN TEACHER EDUCATION

Notes

1. Cinnamond and Zimpher (1990) claim that the instrumental view of reflective teaching as represented in the contemporary teacher education literature results from a reliance upon Dewey's conception of reflectivity. In adopting Dewey's reflective inquiry as an organizing theme for change, they claim that the teacher education community has "limited itself to instrumentalism and individuation for the teacher" (p. 70). They propose Mead's social theory as a substitute for the "Deweyan construction of the reflective process as essentially an individualized phenomenon" (p. 65) and call for a conception of reflection as a function of community.

2. See Lynda Stone's chapter in this volume for an extended discussion of this point.

References

Adler, S. (1984). A field study of selected student teacher perspectives toward social studies. *Theory and Research in Social Education, 12,* 13-30.

Apple, M. W. (1987b). *Teachers and texts.* London: Routledge & Kegan Paul.

Axtelle, G. E., & Burnett, J. R. (1970). Dewey on education and schooling. In J. A. Boydston (Ed.), *Guide to the works of John Dewey* (pp. 257-305). Carbondale: Southern Illinois University Press.

Berger, P. L., & Luckmann, T. (1966). *The social construction of reality.* Garden City, NY: Anchor.

Beyer, L. (1984). Field experience, ideology and the development of critical reflectivity. *Journal of Teacher Education, 35*(3), 36-41.

————. (1988). Training and educating: A critique of technical-mindedness in teacher preparation. *Current Issues in Education, 8,* 21-40.

Carson, T. (1990). What kind of knowing is critical action research? *Theory Into Practice, 29*(3), 158-173.

Cinnamond, J. H. & Zimpher, N. L. (1990). Reflectivity as a function of community. In R. T. Clift, W. R. Houston, & M. C. Pugach (Eds.), *Encouraging reflective practice in education* (pp. 57-72). New York: Teachers College Press.

Clift, R. T., Houston, W. R., & Pugach, M. C. (Eds.). (1990). *Encouraging reflective practice in education.* New York: Teachers College Press.

Cornett, J. (1990). Utilizing action research in graduate curriculum courses. *Theory Into Practice, 29*(3), 185-195.

Cruickshank, D. R. (1985). Uses and benefits of reflective teaching. *Phi Delta Kappan, 66*, 704-706.

Dewey, J. (1904/1964). The relation of theory to practice in education. In R. D. Archambault (Ed.), *John Dewey on education: Selected writings* (pp. 313-338). Chicago: University of Chicago Press.

————. (1913). *Interest and effort in education.* Carbondale: Southern Illinois University Press.

————. (1916). *Democracy and education.* New York: Free Press.

————. (1927). *The public and its problems.* Athens, OH: Swallow.

————. (1929). *Individualism old and new.* New York: Capricorn.

————. (1933). *How we think.* Lexington, MA: Heath.

————. (1939). *Freedom and culture.* New York: Paragon.

Goodman, J. (1989). Education for critical democracy. *Journal of Education, 171*(2), 88-116.

Greene, M. (1989). Reflection and passion in teaching. *Current Issues in Education, 9*, 20-30.

Grimmett, P. P., MacKinnon, A. M., Erickson, G. L., & Riecken, T. J. (1990). Reflective practice in teacher education. In R. T. Clift, W. R. Houston, & M. C. Pugach (Eds.), *Encouraging reflective practice in education* (pp. 20-38). New York: Teachers College Press.

Jordell, K. (1987). Structural and personal influences in the socialization of beginning teachers. *Teaching and Teacher Education, 3*, 165-177.

Kemmis, S., & McTaggart, R. (1988). *The action research planner* (3rd ed.). Victoria, Australia: Deakin University Press.

Lacey, C. (1977). *The socialization of teachers.* London: Metheun.

Richardson, V. (1990). The evolution of reflective teaching and teacher education. In R. T. Clift, W. R. Houston, & M. C. Pugach (Eds.), *Encouraging reflective practice in education* (pp. 3-19). New York: Teachers College Press.

Ross, E. W. (1987). Teacher perspective development: A study of preservice social studies teachers. *Theory and Research in Social Education, 15*(4), 225-243.

————. (1988a). Becoming a teacher: The development of preservice teacher perspectives. *Action in Teacher Education, 10*(2), 101-109.

————. (1988b). Preservice teachers' responses to institutional constraints: The active role of the individual in teacher socialization. *Educational Foundations, 2*(1), 77-92.

————. (1990, April). *Public policy, curricular change and teacher professionalism.* A paper given at the American Educational Research Association annual meeting, Boston.

————. (in press). Critical constructivism and use of knowledge about teaching. *Teacher Education Quarterly.*

Ross, E. W., & Hannay, L. M. (1986). Towards a critical theory of reflective inquiry. *Journal of Teacher Education, 37*(5), 9-15.

Sanger, J. (1990). Awakening a scream of consciousness: The critical group in action research. *Theory Into Practice, 29*(3), 174-178.

Schön, D. (1983). *The reflective practitioner.* New York: Basic Books.

————. (1987). *Educating the reflective practitioner.* San Francisco: Jossey-Bass.

Smyth, J. (1989). Developing and sustaining critical reflection in teacher education. *Current Issues in Education, 9,* 7-19.

Sobol, T. (1990, June). *A new compact for learning: Improving public elementary, middle, and secondary education results in the 1990's.* (Available from the New York State Education Department, Albany, NY 12234).

Tom, A. R. (1985). Inquiring into inquiry-oriented teacher education. *Journal of Teacher Education, 36*(5), 35-44.

————. (1987). Replacing pedagogical knowledge with pedagogical questions. In J. Smyth (Ed.), *Educating teachers: Changing the nature of pedagogical knowledge* (pp. 9-17). London: Falmer Press.

Trumbull, D. J. (1986). Teachers' envisioning: A foundation for artistry. *Teaching and Teacher Education, 2*(2), 139-144.

Zeichner, K. M. (1986). Preparing reflective teachers: An overview of instructional strategies which have been employed in preservice teacher education. *International Journal of Educational Research, 11,* 565-575.

Zeichner, K. M., & Gore, J. M. (1990). Teacher socialization. In W. R. Houston (Ed.), *Handbook of research on teacher education* (pp. 329-348). New York: Macmillan.

Zeichner, K. M., & Tabachnick, B. R. (1985). The development of teacher perspectives: Social strategies and institutional control in the socialization of teachers. *Journal of Education for Teaching, 11,* 1-25.

CHAPTER 12. FACILITATING TEACHER PERSONAL THEORIZING

References

Argyris, C. (1982). *Reasoning, learning and action: Individual and organizational.* San Francisco: Jossey-Bass.

Carr, W. (1980). The gap between theory and practice. *Journal of Further and Higher Education, 4*(1), 60-69.

Carr, W., & Kemmis, S. (1983). *Becoming critical: Knowing through action research.* Victoria, Australia: Deakin University Press.

Clandinin, D. J. (1986). *Classroom practice: Teacher images in action.* London: Falmer Press.

Clark, C., & Peterson, P. (1986). Teachers' thought processes. In M. C. Wittrock (Ed.), *Handbook of research on teaching* (3rd ed.). New York: Macmillan.

Cornett, J. W. (1987). *Teachers' personal practical theories and their influences upon curricular and instructional actions: A case study of a secondary social studies teacher.* Unpublished doctoral dissertation, Ohio State University, Columbus.

Dewey, J. (1922). *Human nature and conduct.* Rahway, NJ: Henry Holt.

Dewey, M. (1938). *Experience and education.* New York: Macmillan.

Elbaz, F. L. (1983). *Teacher thinking: A study of practical knowledge.* London: Croom Helm.

Gadamer, H. (1976). *Philosophical hermeneutics.* Berkeley: University of California Press.

Grundy, S. (1987). *Curriculum: Product or praxis.* London: Falmer Press.

Hammersley, M. (1977). Teacher perspectives, units 9 and 10. In *Open university schooling and society course.* London: Milton Keynes.

Kelly, G. (1955). *The psychology of personal constructs.* New York: Norton.

Kolb, D. A. (1981). Learning styles and disciplinary differences. In A. Chickering (Ed.), *The modern American college.* San Francisco: Jossey-Bass.

Lewis, C. (1955). *Surprised by joy.* New York: Harcourt Brace Jovanovich.

McCutcheon, G. (1988). Curriculum and the work of teachers. In M. Apple and L. Beyer (Eds.), *Curriculum problems, politics and possibilities.* Albany, NY: SUNY Press.

Nash, R. (1973). *Classrooms observed.* London: Routledge & Kegan Paul.

Oberg, A. (1987). Using construct theory as a basis for research into teacher professional development. *Journal of Curriculum Studies, 19*(1), 55-65.

Reid, W. (1978). *Thinking about curriculum.* London: Routledge & Kegan Paul.

Schön, D. (1983). *The reflective practitioner: How professionals think in action.* London: Temple Smith.

Shulman, L. (1987). Paradigms and research programs in the study of teaching: A contemporary perspective. In M. C. Wittrock (Ed.), *Handbook of research on teaching* (3rd ed.). New York: Macmillan.

Taylor, M. (1976). Teachers' perspectives of their pupils. *Research in Education, 16,* 26-35.

CHAPTER 13. REFLECTIVE TEACHING AND THE
PROBLEM OF SCHOOL ORGANIZATION

Notes

1. An exclusively structural analysis of school organization and/or teacher theorizing, of course, is inadequate and incomplete. For a more comprehensive structural and cultural analysis of school organization and Schön's notion of the reflective practitioner, see Skrtic, 1991a, particularly chapters 9 and 10.

2. Virtually all of the material in this chapter on configuration theory (e.g., division of labor, coordination of work, interdependency among

workers) and institutionalization theory (e.g., decoupled structures, decoupled subunits) is drawn from Mintzberg (1979) and Miller & Mintzberg (1983), and from Meyer & Rowan (1977, 1978) and Meyer & Scott (1983), respectively. The other citations that appear in text from this point on are either additional theoretical constructions that support and/or expand upon the basic insights of configuration theory and institutionalization theory, or empirical and interpretive evidence that supports our theoretical claims.

References

Bernstein, R. J. (1983). *Beyond objectivism and relativism: Science, hermeneutics, and praxis*. Philadelphia: University of Pennsylvania Press.

Burns, T., Stalker, G. M. (1966). *The management innovation* (2nd ed.). London: Tavistock.

Burrell, G., & Morgan, G. (1979). *Sociological paradigms and organizational analysis*. London: Heinemann.

Callahan, R. (1962). *Education and the cult of efficiency*. Chicago: University of Chicago Press.

Chandler, M. D., & Sayles, L. R. (1971). *Managing large systems*. New York: Harper & Row.

Clark, D. L. (1985). Emerging paradigms in organizational theory and research. In Y. S. Lincoln (Ed.), *Organizational theory and inquiry: The paradigm revolution* (pp. 43-78). Beverly Hills, CA: Sage.

Cuban, L. (1979). Determinants of curriculum change and stability, 1870-1970. In J. Schaffarzick & G. Sykes (Eds.), *Value conflicts and curriculum issues*. Berkeley, CA: McCutchan.

———. (1983). Effective schools: A friendly but cautionary note. *Phi Delta Kappan, 64*(10), 695-696.

———. (1989). *Managerial imperative and the practice of leadership in schools*. Albany, NY: State University of New York Press.

Dalton, M. (1959). *Men who manage*. New York: Wiley.

Dewey, J. (1897). My pedagogic creed. *School Journal, 54*(3), 77-80.

———. (1899/1976). The school and society. In J. A. Boydston (Ed.), *John Dewey: The middle works. 1899-1924* (Vol. 1, pp. 1-109). Carbondale: Southern Illinois University Press.

———. (1910/1987). The intellectual criterion for truth. J. A. Boydston (Ed.), *John Dewey: The middle works. 1899-1924* (Vol. 4, pp. 50-75). Carbondale: Southern Illinois University Press.

────── . (1910/1989). How we think: A restatement of the relation of reflective thinking to the educative process. In J. A. Boydston (Ed.), *John Dewey: The later works. 1925-1953* (Vol. 8, pp. 105-352). Carbondale: Southern Illinois University Press.

────── . (1916/1980). Democracy and education. In J. A. Boydston (Ed.), *John Dewey: The middle works. 1899-1924* (Vol. 9, pp. 1-370). Carbondale: Southern Illinois University Press.

────── . (1927/1988). The public and its problems. In J. A. Boydston (Ed.), *John Dewey: The later works. 1925-1953* (Vol. 2, pp. 235-372). Carbondale: Southern Illinois University Press.

────── . (1928/1965). Progressive education and the science of education. In M. S. Dworkin, *Dewey on Education* (pp. 113-126). New York: Teachers College Press.

────── . (1930/1988). From absolutism to experimentalism. In J. A. Boydston (Ed.), *John Dewey: The later works. 1925-1953* (Vol. 5, pp. 147-160). Carbondale: Southern Illinois University Press.

Elmore, R. F., & McLaughlin, M. W. (1988). *Steady work: Policy, practice, and the reform of American education.* Santa Monica, CA: The Rand Corporation.

Freire, P. (1970). *Pedagogy of the oppressed.* Trans. by Myra Bergman Ramos. New York: The Seabury Press.

Giroux, H. A. (1988). *Schooling and the struggle for public life: Critical pedagogy in the modern age.* Minneapolis: University of Minnesota Press.

Greene, M. (1978). *Landscapes of learning.* New York: Teachers College Press.

Haber, S. (1964). *Efficiency and uplift: Scientific management in the Progressive Era, 1990-1920.* Chicago: University of Chicago Press.

House, E. R. (1979). Technology versus craft: A ten year perspective on innovation. *Journal of Curriculum Studies, 11*(1), 1-15.

Kloppenberg, J. T. (1986). *Uncertain victory: Social Democracy and progressivism in European and American thought, 1970-1920.* New York: Oxford University Press.

Lazxerson, M. (1983). The origins of special education. In J. G. Chambers and W. T. Hartman (Eds.), *Special education policies: Their history, implementation, and finance.* Philadelphia: Temple University Press.

Lipsky, M. (1975). Toward a theory of street-level bureaucracy. In W. D. Hawley, M. Lipsky, S. B. Greenberg, J. D. Greenstone, I. Katznelson, K. Orren, P. E. Peterson, M. Shefter, & D. Yates (Eds.), *Theoretical perspectives on urban politics* (pp. 196-213). Englewood Cliffs, NJ: Prentice-Hall.

March, J. G., & Olsen, J. P. (1976). *Ambiguity and choice in organizations.* Bergen, Norway: Universitetsforlaget.

Meier, D. (1984). "Getting tough" in the schools. *Dissent, 31*(1), 61-70.

Meyer, J. W., & Rowan, B. (1977). Institutionalized organizations: Formal structure as myth and ceremony. *American Journal of Sociology, 83*, 340-363.

———. (1978). The structure of educational organizations. In M. W. Meyer (Ed.), *Environments and organizations* (pp. 78-109). San Francisco: Jossey-Bass.

Meyer, J. W., & Scott, W. R. (1983). *Organizational environments: Ritual and rationality.* Beverly Hills, CA: Sage.

Miller, D., & Mintzberg, H. (1983). The case for configuration. In G. Morgan (Ed.), *Beyond method: Strategies for social research* (pp. 57-73). Beverly Hills, CA: Sage.

Mintzberg, H. (1979). *The structuring of organizations.* Englewood Cliffs, NJ: Prentice-Hall.

Morgan, G. (1983). *Beyond Method.* Beverly Hills, CA: Sage.

Perrow, C. (1970). *Organizational analysis: A sociological review.* Belmont, CA: Wadsworth.

Pfeffer, J. (1982). *Organizations and organization theory.* Marshfield, MA: Pitman.

Romzek, B. S., & Dubnick, M. J. (1987). Accountability in the public sector: Lessons from the Challenger tragedy. *Public Administration Review, 47*(3), 227-238.

Rorty, R. (1979). *Philosophy and the mirror of nature.* Princeton, NJ: Princeton University Press.

Sarason, S. B., & Doris, J. (1979). *Educational handicap, public policy, and social history.* New York: The Free Press.

Schön, D. A. (1983). *The reflective practitioner: How professionals think in action.* New York: Basic Books.

———. (1987). *Educating the reflective practitioner: Toward a design for teaching and learning in the professions*. San Francisco: Jossey-Bass.

——— . (1988). Coaching reflective thinking. In P. Grimmett and G. Erickson (Eds.), *Reflection in teacher education*. New York: Teachers College Press.

——— . (1989). Professional knowledge and reflective practice. In T. Sergiovanni and J. Moore (Eds.), *Schooling for tomorrow: Directing reforms to issues that count*. Boston: Allyn and Bacon.

Scott, R. W. (1981). *Organizations: Rational, natural, and open systems*. Englewood Cliffs, NJ: Prentice-Hall.

Segal, M. (1974). Organization and environment: A typology of adaptability and structure. *Public Administration Review, 34*(3), 212-220.

Simon, H. A. (1977). *The new science of management decision*. Englewood Cliffs, NJ: Prentice-Hall.

Skrtic, T. M. (1987). An organizational analysis of special education reform. *Counterpoint, 8*(2), 15-19.

——— . (1988). The organizational context of special education. In E. L. Meyen and T. M. Skrtic (Eds.), *Exceptional children and youth: An introduction*. Denver, CO: Love.

——— . (1991a). *Behind special education: A critical analysis of professional culture and school organization*. Denver: Love.

——— . (1991b). The special education paradox: Equity as the way to excellence. *Harvard Educational Review, 61*(2), 148-206.

Thompson, J. D. (1967). *Organizations in action*. New York: McGraw-Hill.

Timar, T. B., & Kirp, D. L. (1988). *Managing educational excellence*. New York: Falmer Press.

Weatherley, R., & Lipsky, M. (1977). Street level bureaucrats and institutional innovation: Implementing special education reform. *Harvard Educational Review, 47*(2), 171-203.

Weber, M. (1922/1978). *Economy and society*. (G. Roth and C. Wittich, Eds.; E. Fischoll et al., Trans.) (2 vols.). Berkeley: University of California Press.

Weick, K. E. (1976). Educational organizations as loosely coupled systems. *Administrative Science Quarterly, 21*(1), 1-19.

——— . (1982). Administering education in loosely coupled schools. *Phi Delta Kappan, 63*(10), 673-676.

Wise, A. E. (1988). The two conflicting trends in school reform: Legislated learning revisited. *Phi Delta Kappan, 69*(5), 328-333.

Woodward, J. (1965). *Industrial organizations: Theory and practice.* Oxford: Oxford University Press.

Zucker, L. G. (1981). Institutional structure and organizational processes: The role of evaluation units in schools. In A. Bank & R. C. Williams (Eds.), *Evaluation and decision making* (CSE Monograph Series, No. 10). Los Angeles: UCLA Center for the Study of Evaluation.

CHAPTER 14. REFLECTIONS ON PRACTICE: IMPLICATIONS FOR ADMINISTRATOR PREPARATION

References

Achilles, C. (1987). *Unlocking some mysteries of administration and administration: A reflective perspective.* Unpublished briefing paper presented to the National Commission on Excellence in Educational Administration.

Ashburn, E. A., Mann, J., & Purdue, P. A. (1987). *Teacher Mentoring: ERIC Clearinghouse on Teacher Education.* Paper presented at the annual meeting of the American Educational Research Association, Washington, DC.

Barnett, B. G. (1987). Principals creating case studies of one another: The peer-assisted leadership program. *Peabody Journal of Education, 63*(1), 174-186.

Baltzell, D. C., & Dentler, R. A. (1983). *Selecting American school principals: A sourcebook for educators.* Washington, DC: ABT Associates for the National Institute of Education.

Berliner, D. (1984). Making the right changes in preservice teacher preparation. *Journal of Teacher Education, 66*(2), 94-96.

Beyer, L. E. (1984, May-June). Field experience, ideology, and the development of critical reflectivity. *Journal of Teacher Education, 35*(3), 36-41.

Cornett, L. M. (1983). *The preparation and selection of school principals.* Atlanta: The Southern Regional Education Board.

Cruickshank, D. & Armaline, W. (1986, October). Field experiences in teacher education: Considerations and recommendations. *Journal of Teacher Education, 37*(3), 34-40.

Dalton, G. W., Thompson, P., & Price, R. L. (1977). The four stages of professional careers: A new look at performance by professionals. *Career Dynamics, 6,* 19-42.

Daresh, J. C. (1986a, Summer). Field-based educational administration training programs. *Planning and Changing, 17*(2), 107-118.

―――. (1986b, Summer). Inservice for beginning principals: The first hurdles are the highest. *Theory Into Practice, 25*(3), 168-173.

―――. (1988, Fall). Learning at Nellie's elbow: Will it truly improve the preparation of educational administrators? *Planning and Changing, 19*(3), 178-188.

Daresh, J. C., & Pape, S. (1987, October). *Internships and other field experiences in the preparation of administrators and other professional educators: A status report.* Paper presented at the annual meeting of the Mid-Western Educational Research Association, Chicago, IL.

Daresh, J. C., & Playko, Marsha A. (1990, April). *Preservice administrative mentoring: Reflections of the mentors.* Paper presented at the annual meeting of the American Educational Research Association, Boston, MA.

Daresh, J. C., & Playko, M. A. (1992). *The professional development of school administrators: Induction, inservice, and applications.* Needham Heights, MA: Allyn & Bacon.

Dewey, J. (1938). *Education and experience.* New York: Macmillan.

Duke, D. L. (1984). *Teaching: The imperiled profession.* Albany, NY: State University of New York Press.

Goodlad, J. I. (1984). *A place called school.* New York: Mcgraw-Hill.

Gousha, R. P., LoPresti, P. L., & Jones, A. H. (1986, October). *Mapping of a dynamic field: Results from the second annual survey of certification and employment standards for educational administrators.* Paper presented at the annual meeting of the Mid-Western Educational Research Association, Chicago, IL.

Kram, K. E. (1985). *Mentoring at work: Developmental relationships in organizational life.* Glenview, IL: Scott, Foresman.

Merriam, S. (1983, Spring). Mentors and protegees: A critical review of the literature. *Adult Education Quarterly, 33*(3), 161-173.

National Commission on Excellence in Educational Administration. (1987). *Leaders for tomorrow's schools.* Tempe, AZ: University Council for Educational Administration.

Posner, G. J. (1985). *Field experience: A guide to reflective teaching.* New York: Longman.

Schein, E. (1978). Establishing a formalized mentoring program. *Training and Development Journal, 37*(2), 38-42.

Sergiovanni, T. J., & Starratt, R. J. (1988). *Supervision: Human perspectives* (4th ed.). New York: McGraw-Hill.

Shapiro, E. C., Haseltine, F., & Rowe, M. (1978). Moving up: Role models, mentors, and the patron system. *Sloan Management Review, 19,* 51-58.

Silver, P. F. (1986). Case records: A reflective practice approach to administrator development. *Theory into Practice, 25*(3), 161-167.

VanVorst, J. R. (1980). *Mentors and protegees among hospital chief executive officers in Indiana.* Unpublished Ph.D. dissertation, Indiana University.

Weindling, D. & Earley, P. (1987). *Secondary headship: The first years.* Philadelphia: NFER-Nelson.

Wright, R. (1989). Student teachers examine and rate classroom discipline factors: Help for the supervisor. *Action in Teacher Education, 10*(2), 85-91.

Zeichner, K. (1985). The ecology of field experiences: Toward an understanding of the role of field experiences in teacher education. In L. Katz & J. Raths (Eds.), *Advances in teacher education* (Vol. 3). Norwood, NJ: Ablex Publishing.

CHAPTER 15. THE PERSONAL AND THE SOCIAL IN EDUCATION

Notes

1. For an elaboration of some of the ideas in this section, see Beyer (1989).

2. This is not to suggest that those advocating more rigorous, systematic, "scientific" procedures and measurements were faithfully representing the actual activities of scientists. It is more accurate to say that those imbued with a faith in science were expressing an ideology of scientism divorced from the contexts in which scientific debates and work take place. Although such contexts may not be totally "self-correcting," they do place limits on the work of practicing scientists that are not necessarily a part of the work of those, like educational theorists, who interpret certain aspects of science within other, quite different, institutional and cultural contexts.

References

Apple, M. W. (1975). The hidden curriculum and the nature of conflict. In W. Pinar (Ed.), *Curriculum theorizing: The reconceptualists*. Berkeley: McCutchan.

————. (1979). *Ideology and curriculum*. New York: Routledge.

Apple, M. W., & Beyer, L. E. (1988). Social evaluation of curriculum. In L. E. Beyer and M. W. Apple (Eds.), *The curriculum: Problems, politics, and possibilities*. Albany: State University of New York Press.

Barone, T. E. (1988). Curriculum platforms and literature. In L. E. Beyer and M. W. Apple (Eds.), *The curriculum: Problems, politics, and possibilities*. Albany: State University of New York Press.

Bellah, R. N., Madsen, R., Sullivan, W. M., Swidler, A., and Tipton, S. M. (1985). *Habits of the heart: Individualism and commitment in American life*. Berkeley: University of California Press.

Bernstein, R. J. (1983). *Beyond objectivism and relativism: Science, hermeneutics, and praxis*. Philadelphia: University of Pennsylvania Press.

Beyer, L. E. (1988). *Knowing and acting: Inquiry, ideology, and educational studies*. London: Falmer Press.

————. (1989). *Critical reflection and the culture of schooling: Empowering teachers*. Geelong, Victoria, Australia: Deakin University Press.

Beyer, L. E., & Apple, M. W. (Eds.). (1988). *The curriculum: Problems, politics, and possibilities*. Albany: State University of New York Press.

Beyer, L. E., Feinberg, W., Pagano, J. A., & Whitson, J. A. (1989). *Preparing teachers as professionals: The role of educational studies and other liberal disciplines*. New York: Teachers College Press.

Clandinin, D. J. (1986). *Classroom practice: Teacher images in action*. London: Falmer Press.

Franklin, B. (1986). *Building the American community: The school curriculum and the search for social control*. London: Falmer Press.

Holmes Group. (1986). *Tomorrow's teachers: A report of the Holmes Group*. East Lansing, MI: Holmes Group.

Kliebard, H. M. (1975). Bureaucracy and curriculum theory. In W. Pinar (Ed.), *Curriculum theorizing: the reconceptualists*. Berkeley: McCutchan

————. (1986). *The struggle for the American curriculum 1893-1958*. Boston: Routledge.

Liston, D., & Zeichner, K. M. (1991). *Teacher education and the conditions of schooling.* New York: Routledge.

MacIntyre, A. (1984). *After virtue: A study in moral theory.* Notre Dame: University of Notre Dame Press.

Marvin, F. S. (1937). *Compte, the founder of sociology.* New York: John Wiley.

Nasaw, D. (1979). *Schooled to order: A social history of public schooling in the United States.* Oxford: Oxford University Press.

Noble, D. D. (1988). Education, technology, and the military. In L. E. Beyer & M. W. Apple (Eds.), *The curriculum: Problems, politics, and possibilities.* Albany: State University of New York Press.

Pagano, J. A. (1990). *Exiles and communities: Teaching in the patriarchal wilderness.* Albany: State University of New York Press.

Rorty, R. (1979). *Philosophy and the mirror of nature.* Princeton: Princeton University Press.

————. (1989). *Contingency, irony, and solidarity.* New York: Cambridge University Press.

Schön, D. (1983). *The reflective practitioner.* New York: Basic Books.

————. (1987). *Educating the reflective practitioner.* San Francisco: Jossey-Bass.

Shulman, L. S. (1987). Knowledge and teaching: Foundations of the new reform. *Harvard Educational Review, 57*(1), 1-22.

Taylor, F. W. (1911). *The principles of scientific management.* New York: Harper & Brothers.

CHAPTER 16. PERSONAL THEORIZING ABOUT
TEACHER PERSONAL THEORIZING

References

Apple, M. W., & Weis, L. (Eds.). (1983). *Ideology and practice in schooling.* Philadelphia: Temple University Press.

Ayers, W. (1989). *The good pre-school teacher.* New York: Teachers College Press.

Bullough, R. V. (1989). *First-year teacher.* New York: Teachers College Press.

Clark, C. M., & Peterson, P. L. (1986). Teachers' thought processes. In

M. Wittrock (Ed.), *Handbook of research on teaching* (3rd ed.; pp. 255-296). New York: Macmillan.

Connelly, F. M., & Clandinin, D. J. (1988). *Teachers as curriculum planners: Narratives of experience.* New York: Teachers College Press.

Dewey, J. (1916). *Democracy and education.* New York: Macmillan.

Eisner, E. W. (1985). *The educational imagination: On the design and evaluation of school programs.* New York: Macmillan.

Epstein, J. (1981). *Masters: Portraits of great teachers.* New York: Basic Books.

Freire, P. (1970). *Pedagogy of the oppressed.* New York: Seabury.

Giroux, H. A., & McLaren, P. (1989). *Critical pedagogy, the state, and cultural struggle.* Albany: State University of New York Press.

Holt, J. (1964). *How children fail.* New York: Delta.

———. (1981). *Teach your own.* New York: Dell.

Hulsebosch, P. (1988). *Significant others: Teachers' perspectives on relationships with parents.* Unpublished Ph.D. dissertation, University of Illinois at Chicago.

Jagla, V. (1989). *In pursuit of the elusive image: An inquiry into teachers' everyday use of imagination and intuition.* Unpublished Ph.D. dissertation, University of Illinois at Chicago.

Kelly, G. A. (1955). *The psychology of personal constructs.* New York: W. W. Norton.

Koerner, M. E. (1989). *Teachers' images of their work: A descriptive study.* Unpublished Ph.D. dissertation, University of Illinois at Chicago.

Kohl, H. R. (1968). *36 children.* New York: Signet.

———. (1978). *Growing with your children.* Boston: Little, Brown.

Kozol, J. (1967). *Death at an early age.* Boston: Houghton Mifflin.

———. (1975). *The night is dark and I am far from home.* Boston: Houghton Mifflin.

Melnick, C. R. (1988). *A search for teachers' knowledge of the out-of-school curriculum of students' lives.* Unpublished Ph.D. dissertation, University of Illinois at Chicago.

Millies, P. S. (1989). *The mental lives of teachers.* Unpublished Ph.D. dissertation, University of Illinois at Chicago.

Paley, V. G. (1984). *Boys and girls.* Chicago: University of Chicago Press.

Rose, M. (1989). *Lives on the boundary: The struggles and achievements of America's underprepared.* New York: The Free Press of Macmillan.

Rudduck, J., & Hopkins, D. (Eds.). (1985). *Research as a basis for teaching: Readings from the work of Lawrence Stenhouse.* London: Falmer Press.

Schön, D. A. (1983). *The reflective practitioner: How professionals think in action.* New York: Basic Books.

Schubert, W. H. (1975). *Imaginative projection: A method of curriculum invention.* Unpublished Ph.D. dissertation, University of Illinois, Urbana-Champaign.

————. (1981). Knowledge about out-of-school curricula. *Educational Forum, 45*(2), 185-199.

————. (1982). Teacher education as theory development. *Educational Considerations, 12*(2), 8-13.

————. (1986). *Curriculum: Perspective, paradigm, and possibility.* New York: Macmillan.

Schubert, W. H., & Ayers, W. (Eds.). (1992). *Teacher lore: Learning from our own experiences.* New York: Longman.

Schubert, W. H., & Schubert, A. L. (1981). Toward curricula that are of, by, and therefore for students. *Journal of Curriculum Theorizing, 3*(1), 239-251.

Schwab, J. J. (1970). *The practical: A language for curriculum.* Washington, DC: National Education Association.

————. (1973). The practical 3: Translation into curriculum. *School Review, 81,* 501-522.

Stenhouse, L. (1975). *Introduction to curriculum research and development.* London: Heinemann.

————. (Ed.). (1980). *Curriculum research and development in action.* London: Heinemann.

Tyler, R. W. (1949). *Basic principles of curriculum and instruction.* Chicago: University of Chicago Press.

van Manen, M. (1986). *The tone of teaching.* Richmond Hill, Ontario: Scholastic.

Weston, N. (1992). *The experienced curriculum in the primary grades: An exploration in student lore.* Unpublished Ph.D. dissertation, University of Illinois at Chicago.

Wigginton, E. (1986). *Sometimes a shining moment: The foxfire experience.* Garden City, NY: Anchor Books.

Willis, G., & Schubert, W. H. (1991). *Reflections from the heart of educational inquiry: Understanding curriculum and teaching through the arts.* Albany: State University of New York Press.

Witherell, C., & Noddings, N. (Eds.). (1991). *Stories lives tell: Narrative and dialogue in education.* New York: Teachers College Press.

Zumwalt, K. (1989). Beginning professional teacher: The need for a curricular vision of teaching. In M. C. Reynold (Ed.), *Knowledge base for the beginning teacher.* American Association of Colleges for Teacher Education. Oxford: Pergamon Press.

CONTRIBUTORS

William Ayers is Assistant Professor in the College of Education, University of Illinois, Chicago. From 1989 to 1990 he was Assistant Deputy Mayor for Education in Chicago, and he currently chairs the Alliance for Better Chicago Schools, a coalition of reform, advocacy, and activist groups. He is interested in urban schools, school improvement, problems of change, and social and ethical issues related to education. He has published in numerous journals, including the *Harvard Educational Review*, the *Cambridge Journal of Education, Educational Leadership*, and the *Journal of Teacher Education*. His book, *The Good Preschool Teacher*, was published by Teachers College Press in 1989.

Betty J. Bennett is Administrative Dean at Oak Ridge High School in Orlando, Florida. She holds a B.A. in elementary education and an M.A. in mathematics education from the University of Central Florida and was a secondary mathematics and computer teacher for nine years.

Landon E. Beyer is Chair of the Department of Education at Knox College. His major scholarly interests are in curriculum theory and practice, the social foundations of education and aesthetic theory and education. Recent publications include *Knowing and Acting: Inquiry, Ideology and Educational Studies* (Falmer Press, 1988); *The Curriculum: Problems, Politics and Possibilities* (SUNY Press, 1988); and *Preparing Teachers as Professionals: The Role of Educational Studies and Other Liberal Disciplines* (Teachers College Press, 1989). He is currently working on a book, to be co-authored with Daniel P. Liston, on the linkages between knowledge and cultural power.

K. Sue Chase is a social studies teacher at Hillard (Ohio) High School. She holds bachelor's and master's degrees in education from Miami University in Oxford, Ohio. She has been a high school social studies teacher for twenty-two years and has presented papers at the annual meetings of the American Educational Research Association and the National Council for the Social Studies.

Jeffrey W. Cornett is Assistant Professor in the College of Education at the University of Central Florida. He has published articles in journals such as *Theory and Research in Social Education, Theory Into Practice,*

311

Science Education, and the *Social Science Record.* His interests include teacher curriculum decision making and ethics in educational research.

John C. Daresh is Associate Professor and Director, Division of Educational Leadership and Policy Studies at the University of Northern Colorado, Greeley. His research, which examines issues in educational administration and supervision, has appeared in such journals as *Theory Into Practice, NASSP Bulletin,* and *Planning and Changing.*

Alan Goins teaches mathematics and science at Lake Mary High School in Lake Mary, Florida. He graduated summa cum laude in 1988 from Duke University with a B.A. in anthropology. He was a contributing writer for *Focus on Physical Science* (Merrill, 1991), a textbook for middle school grades.

Christopher Hammond received a B.A. in English from the University of California, Berkeley, and has taught English and Latin at West Orange High School in Winter Garden, Florida. He is currently working on an advanced degree in American literature at Emory University.

Elizabeth Jakubowski is Assistant Professor in the Department of Curriculum and Instruction at Florida State University. Her research interests include teacher preparation and enhancement, personal constructs, and teacher change. She teaches courses in middle and secondary mathematics education.

Audrey Kleinsasser is Assistant Professor in the College of Education at the University of Wyoming. A former high school English and German teacher, her scholarly interests include teacher knowledge structures, qualitative research methodology, and issues in alternative assessment.

Sarah Ulerick LaMaster is currently a grants specialist at Lane Community College in Eugene, Oregon. Prior to this position, she held faculty posts in science education at Florida State University and the University of Georgia, and in geology at the University of Oregon and University of Minnesota at Morris. She received her Ph.D. in science education from the University of Texas at Austin in 1981. Her special interests are the role of language, metaphor, and belief systems in teacher change.

Gail McCutcheon is Associate Professor of Education of the Ohio State University in Columbus, where she teaches and does research on curriculum, action research, and qualitative inquiry. She taught third and fourth grades in New Mexico and New York for more than eight years, received her B.A. from the University of New Mexico, her M.A. from Bank Street College, and her Ph.D. from Stanford University in California.

Janet E. McDaniel is Assistant Professor of Education at California State University, San Marcos, where she directs the middle grade teacher education program. Her scholarly interests include middle grade teaching and curriculum, school-university partnerships and social foundations of knowledge in teacher education. She has recently published articles in *Social Education* and *Teacher Education Quarterly*.

Patricia Miller is Teaching Specialist for the Office of Substance Abuse Prevention and Intervention in Wichita Public Schools, USD#259. She holds a bachelor's degree from Emporia State University and a masters in education from Wichita State University.

Sharon L. Pape is Assistant Professor in the Department of Curriculum and Instruction at Southern Illinois University in Carbondale. Her research focuses on teacher education, particularly novice teachers' thinking about classroom curriculum and instruction.

Walter C. Parker is Associate Professor of Social Studies Education at the University of Washington in Seattle. His research on teacher personal theorizing, the social studies curriculum, and civic intelligence has appeared in numerous books and journals. His recent book is *Renewing the Social Studies Curriculum* (ASCD, 1991).

E. Wayne Ross is Associate Professor of Education at the State University of New York at Binghamton, where he teaches courses in social education and curriculum theory. His research focuses on the influence of social and institutional contexts on teachers' practice and reflective thinking in social studies teaching and teacher education. He has published articles in numerous journals, including *Theory and Research in Social Education, Journal of Teacher Education, Educational Foundations*, and the *Journal of Educational Research*.

William H. Schubert is Professor of Education at the University of Illinois-Chicago. He is a former president of the Society for the Study of Curriculum History and is currently president of the John Dewey Society. He is Director of the Teacher Lore Project. He has published numerous articles on curriculum theory and history, inquiry paradigms, and curriculum development. His recent books are *Curriculum Books: The First Eighty Years* (University Press of America, 1984); *Curriculum: Perspective, Paradigm and Possibility* (Macmillan, 1986); and *Reflections from the Heart of Educational Inquiry: Understanding Curriculum and Teaching Through the Arts*, with George Willis (SUNY Press, 1991). He is currently working on several books on teacher lore, teachers and learners as curriculum developers, and curriculum history.

Debbie Schrock has taught biology for eleven years, the past nine years at Andover (Kansas) High School. She holds a B.S. from Fort Hays State University and a masters of science in education from Wichita State University.

Thomas M. Skrtic is Professor of Special Education at the University of Kansas, where, in addition to his primary work in special education policy and administration, he teaches in the areas of curriculum and instruction and educational inquiry. His most recent book, *Behind Special Education*, is a critical analysis of professional culture and school organization in American public education. His research interests include philosophical pragmatism, organizational theory, and educational reform.

Lynda Stone is Assistant Professor in the Educational Foundations Department at the University of Hawaii. Her research focuses on the broad forms of knowledge from which we educate and on postmodern philosophical perspectives on education.

Kenneth Tobin is Professor in the Department of Curriculum and Instruction at Florida State University. His research addresses issues in science teaching and curriculum. He has published numerous scholarly articles in journals such as *Review of Educational Research, Teaching and Teacher Education, Journal of Curriculum Studies,* and *Science Education*. His most recent books include *Exemplary Practice in Science and Mathematics Education* (with Barry Fraser) and *Windows Into Science Classrooms: Problems Associated with Higher-Level Cognitive Learning*, a collection of ethnographic studies of science classrooms published by Falmer Press.

Stephen J. Thornton is Associate Professor of History and Education and directs the doctoral program in social studies education at Teachers College, Columbia University. His scholarly interests focus on how social studies teachers make sense of the curriculum and their students. He has published in a variety of journals, including the *Elementary School Journal* and the *Journal of Curriculum and Supervision*. His "Teacher as Curricular-Instructional Gatekeeper in Social Studies" appeared in *Handbook of Research on Social Studies Teaching and Learning* (Macmillan, 1991).

Linda P. Ware is a doctoral candidate at the University of Kansas, Department of Special Education, and a consultant for the Northeast Kansas Education Service Center. Her research interests include teacher-initiated change, technology integration, curriculum revision, and school reorganization. Her dissertation is a naturalistic study into the cultural and structural conditions of educational innovation.

NAME INDEX

SUBJECT INDEX

Acculturation, 247
Action Research, 144-145, 188-190
Adhocracy, 214-218
Administrator preparation, 220-222
Assumptions, reconstruction of, 267
Autobiography in teaching, 45-49

Behaviorism. *See* Educational psychology
Beliefs, 24
Bricolage, 19, 97-114, 265. *See also* Levi-Strauss; Parker, W. C., and McDaniel, J. E.
Bureaucracies: machine, 209-214; professional, 209-215

Case Study method, 56, 100
Change strategy, 126, 172-174
Classroom culture, 55-62
Classroom laboratory, 11. *See also* Dewey, J.
Cognitive: inventions, 107; restructuring, 135; science, 6, 9; tools, 81, 106
Cognitive process research. *See* Process product research
Cognitive theory, model of, 194
Collaboration, 215, 218, 260
Communication, genuine, 18
Communicative competence, 202
Configuration theory, 209-211

Constant-comparative method, 101-102
Construct: meaning, 28; personal, 68, 262. *See also* Meaning
Constructivism: as epistemology, 126-127; 131; radical, 166-168
Constructivist: learning theory, 197-199; perspective, 67, 71; social studies, 89, 91, 92
Contextual restraints on theorizing, 250
Cooperating teacher, 61
Cooperative learning, 165
CoRT Program, 101. *See also* deBono, E.
Coupling, 210-211
Cricial self reflection, 16, 188. *See also* Reflection
Critical theorizing, 249-254. *See also* Curriculum theorizing
Curriculum: as experience, 10-12, 248; as lived situations, 40; coverage of content, 90-91; instructional choice, 89, 94, 95; invention, 98, 99, 112; non school, 268-269; theorizing, 266-268
Curriculum development: center to periphery model, 97, 112; factory model, 248; interactive planning, 200-202; models, 143, 145; preactive planning, 199-200